HISTORIES
OF
Dirt

HISTORIES OF
Dirt

Media and Urban Life in Colonial and Postcolonial Lagos

STEPHANIE NEWELL

Duke University Press
Durham and London
2020

Printed in the United States of America on acid-free paper ∞
Designed by Drew Sisk
Typeset in Adobe Caslon Pro, ITC Caslon 224,
and Folio by Copperline Books

Library of Congress Cataloging-in-Publication Data
Names: Newell, Stephanie, [date] author.
Title: Histories of dirt : media and urban life in colonial
and postcolonial Lagos / Stephanie Newell.
Description: Durham : Duke University Press, 2020. |
Includes bibliographical references and index.
Identifiers: LCCN 2019013463 (print)
LCCN 2019016769 (ebook)
ISBN 9781478007067 (ebook)
ISBN 9781478005391 (hardcover : alk. paper)
ISBN 9781478006435 (pbk. : alk. paper)
Subjects: LCSH: Public health—Nigeria—Lagos. | Urban
health—Nigeria—Lagos. | Sanitation—Nigeria—Lagos. |
Environmental health—Nigeria—Lagos.
Classification: LCC RA566.5.N6 (ebook) |
LCC RA566.5.N6 N494 2020 (print) | DDC 362.109669/1—dc23
LC record available at https://lccn.loc.gov/2019013463

Cover art: *Show Me You Love Me*. Performance by
Yusuf Durodola. Photograph by Benjamin Oladapo.
Akoka, Lagos, Nigeria, 2016. Courtesy of the artists.

DUKE UNIVERSITY PRESS GRATEFULLY ACKNOWLEDGES
THE MACMILLAN CENTER FOR INTERNATIONAL AND
AREA STUDIES AT YALE UNIVERSITY, WHICH PROVIDED
FUNDS TOWARD THE PUBLICATION OF THIS BOOK.

CONTENTS

ABBREVIATIONS

APC	All Progressives Congress
CFU	Colonial Film Unit
ERC	European Research Council
ES	Elementary School Student interviewee
f	female interviewee
FGD	Focus Group Discussion
GRA	Government Reserved (or Residential) Area
HIR	High-Income Resident interviewee
HPU	Health Propaganda Unit
HS	High School Student interviewee
IDH	Infectious Diseases Hospital
LAWMA	Lagos Waste Management Authority
LIR	Low-Income Resident interviewee
LSHTM	London School of Hygiene and Tropical Medicine
m	male interviewee
mf	two-person interview with a man and a woman
MIR	Middle-Income Resident interviewee
Misc	Lagos resident with general trade/profession
MW	Media Worker interviewee
n	gender of interviewee unspecified or nonbinary

n.d.	no date
NGO	nongovernmental organization
NNA	Nigerian National Archives (Ibadan)
NOA	National Orientation Agency
n.p.	no page
OH	Oral Historian interviewee
PDP	People's Democratic Party
PHU	Public Health User interviewee
PHW	Public Health Worker interviewee
PRO	Public Record Office, National Archives, London (Kew)
PrWW	Private Waste Worker interviewee
PSP	Private Sector Participation
PWW	Public Waste Worker interviewee
SG	School Gatekeeper interviewee
TS	Student in Tertiary Education interviewee
UAC	United Africa Company (Unilever Archives and Records)
UAC LBC	United Africa Company Leverhulme Business Correspondence
WAI	War Against Indiscipline

AUTHOR'S NOTE

Interviews and Focus Group Discussions

Numbers 7–44 were conducted and transcribed by John Uwa. Numbers 45–58 were conducted and transcribed by Jane Nebe. Numbers 59–121 were conducted and transcribed by Olutoyosi Tokun. All other interviews were conducted and transcribed collectively by the team.

Orthography

Full diacritics have been used for Yoruba words and phrases inside quotations, including places and names. Only subdots have been used for proper nouns outside quoted material, as is the current convention; these have not been inserted if authors do not use subdots for their own names.

The Cultural Politics of Dirt in Africa (Dirtpol) Project

In September 2013, the Cultural Politics of Dirt in Africa project team, funded by the European Research Council, set out to understand practical as well as cultural, political, and historical aspects of urban living through people's perceptions of waste management, public health, migration, public morality, environmental hazards, neighborliness, and town planning in two African cities, Lagos and Nairobi. One of the motivations for this interdisciplinary comparative project was a report published by the United Nations that estimated an increase in African urban dwellers from 414 million to more than 1.2 billion by 2050.[1] According to the UN, African city-dwellers were set to outnumber rural populations for the first time in history. Furthermore, they estimated that 40 percent of the continent's one billion people lived in urban areas, 60 percent of whom inhabited dwellings with inadequate sanitation and poor water supplies.[2] We speculated that the topic of dirt might have a great deal to offer researchers with an interest in people's self-understandings in urban contexts, and that discourses of dirt may have cultural histories meriting detailed examination.

As principal investigator on the grant, I assembled a team of researchers in Lagos and Nairobi and designed the research topics for the group to take into fieldwork. Through regular meetings, we worked together to develop a set of interview questions that would probe how particular urban spaces came to be regarded as dirty or full of dirt, and how certain objects and subjects came to be labeled using categories related to dirt. The regional coordinator of the project in Lagos, Patrick Oloko, and the six project researchers in Lagos and Nairobi—Jane Nebe, Olutoyosi Tokun, and John Uwa in Lagos, and Ann Kirori, Job Mwaura, and Rebeccah Onwong'a in Nairobi—came from disciplines as diverse as literary studies, media studies, education, public health, environmental studies, and biological sciences.

With a background in West African cultural history, I had noticed that dirt permeated discussions of everyday urban life in British colonial archives and African-owned newspapers in the late nineteenth and early twentieth centuries. Dirt seemed to be more than an empirical substance in these discussions: it was an idea—or a complex set of representations—that shaped people's perceptions of one another's cultures and bodies and influenced their attitudes toward waste, urbanization, ethnicity, and health. Through the Dirtpol project I wanted us to find out if and how ideas about dirt continued to shape people's perceptions of the urban environment, and in what ways popular narratives and mass media contributed to the formation of public opinion about the dirt or dirtiness of others.

The Dirtpol project aimed to situate African discourses about dirt in relation to urbanization as produced and understood by urban residents themselves. In short, we wanted to find out about local understandings of "dirt," an English word chosen for the wide range of African-language words, phrases, and connotations it broadly encompassed, as well as for its own rich array of connotations in Anglophone contexts as an entry-point into people's responses to urbanization and the environment.[3]

Dirtpol began as a tale of two cities, proposing a comparative historical study of Nairobi and Lagos as two African cities with superficial similarities such as comparable positions in World Bank indicators of poverty ratios, life expectancy, and urban development. Both cities contain a plethora of unplanned spaces in which the majority of residents depend for their survival on informal networks of financial and social support, as well as planned urban spaces such as municipal rubbish dumps, public parks, and gated private housing estates. As scholars have noted, the popular narratives and commentaries generated within these urban spaces give rise to common themes in Kenyan and Nigerian popular media shared with many other African cities about people's lifestyles, political corruption, poverty and wealth, immigration, class, spirituality, pollution, and the environment.[4]

But very quickly Lagos and Nairobi started to populate our topics in different ways, not least because the beginning of fieldwork in February 2014 coincided with the outbreak of the Ebola virus in West Africa. From February onward, the Nigerian media and public discussion were dominated by Ebola stories. Ebola exemplified many themes of the project, but it had a further distorting effect on the comparative framework. The content of interviews and focus group discussions diverged significantly across the continent: in Lagos basic urban practices such as shaking hands, entering a bank, visiting a barber's shop, and queuing for public transport became sources of extreme interpersonal anxiety, while in Nairobi life continued as before, with one or two popular songs circulating about the socially disruptive effects of Ebola in the west of the continent.[5]

Besides the obvious differences generated by such crises to the stories about urban encounters that residents tell in Lagos and Nairobi, residual differences in the two countries' colonial and postcolonial histories also have an impact on the shape of present-day urban cultures and the interrelationships of residents. Dirtpol researchers' fieldwork showed how what appeared on the surface to be broad common themes masked localized differences that generated vital gaps of noncomparison with implications for comparative historical studies as well as cultural studies. Whether one's chosen theme is dirt, cleanliness, sexuality, gender, or another of the multifarious "ways in" to comparative cultural history, the primary challenge for scholars adopting a themed approach is to preserve the cultural complexity of their chosen global cities while also creating space for nonreductive historical and transnational comparisons.

Key methodological questions accompany this type of project and are raised throughout the chapters that follow: Are global cities better studied in comparison with one another within assumed global (or postcolonial) networks? Or are they better studied in their specificity as singular cultural entities, not comparable by too many factors for their superficial similarities to be productive? My decision to focus on Lagos in this book, rather than on Lagos in comparison with Nairobi, arose from the complex intellectual and practical problems described above in combination with my longstanding immersion in Nigerian cultural history. Throughout the book, however, I try to situate Lagos within continental political and cultural currents.

The Dirtpol project could not have been undertaken by any one individual, but each of us developed a different understanding of the project as a whole. Patrick Oloko published on contemporary Nigerian newspapers' fascination for "wasted bodies," that is, people abandoned on municipal dumpsites around Lagos; John Uwa published on the history of fecal waste removal in Lagos and its literary representations; all of the project researchers gave presentations at workshops in Nigeria and the United States.[6]

This book represents my interpretation of the interview material produced by the research team in Lagos in tandem and juxtaposition with my own archival research. In examining local and transnational concepts of dirt from the period of European colonial expansion in the 1880s to the present day, the book tries to position contemporary Nigerian media and public health debates in relation to the country's long history of intercultural encounters with the Global North and other parts of the world. Not least as a consequence of the transnational circulation of mass media such as newspapers since the 1880s and films since the 1920s, the book is comparative across regions as well as periods. The first half draws on material I gathered in African newspaper and colonial public health archives. Here, I struggle to retrieve African perspectives from written colonial archives imbued with racist assumptions about the inferiority of "natives" in matters of sanitation and public health. By contrast, chapters 6, 7, and 8, which draw on in-depth interviews and focus groups conducted by Olutoyosi Tokun, Jane Nebe, and John Uwa with contemporary Lagosians, is packed with the voices and opinions of contemporary urban dwellers as they comment in English and African languages on topics ranging from waste disposal to homosexuality.[7]

The vitality of these interviews with urban residents contrasts starkly with the limited presence of Africans as speaking subjects in the colonial archives, a topic discussed in detail in chapter 5, where I reflect on whether or not it is possible to bridge such a chasm in a meaningful way. The sources for chapters 6, 7, and 8 were living people, interviewed by local Nigerian researchers.[8] As such, research for the second half of the book necessitated a new set of approaches and generated different ethical, methodological, and practical challenges from those I faced in newspaper and government archives. The shift from cultural history to the study of contemporary cultures, and from archival documents to the analysis of interview transcripts, involved a considerable change in my methods and orientation, not least from the individual context of archival research to the collaborative context of interviews undertaken by members of the team, working singly or together. No matter who conducted and transcribed the interviews, each document involved collective interpretation, commentary, and consultation—and on several occasions debriefing—during weekly team meetings and one-on-one video conference calls, and in the weekly reports each team member circulated to the group.

Where the first half of the book complains about the "whiting-out" of Africans from British colonial files, and the irretrievability of Afrophone audiences from written midcentury media commentaries, the second half of the book involves challenges relating to the translation and transcription of Yoruba and Nigerian Pidgin interviews into English, as well as debates about uses of English words to describe highly localized theories of personhood.[9] When transcribing material, I did not want us simply to turn voices into texts for close analysis: I hoped we could find ways to transfer the nuanced, carefully intoned, and often doubly meaningful local categories for dirty bodies, objects, and environments into English on paper without reducing them simply to versions of the English word "dirt." Without assuming that people's views can be retrieved in an unmediated form from digital voice recordings, I wished as far as possible to retain the subjective qualities of interviews and to preserve the personalities—of the interviewers as well as the participants—that often get lost in the written archive. For that reason, in chapters 6, 7, and 8 the vital mediating presence of the Nigerian researchers is emphasized alongside the individuality of interviewees.

The connection between the two halves of the book is not made through anachronistic assumptions that present-day Lagosians somehow speak for, fill in the gaps, or represent African urban residents from a century ago. Connecting these different research contexts is the question of how public opinion is shaped over time. The individuality of interviewees in the second half of the book offered me a model for listening out for local critical commentaries and individual voices in the archives, albeit in the nonverbal forms described in chapter 4.

In approaching the transcripts of interviews and focus group discussions, I wanted to understand the *cultural politics* of dirt: that is, the ways in which dirt signifies politically through complex cultural networks in urban Africa, and the ways in which urban identities and relationships may be marked and transformed over time by categories denoting dirt. By developing a historicized understanding of public opinion during a long twentieth century of intercultural encounters in Africa, I wanted to ask about the ways in which public opinion and popular media feed into wider narratives of African social and political history. In this book, I identify and reflect on Nigerian representations and understandings of dirt in a historical perspective in an effort to trace pathways from mediated perceptions and opinions to political and social outcomes at the street level, and back to the media once again. These processes constitute what I am calling public opinion, which arises in reaction to materials circulating in the public sphere but not exclusively as their outcome. As this book will suggest, dirt is a particularly useful tool to access public opinion in global cities, not least because the histories of dirt continue to influence the terminology through which people and the media interpret one another today.

ACKNOWLEDGMENTS

In the six years it has taken to research and write this book, I have built up debts of gratitude to numerous people.

Fieldwork for chapters 6, 7, and 8 was conducted by the Cultural Politics of Dirt in Africa (Dirtpol) research team based at the University of Lagos: Olutoyosi Tokun, John Uwa, and Jane Nebe, supervised by Patrick Oloko. They organized, translated, and transcribed more than 120 interviews in schools, health clinics, waste-processing sites, and surrounding communities, helped by the project coordinator, Claire Craig at Sussex University. In Nairobi, Job Mwaura, Ann Kirori, and Rebeccah Onwong'a added a valuable comparative dimension to the project between February 2014 and June 2015. Discussions with the team, alongside their blogposts for the project website, weekly reports, presentations and, in two cases, publications, have inspired my thinking throughout this book. I hope I have done justice to their incredible work and team spirit, and I remain indebted to them as collaborators, colleagues, and friends.

Senior managers at the University of Lagos during the 2013–17 research period offered warm encouragement and support: especial thanks are due to Professor Rahman A. Bello (vice chancellor of the University of Lagos), Professor Babajide Alo (deputy vice chancellor [DVC], Academics and Research), Professor Duro Oni (DVC, Management and Services), Professor Akin Oyebode (director of the Office of International Partnership), Dr. Oluwatoyin Ipaye (registrar), Dr. Lateef Odekunle (bursar), Professor Toyin Ogundipe (director of Academic Planning), and Professor Muyiwa Falaiye (dean of Faculty of Arts). The project would not have got off the ground without the University of Lagos accountant, Funmi Adekunle, whose good-humored commitment to the smooth functioning of the grant ensured success at every stage. At the University of Sussex, the research support team deserves heartfelt thanks, most especially Amelia Wakeford and Julian Golland, who provided tireless assistance with project management between 2012 and 2015. At Yale University, warm appreciation goes to the managers and staff of the MacMillan Center for International and Area Studies for supporting the transition of the project from the U.K. to Yale.

Karin Barber's brilliance as a scholar of Yoruba cultural history and print cultures inspired my thinking at many stages of the project, and her perceptive feedback and questions about key terms helped me to interrogate my ideas along the way. Conversations with Louise Green and participants in the three Dirtpol workshops at the University of Lagos, Stellenbosch University, and Yale University helped to shape the overall structure of the book. I am also grateful to Oluseye Adesola for his assistance with Yoruba translation, and to the Yoruba linguists and oral historians who generously gave their time to be interviewed for this book.

Many thanks to staff at the Nigerian National Archives, Unilever Archives and Records, and the Public Record Office (U.K.) for their assistance in providing files, images, and information. Interviews in government schools and waste disposal sites were made possible with permission from the Ministry of Education (Lagos) and the Lagos Waste Management Authority (LAWMA) respectively, who kindly granted the research team permits to work in public sector environments. The Dirtpol project was funded by the ERC (AdG 323343) between September 1, 2013, and June 30, 2015. From July 1, 2015, to December 31, 2016, the project received generous funding from the Whitney and Betty MacMillan Center for International and Area Studies at Yale University, specifically the Edward J. and Dorothy Clarke Kempf Memorial Fund and the Stephen and Ruth Hendel '73 Fund for Innovation in Africa. Research for chapter 4 would not have been possible without the outstanding resource provided by the Colonial Film Database (http://www.colonialfilm.org.uk/).

Small parts of the preface were published as "Researching the Cultural Politics of Dirt in Lagos" in *Theorizing Fieldwork in the Humanities: Undisciplined Approaches to the Global South*, edited by Shalini Puri and Debra A. Castillo (Basingstoke, U.K.: Palgrave Macmillan, 2016), 193–211; and in S. Newell et al., "Dirty Methods as Ethical Methods? In the Field with 'The Cultural Politics of Dirt in Africa, 1880–Present,'" in *Routledge In-*

ternational Handbook of Interdisciplinary Research Methods, edited by Celia Lury et al. (London: Routledge, 2018), 248–65. Small parts of the introduction were published as "Dirty Familiars: Colonial Encounters in African Cities," in *Global Garbage: Urban Imaginaries of Waste, Excess, and Abandonment*, edited by Christoph Lindner and Miriam Meissner (New York: Routledge, 2015), 35–51. Parts of chapters 4 and 5 were published as "The Last Laugh: African Audience Responses to Colonial Health Propaganda Films," *Cambridge Journal of Postcolonial Literary Inquiry* 4 (3): 347–61, 2017. Other parts of chapter 4 were published in 2018 as "Screening Dirt: Colonial Film Audiences and the Problem of Spectatorship," *Social Dynamics* 44 (1): 6–20.

Above all, this book would not have been possible without the generous participation of Lagosians in focus group discussions and interviews. I am grateful to the schoolchildren and teachers, waste management professionals, health service providers and users, media workers, oral historians, and many residents of the city whose voluntary participation in the project and perceptive commentaries form a vital core of knowledge in the book.

INTRODUCTION

While traveling with William Hesketh Lever and others on a lengthy tour of inspection of Lever Brothers' numerous trading stations in West and Central Africa in the mid-1920s, Thomas Malcolm Knox (1900–1980), secretary to Lord Lever, adopted an interpretive framework that is both depressingly familiar today in antihumanist discourses, and richly descriptive of the economic and emotional relationships between strangers in multicultural urban environments. The city of Lagos, Knox noted, "turns out to be a town of unspeakable squalor. It is no wonder that it is the nurse of disease. Filth everywhere."[1] For Knox, the source of filth was easy to identify, for "everything reeks of dirty natives."[2] Yet this same city, he recognized, "is the representative of a much higher state of civilization" than the "squalid" African trading posts he recently visited in the hinterland of the Belgian Congo, for Lagos boasted European shops built to supply local consumers with household products manufactured in Europe using raw materials exported from Africa's "uncivilized" interior.[3]

Several scholars have commented on the circular, self-serving nature of the connection between cleanliness and civilization in the writings of European travelers during the colonial period.[4] Perceived and narrated through "imperial eyes," the figure of the "dirty native" legitimized European cultural and economic expansion into the most intimate corners of Africans' daily lives.[5] For European traders and government officials alike, "dirty natives" were far more dangerous than objects discarded by the wayside, or trash, and necessitated regimes of sanitation and urban racial segregation. In countless colonial-era travelogues and memoirs by white British men, the same rhetoric of difference is mapped onto the bodies and beliefs of others through a spectrum of dirt-related words, facilitating the same dead-end conclusions about the inferiority of African cultures each time. In the 1870s, for example, the trader John Whitford described Lagos as "a filthy, disgusting, savage place and unsafe to wander about in the streets."[6] All across West Africa, local populations were "filthy" in his view, not because of a lack of soap and water, but because the unfamiliar appearance of people and foodstuffs elicited strong feelings of revulsion in him, not least the "hideously ugly" women who possessed "strong limbs developed by hard work, which should pertain to a man only."[7] Other traders adopted the same tropes as Whitford and Knox, describing local people's unfamiliar clothing and physiques in visceral terms that conveyed their nausea as if it were a natural sense perception rather than a reaction to the culturally challenging norms of others. As one anonymous trader wrote of Nigerian villagers in the 1920s, "not only did their bodies give off a horrible smell, but their hair was tousled like dirty rope, and their skin a dull black. The bits of cloth around the loins were pregnant with filth."[8]

These expressions of disgust at the supposed uncleanliness of others offer historically specific examples of a reactionary discourse that persists into the twenty-first century, forming one of the pivots on which this book turns. Understanding these strained and failed cross-cultural relationships in past decades can help us to contextualize the antihumanist currents that persist in contemporary debates about multiculturalism and toleration in global urban environments. Whitford's identification of African women as "ugly" in the 1870s, Knox's disgust at the strangeness of others in the 1920s, and the similar reactions of numerous other European travelers and traders in Africa in the late nineteenth and early twentieth centuries provide us with a historically situated prologue to an unpalatable side of discourses about globalization and urbanization that persist in the present day.

In spite of his protestations of loyalty to judgments based on the observation of "empirical phenomena" in Africa, Knox's disgust and repulsion were not focused on unclean streets or unwashed bodies but on what was unrecognizable to him.[9] In Jebba, Nigeria, for example, he described how "we stopped at various native stalls and examined their wares—capsicum (pepper of a particularly strong variety), chop of various sorts, extraordinary and repulsive stuff all of it";[10] at the market in Zaria, in northern Nigeria, he found that "the meat presents the most disgusting appearance. It is covered with flies and vermin and even were these absent seemed to consist mainly of the least savoury looking parts of animals."[11] Also at the Zaria market, he found that "the knick-knack stalls were the most curious of all. Little bits of stick, a few knobs of ginger, little bits of stone, a tooth pick or two, all apparently things of little or no use."[12]

The association of dirt with "useless" matter demonstrates the ways in which dirt, as a category, names matter that is no longer regarded as having economic, social, or productive value, and is not therefore recognized as part of human social systems. In Knox's case, the "useless" matter comprised locally manufactured African products, the purpose of which he simply failed to recognize. These products were useless because he wished to supplant them with imported alternatives. All the way from Casablanca to the interior of Congo, the marked preference of local people for locally produced commodities—unrecognizable to the traveler—rather than imported commodities purchased from the European companies operating in the region filled Knox with revulsion, and rendered local people nauseating "others" who resisted assimilation into the global economy represented by European traders. Their visceral responses had little to do with dirt as an empirical substance and more to do with white traders' subjective reactions to local consumption practices. What revolted Knox was the entire public habitus: the busy local streets and the messy, protuberant local commodities displayed for sale in the markets. What revolted him, in short, was the presence of the foreign body as a consuming entity that participated in a cash economy but desired merchandise that was completely alien to his own trade interests. The powerful feelings of revulsion that he experienced marked the moment at which he recognized the other's humanity as a consuming subject—eating, drinking, socializing, purchasing goods—and instantaneously dismissed the other's tastes as unpalatable to himself and, crucially, beyond his economic control.

The examples of Whitford and Knox illustrate how dirt is far more than an empirical substance: it is also an interpretive category that facilitates moral, sanitary, economic, and aesthetic evaluations of other cultures under the rubric of uncleanliness. Operating through categorical oppositions between the (clean) self and the (filthy) other, dirt has a place in histories of reactionary social and political thought. Dirt sticks: it attaches to bodies and ranges from colonialist understandings of "native" domestic hygiene through to contemporary rejections of nonbinary sexualities and global media representations of poverty in postcolonial cities. As a category of interpretation, dirt has a vibrant historicity that reverberates through the decades, changing with the times, but permeating how the bodies of strangers are produced by those with the power to tell stories and to be heard in contemporary global contexts.

Knox's dystopian vision of an Africa—with "children romping heedless of the endless flies and vermin," where "thoroughly repulsive" people and "degenerates" live in "dirt, grit, dust," where "deformed men and crippled children" intermingle with "people wandering about suffering obviously from loathsome and unspeakable diseases"—is an iteration of reactionary Western responses to African urban environments during periods of famine or epidemic.[13] With its remarkable staying power, this deployment of the category of dirt has marked the status and proximity of an other whose presence is embedded in the desire for exclusion or segregation on the part of observers. Whitford's and Knox's descriptions conform to theorizations of dirt as that which society expels, excretes, or treats as abject or excessive.[14] Their interpretive framework matches Mary Douglas's resonant assertion that dirt marks the limits of a society's understanding of itself, signifying people's need to withdraw from any habitus that is perceived to be dirty, and, in reaction, to reassert their own social and behavioral boundaries.[15] For Douglas, as Richard Fardon notes, "ideas of impurity and danger hold members of a society to account to one another, and they do so with a character and intensity that stems from and rebounds back upon that particular form of society."[16] From this perspective, dirt represents a type of excess that can never be valued or conceived of in positive ways. For Knox and his peers, dirt signified disorder, inefficiency, unfamiliar bodies, and the unrecognizable; as a discursive category, it mediated between the margins and the mainstream, facilitating the expulsion of particular types of matter from the realm of social approval.

Several scholars have noted how dirt was a key ingredient in the making of imperial identities and in the marketing of imperial products to global consumers in the colonial era (fig. Intro.1).[17] Out of it grew new global markets to the extent that, in one advertisement at least, soap as a commodity replaced the Victorian moral principle that "cleanliness is next to godliness." A famous advertisement from the Pears Soap Company in 1890 starkly reminded consumers, via a misquotation from Justus von Liebig, that "the consumption of soap is a measure of the wealth, civilisation, health, and purity of the people" (fig. Intro.2).[18] Significantly, this advertisement was printed on the back cover of a special "Stanley Edition" of the *Graphic* celebrating the recent Emin Pasha Relief Expedition led by Stanley from 1886 to 1889. Through numerous vivid drawings of Stanley's expedition from the east coast of Africa into the interior of the continent, the

Lux Will Wash Locks.

[Photo by M. Frost, Biddenden.

Here is a lady of colour, hailing from Africa, preparing to wash her luxuriant locks in Lux, which, of course, is famous as a shampoo soap. The jolly subject of the photograph uses Lux regularly, and, judging by the crop shown around her head, it acts as a fine tonic for the hair.

FIGURE INTRO.I. Advertisement for Lux. *Progress Magazine: The Magazine of Lever Brothers and Unilever Ltd*, July 1925, n.p. Reproduced with kind permission of Unilever from an original in Unilever Archives.

FIGURE INTRO.2. Advertisement for Pears Soap. *The Graphic*, April 30, 1890, 36. Author's collection.

special issue illustrates the contrasts between the moral authority, bravery, and leadership of British men, and Africans' lack of control, made evident not least by their lack of clothing (fig. Intro.3). Appearing in the wake of these images and reports, the Pears Soap advertisement on the back cover is a tangible by-product of the "dirty native" ideology.

The first two chapters of *Histories of Dirt* ask about the extent to which the imperial culture's myths and beliefs about the supposedly dirty tastes, habits, and practices of Africans were carried over into the practical application of scientific discoveries, legitimizing racial segregation in the name of public health. The archival materials examined in these chapters reveal how British West Africa narrowly escaped formal racial segregation of the type successfully imposed by town planners in East and South African British colonies in the first two decades of the twentieth century.

Colonial town planning did not, however, avoid institutionalized racism at the levels of the interpretation of science and the implementation of policy. A homogeneous African "native" was produced in West African public health discourse in the early twentieth century, standing in for or, in the case of malaria, replacing political responses to the problems of sanitation and disease. As the archives examined in chapters 1 and 2 indicate, in the face of white traders' fears of contamination from African residents, and in the absence of funds for what Dr. Henry Strachan of Freetown termed "sanitary salvation" in colonial cities, British West African governments carefully considered adopting a formal policy of racial segregation in order to protect Europeans from the panoply of tropical diseases and global "filth diseases" associated with urbanization, on the one hand, and the proximity of "natives," on the other.[19]

These two chapters discuss how British officials wished to transform Africans into recognizably clean and healthy subjects through legislation backed by teams of sanitary inspectors with powers to enforce municipal rules.[20] In a manner similar to that of the European travelers and traders in the late nineteenth and early twentieth centuries, British officials in West Africa used their own moral and material categories of dirt to develop a set of criteria that marked the boundary between unacceptable and acceptable local domestic behaviors. Government intervention was deemed legitimate and necessary in the case of "dirty" local practices in expanding African cities, not only to protect European officials from contagion, but also to protect Africans from themselves.

How African urban residents reacted to these public health measures—and the opinions that underwrote them—is a key concern in this book.

FIGURE INTRO.3. "Forest Dwarfs Eating Snakes." *The Graphic*, April 30, 1890, 10.
Author's collection.

The viewpoints of educated local elites are preserved in the ample newspaper archives of the colonial period. In spite of substantial differences of opinion among themselves on the topic of home rule, when it came to town planning in the early twentieth century, Nigerian newspaper editors were unanimous in their adoption of government public health frameworks. While the radical, Afrocentric press published outspoken criticisms of colonial failures to implement town-planning schemes that would benefit the majority and responded to racial discrimination with calls for self-rule, conservative and pro-British newspapers such as the *Nigerian Pioneer* and the government-backed Nigerian *Daily Times* published regular polite requests for sanitary improvements and offered advice about the sources of filth in Nigerian towns. In spite of the pseudo–racial science that underwrote colonial public health policy, discussed in chapters 1 and 2, for a variety of reasons none of the Anglophone African newspapers rejected public health discourse per se. But, as chapter 3 shows through a case study of the conservative *Nigerian Pioneer*, editors worked hard to replace colonial racializations of dirt with other explanations for "native" filth, swapping out one maligned category of person for others and, in the process, splitting and contesting the hegemonic African produced by colonial discourse.

Focusing on the *Nigerian Pioneer* during the bubonic plague epidemic of 1924–31, chapter 3 asks how and why a newspaper owned and edited by an unofficial African member of the Legislative Council and a key participant in municipal affairs offered such sparse underreporting of this critical epidemic.[21] In highlighting the work of the conservative *Pioneer* rather than its radical and anticolonial peers, this discussion underscores the ambivalent role of imperial loyalists—regarded as collaborators by their anticolonial rivals—who attempted to retain positions of social and political power during the period that witnessed the rise of "new imperialism" in British colonial policy. The extent to which these members of the educated elite used the press to displace the discourse of dirt from the colonial figure of "the native" and shift it onto other urban bodies is the focus of discussion in this chapter, with the aim of determining whether, and how, they changed the terms of the colonial discourse of dirt.

Not all concepts relating to dirt produce the adverse standpoints described above. In the early twentieth-century examples discussed at the start of the book, as much as in the midcentury examples in chapters 4 and 5, and the early twenty-first-century examples in the concluding chapters, the identification of urban dirt often opens up spaces for curiosity and speculation on the part of observers, as well as failures to comprehend other people's behavior. *Histories of Dirt* is characterized by people's efforts to create narratives that attempt to understand the motivations and behavior of people labeled "dirty." Within and behind discourses of disease eradication, public health, and moral sanitation lie their speculative stories about dirt, often incompatible with and uncontainable by mainstream ideological oppositions between health and filth, and often resisting the binary, aggressive "dirty othering" performed in mainstream and official media. Time and again, this book finds that people pour their imaginations into stories about the dirt of others, even as they ostensibly endorse a desire for cleanliness or purity. So frequent and sustained are these moments of curiosity and creativity in conjunction with the discourse of dirt that, as many chapters will demonstrate, the category of dirt begins to stand for the failure, rather than the achievement, of the ideological processes of othering it manifestly endorses.

In the long twentieth century covered by this book, Nigerian urban identities and relationships are shown to be marked and transformed by changing categories denoting dirt as people's perceptions of who and what are useful and good shift over the decades. Moving from early twentieth-century colonial archives in the first three chapters to Nigerian media and midcentury audience research in chapters 4 and 5, and, finally, to interviews and focus group discussions with contemporary Lagosians in chapters 6 to 8, the book offers an increasingly localized account of diverse historical actors' perceptions of dirt in urban environments.[22] Whereas the opening chapters turn to Anglophone African newspaper producers and consumers in the early twentieth century for examples of local reactions to externally imposed categories of dirt, and while the middle chapters attempt to retrieve rural Nigerians' responses to colonial public health media from the written archives of the 1940 and 1950s, the final part of the book turns to a multicultural living archive of urban residents in order to pursue the question of the extent to which Lagosians process official and media messages through their own aesthetic, spiritual, moral, economic, and political value systems.

A key question relates to appropriate methods for researching Lagosian cultural history in archives that often exclude African subjects and filter local perspectives through a racist colonial optic. The possibility of finding non-Eurocentric methods for approaching historical sources that are saturated with British colonial constructions of Africans is a central problem in the book. How can local residents' values and opinions be identified in Anglophone archives whose authors were British government officials, often with powerfully anti-African visions of how urban environments should look in order to be free from what they identified as dirt? The book as a whole attempts to prioritize African responses to government policies in tension with official representations of public health initiatives. In so doing, it attempts to chart a path through voluminous colonial archives by focusing on Africans as media consumers, commentators, interpreters, householders, and producers of public opinion.

In attempting to read for African perspectives, the book evaluates not only the cultural histories of specific "dirty" discourses, but also the theoretical and methodological directions that the concept of dirt generates as a starting point for comparative historical case studies over a long twentieth century. This includes a consideration of problems relating to the translation, or translatability, of the variety of local language concepts relating to dirt, which change over time and get lost in transcription. Rather than wishing to retrieve impossibly pristine African subjects from the written archives, the book tries to identify colonial mediations of African subjectivity and African responses to these mediations. Examples of African reactions to media—albeit untranslated and nonverbal—are pulled from colonial files and strung together into a series of questions about how mass media texts such as public health movies and newspapers contributed to local perspectives on dirt and urbanization. Colonial public health policy, town-planning initiatives, and propaganda films are treated as contributing to African public opinion in public spaces that include people's preexisting practices and values. Underlying this method is the conviction that in West Africa, as elsewhere, "public opinion has a life of its own."[23]

Chapters 6 to 8, with their attention to over 120 interviews with people from diverse age groups and backgrounds, demonstrate how actively ordinary Lagosians create narratives through which they mediate and judge mainstream media material. Time and again, the interviewees for this book treated news stories not as stopping points but as templates to be embellished with individualized accounts of dirty behavior. In the process, as these chapters suggest, interviewees often produced empathetic and ventriloquistic accounts of people who are popularly labeled dirty, such as *agbépòò* (night-soil workers), or stigmatized in mainstream political and religious discourse, such as people with nonbinary sexualities.

Dirt has been a potent category in Eurocentric representations of Africa for more than a century and remains a source of such fascination for Western publics. To adopt it as a research theme runs the risk of perpetuating, rather than countering, simplistic binary oppositions that support negative Eurocentric stereotypes of the continent.[24] As demonstrated by the widespread discontent among Nigerian viewers of the BBC's three-part documentary *Welcome to Lagos*, screened in 2010 and discussed in more detail in chapter 7, which represented Lagos through exclusive attention to waste workers and so-called slum dwellers, the vector of dirt risks distorting and misrepresenting the complex totalities of people in postcolonial cities. As an outsider's way of seeing the other, the category of dirt risks skewing other outsiders' views of people, places, and objects, magnifying the "worst" features of other cultures and ignoring their complexities in favor of stark oppositions with whatever is perceived to be clean.

Whether they be the "natives" of colonial discourse or the LGBTQ+ bodies of contemporary homophobias, bodies officially marked as dirty become ripe for removal. For good reason, therefore, until recently Africanist scholars in the arts and humanities have tended to avoid the topic of dirt in studying the continent's cultural and social histories.[25] With significant exceptions in anthropology, where disgust has been a prominent topic since the work of Mary Douglas in the 1960s, and in the study of African visual cultures, where aesthetic revaluations of "trash" have become the subject of considerable recent interest in film studies and art history, scholars with an interest in the politics and aesthetics of dirt in Africa have tended to focus on purification, soap, and sanitation in their discussions of social history and the postcolonial city.[26] Can a politics and poetics of dirt be composed for West Africa that avoids the Eurocentrism of Knox and his peers, while acknowledging the impact of colonialism in the history of postcolonial cities?

This book recognizes the tenacity of dirt as a Eurocentric category for the negative evaluation of people, objects, and places, but it also seeks to historicize dirt in dynamic multicultural contexts and disconnect it from a binary relationship with cleanliness. Dirt is a discursive field in its own right with histories that may be traceable to colonial encounters, but neither begin nor end in the deadening logic of the travelers and traders described in preceding pages. In Lagos, a multitude of words exists in Yoruba, Nigerian Pidgin, English, and other languages to describe dirt and dirtiness, dating back well before the colonial encounter. As chapters 6, 7, and 8 will show, people's interpretations of sexual and (im)moral activities, ethnic otherness, environmental pollution, waste management, physical contagion, and contamination combine with positive evaluations of dirt through proverbs about waste and vermin, and applause for the transformation of trash into useful and valuable new commodities. At a practical level, Lagosians' responses to globalization include frugality and the recycling of trash, changing their relationship with waste in ways that prevent the materialization of disgust. Likewise, the artistic transformation of rubbish into beautiful, symbolic, or useful objects also breaks the cycle of colonialist conceptualizations.[27]

Put simply, dirt should not be regarded only as the binary opposite of cleanliness or purity: it is a dense cultural category with histories of its own, through which locally situated understandings of identity and interpersonal relationships may be filtered. If dirt is often used as a category in official discourses to mark a reactionary desire for the removal (or symbolic "cleaning up") of the targets it identifies, this book will show how dirt is greater than this usage and plural in a manner that exceeds black-and-white hegemonies. When Lagosians' opinions and languages are added to the melting pot of colonial and postcolonial urban interactions, a proliferation of additional connotations and concepts arise around the category of dirt, sometimes providing respite from (post)colonial discourses of animosity and antihumanism.

A focus on dirt helps to make visible how people produce and make use of supposedly natural, universal, biological concepts in response to specific and changing types of urban encounter, and how these concepts change over time. Chapter 7, for example, historicizes public opinion about hitherto stigmatized professions such as refuse and sewage removal, particularly in relation to how urban residents' perceptions were transformed by a combination of public relations interventions and investments in waste management infrastructure in Lagos in the early twenty-first century. The emphasis throughout the book is on the ways in which urban publics are informed by mediated visions of the city and the urban environment, whether through religious doctrine, newspapers, movies, social media, and advertisements, or through discussions, disagreements, and the exchange of opinion.

Public opinion is complex and nebulous, but it is not detached from the publics whose opinions it proclaims, nor is it from the different types of media and communication that contribute to urban dwellers' attitudes and values at different historical moments. Rather than adopting a simple model of audience reception through which mass media consumers are regarded as readily influenced by messages from mainstream, official, and online sources, this book provides evidence throughout that Nigerian audiences articulate independent lines of reasoning as they interpret the environments in which they live and work. As shown in chapters 6 to 8, religious institutions and the media play a crucial role in helping urban residents to double-check the truth and accuracy of their perceptions and judgments about their own and others' "dirty" behavior, but people form opinions in collaboration with these messages as active media consumers who configure interpretive systems on the ground, among themselves. In this space of public opinion, urban residents are commentators as well as media consumers whose independent responses can be traced back over more than a century of intercultural encounters in West Africa.[28] Indeed, in discussing the urban environment and their perceptions of dirt, the Lagosians we interviewed often situated themselves at one remove from public opinion, checking their individual actions and attitudes against it, using it as gauge of socially acceptable behavior and a reference point when asked to describe what they regarded as dirty professions or dirty behavior.

This book is as much about local audiences in diverse historical settings as it is about the different media texts they consume over time. The emphasis on grassroots African opinions and interpretations of media is designed to seek out counternarratives to colonial—and, to some extent, middle-class West African—definitions of dirt, and to continue the methodological experiment started by historians such as Ann Laura Stoler and Antoinette Burton, who decentralize official archives, and seek alternative methods and sources for compiling cultural histories of Europe's imperial territories.[29] Lagosians' opinions about urban relationships are at the forefront of the study, including public responses to international media portrayals of Lagos as one of the "least livable cities in the world" and the BBC's documentary *Welcome to Lagos*.[30]

In the face of archival constraints for this type of research, my overarching aim is to consider a history of urbanization from the perspectives of non-elite and sub-elite urban residents alongside elite Africans and colonial and official commentators.[31] Using a range of historical examples— from debates about sanitation and town planning in African newspapers to Colonial Film Unit strategies for communicating health and hygiene messages to intended audiences—the book asks about the ways in which ordinary, daily texts about public health and the urban environment have contributed to the identification of dirt in the urban imaginaries of Lagosians over the decades. If the study necessarily depends on British colonial archives as a historical starting point, it tries to problematize the information such archives yield by attempting to read them for African perspectives: Anglophone sources are scoured for instances of African praxis and the presence of local opinions, and contrasted with African sources, wherever available, on the same topics from the period. In this way, the book tries to honor the project called for by Andreas Huyssen, to develop "deeper knowledge about the ways in which modernity has historically evolved in the cities of the non-Western world, what urban constellations and conflicts it has created there, and what such developments might mean today for city cultures at large."[32]

1

European
Insanitary Nuisances

Lagos is a multiethnic coastal city with a history of trade and migration closely connected to the transatlantic slave trade and its abolition.[1] With the British annexation of Lagos in 1861, and with passenger and cargo ships plying the West African coast well into the twentieth century, the city formed the last port of call in a network of trading posts along the West African littoral, including Freetown, Monrovia, Sekondi-Takoradi, and Accra.[2] With its regional status as the "Liverpool of West Africa" came inward migration from many parts of world, including western Europe, Syria, Brazil, and other parts of Africa.[3] The population of Lagos expanded from 41,847 in 1901 to 73,788 in 1911, further rising to 98,303 in 1921 and 126,474 in 1931 as the town and its boundaries expanded.[4]

In the Township Ordinance of 1917, Lord Frederick Lugard (1858–1945) established Lagos as a "First-Class Township," ranked thus not by its infrastructure but by its number of European inhabitants, including the influential white trader community.[5] Through their chambers of commerce in Lagos (est. 1888) and Liverpool (est. 1774), white traders complained continuously to government about what they saw as a proliferation of poor-quality, unplanned, overcrowded, and insanitary dwellings springing up all over town with the potential for the uncontrollable spread of disease and a host of other "sanitary atrocities."[6] Many government officials agreed: in the binary racial logic of colonial town planning in the early twentieth century, "unsanitary native villages block[ed] the way to European expansion on healthy sites."[7] Even the most ostentatiously wealthy Africans—the "better class natives"—were regarded as incapable of constructing a "hygienic home" according to the Eurocentric way of seeing towns, simply because "the *native idea* of a dwelling house, even costing over £1,000 is not as a rule in accordance with hygienic principles."[8]

Lagos was never a European outpost or transport depot like Nairobi in the early twentieth century: the city always contained large numbers of what the Nigerian Medical and Sanitary Department inappropriately classified as "non-official Natives," that is, African residents not in government employment. These were the "*Ọmọ Èkó*" (Yoruba indigenes; lit., "children of Lagos"), "*Ará Èkó*" (Yoruba outsiders who live in Lagos), "*Ará Òkè*" (Yoruba uplanders), "*Àlejò*" (strangers/visitors), "*Àjòjì*" (strangers from another country), and "*Ọbáléndé/Ọbáléwandé*" (Yoruba: "the Ọba chased me/us to this area," people living in the Hausa quarter of town).[9] The city's quarters included precolonial areas (Ìsàlẹ̀ Èkó, Offin, Ereko, and Oko Faji) and ethnically identifiable areas (Yoruba, "Saro," Brazilian, and Muslim settlements).[10] Taken together, these were, in Liora Bigon's words, "far from being an incarnation of a system of disciplinary power in terms of urban form."[11] Except for the "European Quarter" comprising Broad Street down to the Marina, and the Government Reserved Area (GRA) at Ikoyi between the 1920s and the 1950s, white residents had to fit themselves into the existing urban infrastructure of a cosmopolitan city that preexisted their arrival by many decades (fig. 1.1). Notably, the first European settlement was a dumpsite known as Ehingbeti, used by local residents for waste and defecation and "therefore beyond the pale of respectability."[12] In the 1860s the British displaced numerous "wretched native tenements" from the "filthy beach" and surrounding areas in order to build wide streets, a promenade, and "brick stores, with comfortable luxurious dwellings above," as well as barracks, a racecourse, a courthouse, a cemetery, and other visible structures of British urban occupation.[13]

British health and sanitation officials in the early twentieth century did not celebrate the creative ingenuity of inhabitants eager to experience and absorb the modernity of the expanding African city; nor did they marvel at new arrivals' capacity to survive with kith and kin on extremely low incomes, forming credit networks, sharing childcare and domestic tasks, and participating in countless other ways in an "art of citizenship" that contrib-

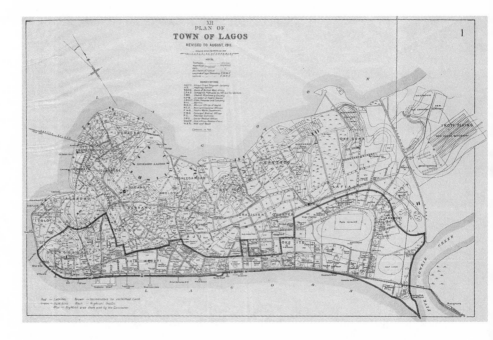

FIGURE 1.1. "Plan of Town of Lagos," showing night-soil areas and location of latrines, including information about different quarters of town. PRO CO 147/651, "Plan of Town of Lagos Sanitary Report 1013: Map 1," *Plan of Town of Lagos Revised to August 1911.* Reproduced with kind permission of The National Archives (U.K.).

uted to later urban theorists' suggestion that "people are infrastructure" in global African cities.[14] Rather, in the first two decades of the twentieth century, the relatively unplanned and mixed urban spaces that had hosted previous decades of African-European contact as inhabitants, traders, churchgoers, educators, and bureaucrats came under scrutiny by the emergent and newly constituted public works departments, town councils, government health boards, and sanitary inspectorates, all on grounds of public health and sanitation.[15]

This chapter seeks to understand the cultural processes by which Lagosians came to be regarded by British officials as sources of contagion and dirt in the early twentieth century, and how, as an undiscerning racial ideology grew to dominate municipal policy decisions in Lagos and other West African cities at the turn of the century, the daily practices of urban residents challenged, withstood, or simply bypassed the colonizer's scientific and at times messianic vision of how colonial cities should be laid out and managed.

The topic of racism in colonial town planning has preoccupied historians of African public health and urbanization since Megan Vaughan's pioneering study of the ways biomedicine in East and Central Africa "constructed 'the African' [as . . .] an object of knowledge," and redefined spaces of sickness and health, particularly in relation to the remapping of towns.[16] Numerous scholars since Vaughan have pointed out that a new way of seeing African cities and their inhabitants through the prism of tropical hygiene occurred in the early twentieth century, as British ideas about municipal government and town planning from the Victorian era were grouted with imperial ideology and exported to the colonies.[17]

How these European imaginaries and sources came to be attached to African bodies remains a key question in this chapter, as in other scholars' work, because in displacing dirt onto a homogenized African subject, and in holding that representative figure individually accountable for public health failures through his or her "natural uncleanly habits," British officials failed to recognize several factors: first, the cultural diversity of coastal cities with constant in- and outflows of migrants from numerous social and cultural backgrounds; second, the numbers of educated Africans for whom Victorian principles of sanitation had become goals for municipal modernity; and, third, their own structural and bureaucratic roles as curators of the very environments in which the most dangerous types of "filth disease" could thrive.[18] Rather, they preferred to blame the recipients of their public health messages for failing to understand the complexity of the science. As one British official patronizingly put it in the 1910s, "The whole theory of public hygiene in West Africa must be puzzling to the uneducated native but this is a difficulty which can only be cured by time and patience."[19]

Scholars with expertise in historical epidemiology, critical race theory, and imperial urban history have noted these conjunctions and displacements many times over.[20] As yet relatively unexamined are the ways in which culturally specific perceptions of the environment among the diverse populations of West African towns—not just the ruling and educated elites—shaped the reception (not the implementation) of colonial public health initiatives. The tensions between the singular "native" as a construct of colonial discourse and urban dwellers' diverse understandings of urban hygiene is palpable at many levels in the sources consulted for this chapter. Such tensions destabilize the absolute power one might otherwise attribute to public health officials based on the rhetorical strength of their reports. One should not, in other words, believe the "devious discourse" preserved in the documents that officials submitted to the imperial filing system.[21]

Especially in its early days, as David Gordon observes in his medical history of King William's Town, South Africa, in the 1850s, "the story [is . . .] of the vicissitudes of an encounter between Europeans and Africans struggling to control knowledge and resources of healing techniques in the context of changing political alignments."[22] In this respect, the interesting question is not about the way "the native" was fabricated and woven into popular discourse by the colonial authorities, but how and why colonial ideas about dirt succeeded in some quarters, and failed in others, to attach to urban dwellers' bodies, and the ways in which these ideas were mediated among different sectors of the African urban population.

The new discourse of tropical hygiene in the early twentieth century was part of a set of historically specific struggles for power, land, and resources that included local agents such as chiefs and customary authorities, educated professionals, newspaper editors, teachers, sanitary workers, traders, and churchgoers alongside the main European socioeconomic groups in West African cities such as government officials, produce traders, and missionaries.[23] In itself, colonial public health comprised a dynamic political space where control was exercised by and through multicultural actors ranging from the greatly feared *woléwolé* (Yoruba: African sanitary inspectors) who had the power to evict people from their homes through to the chief medical officers in colonial towns.[24]

Public health legislation and policies were as much about building state institutions and creating governable subjects as they were about improving local residents' living conditions, and the colonial archives highlight this side of the story.[25] Often borrowed from India, where "filth diseases"— diseases of the poor—recurred in cities, these regulations and ordinances laid out a plethora of measures for dealing with urban "nuisances" such as unapproved building works, illegal cesspools, and overcrowded lodgings.[26] From the outset, the rules were invasive, including the right of entry for sanitary officers into people's homes and the removal of material deemed to be "rubbish" from dwellings and compounds.

This was an era of sanitary micromanagement in Britain's colonies, with officials stepping over the threshold into people's personal spaces to prohibit animal slaughter and the burial of family members within compounds, and to stipulate the minimum distance between dwellings on private land.[27] By the late 1920s in Lagos, after two decades of "re-planning, development and improvement" ordinances, the Municipal Board of Health in Lagos could boast of its powers to impose renovation or demolition orders on any building deemed "unfit for human habitation."[28] City

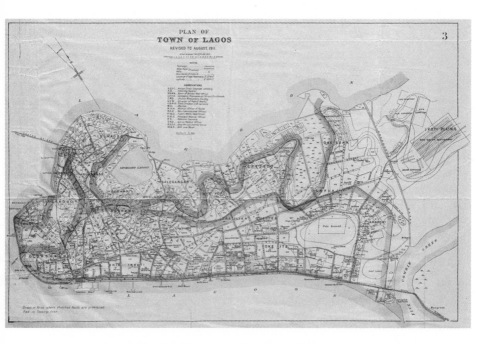

FIGURE 1.2. "Plan of Town of Lagos," showing area where thatched roofs were prohibited. PRO CO 147/651, "Plan of Town of Lagos Sanitary Report 1013: Map 3," *Plan of Town of Lagos Revised to August 1911.* Reproduced with kind permission of The National Archives (U.K.).

maps meticulously laid out sectors where thatched roofs were prohibited and where water pumps and public latrines were located (fig. 1.2).[29]

In practice, however, the regulations were chaotic and contradictory, involving multiple departments, medical professionals, and administrators, sometimes in open rivalry with one another.[30] Rules were often flouted by chief sanitary inspectors themselves, and the powers conferred on *wolé-wolé* created conditions for malpractice: throughout the municipality, accusations of harassment by officials were rife. But this lack of coherence at street level also enabled widespread local disregard for the rules, and out of this disregard one can build parallel histories of colonial public health that give space to African urban residents as rational actors.

Fecal Positions

In one particular area of public health more than any other, African urban residents were homogenized as a group by the colonial authorities and blamed for the sanitary risks they allegedly created. By refusing to use designated municipal latrines in contexts of urban overcrowding, and in preferring to use "the bush" for defecation, Africans were continuously blamed by medical officials for creating conditions ripe for parasites, bacteria, and the "filth diseases"—tuberculosis, cholera, smallpox, typhoid, and bubonic plague—to spread rapidly from person to person.[31] "What we have been doing in Lagos of late," explained Sir William MacGregor, a qualified physician and governor of Lagos Colony (1899–1902), "is increasing the number of public latrines. In respect of these we require to use a very large quantity of disinfectants, and I am afraid from what I hear we do not use sufficient at the present time."[32] Over in Cape Coast, colonial Ghana, Dr. Matthew Logan Taylor of the Liverpool School of Tropical Medicine reported, "There are very few cesspits, public latrines having been erected throughout the town; but as the number of these is insufficient for the requirements of the population the natives make use of the beach and the bush."[33] By 1913 the situation was no better. Gold Coast governor Sir Hugh Clifford (1912–19) reported, "The construction and maintenance of public latrines ought rightly to form part of the duties of the Accra Town Council [but . . .] that body is not possessed of funds sufficient to cope with this public necessity."[34]

Colonial sanitary officials produced reports on all aspects of their work, leaving behind a thick paper trail of their engagements with urban populations. These archives are packed with examples of African noncompliance with municipal building regulations and sanitary rules. Indeed, the archives contain so many examples of enduring local architectural, building, hygienic, and domestic practices between the 1900s and the 1920s that, if one reads against the dismissive Eurocentric tone pervading the documents, it is possible to assemble the fragments of nonelite Lagosians' urban lives in the early twentieth century into a sketchy picture of domestic environments outside the colonial optic.[35] Unlike the African-owned newspapers discussed in more detail in chapter 3, where editors and correspondents often enthusiastically endorsed municipal infrastructure projects such as the provision of drains, roads, latrines, water pipes, and subsidized housing, and held colonial and metropolitan authorities to account for the nonimplementation of public health initiatives in their cities, the documents available in the official archives contain hints about existing local practices, almost always framed in critical, dismissive terms as requiring transformation. The presence of the "native" body in the archives disrupts the ostensibly rational public health discourse of ordinances designed to prevent a repetition of the atrocious living conditions endured by British working classes in industrial cities.

With few exceptions, colonial officials saw African cities as straining under the weight of uncontrollable in-migrations of newcomers looking for opportunities—not all of them legitimate—in the urban cash economy. From this typically elitist perspective on urban expansion, Lagos, like so many other colonial African cities, appeared to be increasingly susceptible to diseases spread by the combination of incomers' traditional prejudices and residual poor health, ignorance, and lack of education, over against the healthy modern lifestyles of the policy-making elites. In his report on the sanitary condition of West African towns, delivered to the Colonial Office in 1909, the influential medic, advocate of racial segregation in colonial towns, and sanitary champion after whom a latrine was named, Professor W. J. Simpson, advocated "complete control of streets, buildings, and open spaces" by colonial governments to prevent local people from "the construction of their huts and houses on unsuitable sites and in such a manner as to be unhealthy [and . . .] congested."[36] Simpson praised Lagos for being "well laid out in its European and Brazilian quarters, and in a few of the parts occupied by the better class natives, but the remainder, with the exception of a few good streets here and there, is very much congested and in many parts consists of a conglomeration of huts and houses and a labyrinth of narrow lanes."[37]

In towns and cities throughout British West Africa in the early twentieth century, resident African populations quietly resisted the spatial politics and control of bodies produced by Western public health interventions. "We generally observe two things about municipalities," wrote Ronald Ross in his reflections on sanitation in Nigeria in 1922: "the excellence of their sanitary by-laws and the completeness with which the public ignores them."[38] "The Natives are urged to keep their towns clean but in most cases they pay little attention to such except when they expect a visit from the DC," complained the chief medical officer of Lagos in 1909.[39] The governor of Gambia, Henry Lionel Galway (1911–14), agreed: "The majority of [Africans . . .] really seem to prefer living in insanitary surroundings, and are very averse to the introduction of additional sanitary precautions."[40] If a municipal ordinance was deemed impractical or expensive, local residents would ignore it.[41] As the senior sanitary officer for Lagos stated, "Having to deal with a people who have, to all intents and purposes, no belief in practical sanitation renders the matter [of European health in West Africa] more difficult to deal with, and makes it all the more necessary to take every precaution which is possible."[42] Reviewing all this evidence in 1913, the secretary of state for the colonies concluded that in cities like Lagos with "a large and old-established native population," residents "tend to obstruct effective measures" for sanitation.[43]

Disobedience, disregard, obstruction, disrespect, aversion: these terms recur in reports sent to London by senior officials in the early years of the twentieth century. As Dr. Logan Taylor of Sierra Leone commented about West African urban residents at the turn of the century, "Natives do not see the necessity for cleanliness, being quite content to remain as they are."[44] If colonial sanitation was about establishing colonial modes of governmentality alongside new ways of living among urban populations, the public health regime of the early twentieth century can be seen to have produced urban residents who resisted the rules and regulations, and had "little or no respect for Western values."[45] African urban residents, according to R. H. Kennan, senior medical officer of Sierra Leone, were "not infrequently easily led, but difficult to drive, particularly on account of the power of traditional prejudice, [and] partly because of the inadequate means of compulsion available at the command of the executive."[46]

With insufficient labor, finance, or public will behind them, the multitude of public health regulations proved to be ineffectual until the 1920s. Townspeople would have been perfectly aware—from visual evidence if not from the repeated complaints in annual reports from sanitary officers between 1900 and the 1910s, reprinted and debated in the African press—that local inspectorates lacked the personnel and resources to enforce the rules. Tensions between municipal rules and the daily lives of urban Africans surfaced repeatedly in relation to house building, the disposal of waste, defecatory practices, and the keeping of animals and perishable goods. Local residents offered many reasons for noncompliance with town council regulations: in some cases, the rule-breakers insisted their villages were outside the boundaries set by town councils, rendering them exempt from jurisdiction; in other cases, residents claimed outsider status on religious grounds or as immigrants from other countries to do "pretty much as they please[d] in the way of building new houses, wells etc."[47] Common sense and practical considerations combined with cunning to obstruct local obedience to regulations that few personnel were there to enforce.

Seeing West African towns through the Eurocentric framework of sanitation, colonial reformers failed to allow for the complexity of locally defined spaces, and they rarely acknowledged that particular areas of town, or particular categories of resident, might be more vulnerable than others to diseases associated with poverty, labor, ethnic stigmatization, and overcrowding.[48] At one level, their observations that local residents obstructed European public health efforts are accurate: numerous Lagosians simply did not comply with the new rules. But the interpretive frameworks and conclusions adopted by government officials and their supporters—that Africans per se were to blame for poor urban sanitation and required coercive or persuasive reeducation by those who knew best—failed to explain the structural and behavioral reasons why many ordinary Lagosians (and their contemporaries in other colonial African cities) did not always comply with governmental sanitary missions against local domestic practices. If public health messaging was in the best interests of everybody, why did some urban publics choose to ignore it and continue as before, rejecting the new messages and abiding by alternative codes of behavior?

If one reads British town-planning documents for the very rationale their authors dismissed as "ignorance" and "prejudice," it is possible to identify alternative values at street level, as well as the presence of economic and other explanations for disease that militated against the local uptake of health measures. Open-air defecation in scrubland and along the shoreline would have minimized and scattered the risk of infection, whereas single-site latrines with multiple users were laboratories for bacteria, parasites, and a panoply of other diseases.[49] If a chief cause of the spread of "filth diseases" was infected excrement, one can identify a clear rationale for urban residents' disregard for the rules in believing that excreta scattered above ground formed a less potent risk than their concentration in dirty latrines.[50] This is not to suggest that an African urban population was free of disease, or that European epidemiology failed to bring benefits that were recognized locally, but that African dwellings and domestic practices were not nearly as lethal as represented by many white urban residents in the colonial period. For urban residents who wished to avoid the outlay of scarce resources on the installation and maintenance of toilets, free-range defecation was second-to-none. Ross admitted as much at the conference on sanitation between influential British produce traders with interests in Lagos and Sir William MacGregor, governor of Lagos, in 1903. In response to the traders' complaints about the public health hazard of unburied excreta, he commented that "[you] complain that the soil is soaked with sewage, but I doubt whether this causes the number of deaths attributed to it. The organic matter disappears in a very short time, when exposed to the heat of a tropical sun."[51] Three decades later, in the context of transformed urban environments with significant government investment in public health infrastructure, inspection, and education, this confession remains as tenacious as ever: "It is shameful to have to own it, but the more primitive a village the cleaner it usually is."[52]

An incriminating admission runs through the public health archives in the first two decades of the twentieth century. Whether describing the overflowing (or nonexistent) sewers and drains in colonial cities, or the inadequate (or nonexistent) public latrines with dirty facilities shared by too many people, or the insufficient public funding for clean water supply, municipal rubbish clearance, and the disinfection of latrines and sewers, time and again the origin of urban "filth diseases" was traced to systemic failures in government rather than to local African (mal)practices. From their own accounts, sanitary officials found that the sources of filth and contagion often originated in the very measures that were regarded as the solution to Africans' supposed lack of sanitation.[53] "Most of the tenants of the houses say that their rubbish has not been removed for years," Ross reported on his visit to Freetown in 1902.[54] "One bullock cart is all they possess for removing the refuse from the dustbins," confirmed Logan Taylor in his inspection of Freetown for malarial larvae.[55] In 1900, fifty-one of the fifty-three public wells in Lagos were found to contain bacterial contaminants known to cause dysentery.[56] In Freetown, a public health disaster was caused by the government's failure to maintain existing infrastructure: on visiting the city in the rainy season, Ross found "the faulty nature of the municipal drains" was to blame for a "shocking . . . condition of affairs" in which "the streets were practically marshes," endangering public health.[57] Cape Coast in colonial Ghana was no better. In his "Report on the Sanitary Conditions of Cape Coast Town," Logan Taylor highlighted the poor condition of the drains and the "objectionable" state of the thirteen pan latrine sites available for public use. "Great carelessness exists in regard to the cleaning of the latrines, the warders often leaving them in a very filthy condition and blaming the matter on the scavengers whose duty they say it is to come after them and clean up."[58] Additionally, "indiscriminate building has been going on for a long time and no notice seems to be taken of it."[59] Meanwhile, in Lagos, two prominent African doctors—Oguntola Sapara and J. M. Dalziel—presented a conference paper in 1918 that "incriminated overcrowding, defective ventilation and mass ignorance, for which they prescribed corrective measures, not only to combat tuberculosis in particular, but in general to improve the environmental sanitation of Lagos."[60]

This counter-reading of the public health archive was present from the outset of colonial town planning. The proliferation of diseases like tuberculosis in tropical cities had everything to do with the rapid urbanization accompanying colonial contact, compounded by the lack of investment in public health infrastructure.[61] In 1901, a commission of inquiry into infant mortality under Sir William MacGregor, governor of Lagos from 1899 to 1904, recognized that the "filth diseases" were exacerbated by practices introduced from overseas, incubated in urban areas through multiple municipal failures to provide facilities and infrastructure for African urban laborers. MacGregor's commission found that, among the indirect causes of child death, were "local conditions [in . . .] certain parts of this Town," including "over-heating of their house by day and by night through the use of corrugated iron alone for the roofs," and "crowding together of a lot of small houses preventing any ventilation."[62] The "great white plague" of tuberculosis lurked just around the corner of such homes.[63]

An outcome of the colonial (mis)recognition of West African building materials as harboring vermin and disease was that houses made of local materials such as timber, shingle, bamboo, and adobe were demolished and replaced with houses "built in rows behind one another on sidelong ground," with corrugated iron roofs and concrete.[64] As MacGregor recognized in 1901, these were hotter and unhealthier than the dwellings they replaced. By the mid-1940s, the consequences of mass-produced urban housing built to European standards were apparent. In his inquiry into West African governments' provision of housing for the urban labor force, Major (Sir) Granville St. John Orde Browne (1883–1947) described the previous thirty years of colonial building projects as "iron and concrete Government cells," and "recommend[ed] strongly that the Colonial Governments should get away from the [construction of . . .] rows of concrete cells with iron roofs," which are "entirely unsuitable to local conditions."[65]

Officials admitted that a lack of investment combined with too few facilities and staff to pose major obstacles to sanitary progress. Logan Taylor stated in 1902, "It is these insanitary conditions more than purely climatical influences that are to blame for the unhealthiness of the West Coast."[66] As Doctors Sapara, Dalziel, and Logan Taylor all recognized, Eurocentric town planning ideals from 1900 onward reproduced some of the dystopic, insanitary spaces that characterized "slumland" in Victorian-era British inner cities and contributed to the environmental problems of subsequent years.[67] In the absence of mass sewage and drainage provision, within a short space of time these square houses built to European blueprints with tin roofs and multihousehold shared latrines duplicated the worst features of British inner cities.[68]

European officials' displacement of responsibility onto African urban subjects for the incubation of urban disease characterizes colonial public health initiatives from the early 1900s to the early 1950s to the extent that it can be regarded as a constitutive feature of public health policy in West Africa.[69] Blaming service users rather than service providers, and attempting to produce behavioral change through legislation and propaganda, health officials failed to see dirt and contagion as systemic, as integral to the colonial vision of African cities, and as produced in large part by the development of the conurbations that were integral to the "three Cs" of colonialism (Civilization, Commerce, and Christianity). Such systemic and institutional culpability was masked at all levels by political officers' enforcement of rules and insistence on behavioral change among individual Africans at street level. Urban populations were held to blame: "If each and every person in this town [Lagos] will only be strictly clean in his or her house, food, drinking, clothing and habits, and . . . if every one do his or her best in this direction, more good will be accomplished in Sanitation in one year than can otherwise be brought about by years of evaded and opposed Sanitary Legislation."[70]

In their reports, British sanitary officers were quick to list the African domestic behaviors responsible for incubating contagious diseases, encouraging vermin, and harboring malarial mosquito larvae. Of especial concern were swish pits left to gather water, or used for the disposal of household refuse, after the extraction of clay to make bricks and plaster for buildings; "fetish pots" dedicated to Eṣu and other Yoruba deities, and water storage vessels exposed in compounds with ill-fitting lids; unburied excreta on the surface of common land and shorelines near crowded urban settlements; animals kept in the vicinity of dwellings; the use of bamboo and palm thatch—considered to be a vermin magnet as well as a fire hazard—rather than corrugated iron for the roofs of close-packed dwellings; pit latrines and cesspools situated in or near domestic quarters; and organic and inorganic refuse discarded near people's homes.[71]

European residents persistently regarded their poorer, cash-strapped African neighbors as more dangerous to public health and less clean than their own superior households, with money for imported commodities such as soap. "I . . . have the ill-fortune to occupy quarters in the center of what is recognized as a public latrine," complained Sir Hugh Clifford, governor of colonial Ghana in 1913, of his residence, the old Christiansborg slave fortress surrounded by a shoreline used for defecation by locals in the absence of public latrines.[72] At the "Sanitation of Lagos" conference convened in 1903 by Liverpool and Manchester produce traders, the governor was presented with a catalogue of accusations against locals for their contaminating behavior. One trader, M. E. Cohen claimed that, "with regard to native dwellings[, there] is one close to our house in Lagos, and there can be no doubt that the dirt and the smell arising from them are not only a nuisance, but are injurious to the health of Europeans."[73]

Yet health inspectors' reports often directly contradict this connection of cleanliness with European dwellings, and dirt with African homes. Poorer African households generally produced organic, compostable waste that rotted rapidly, if pungently, in the tropical climate, in contrast to imported tins, cans, and bottles of Western produce that, when discarded, provided habitats for mosquito larvae to thrive. In this respect, the consumption of imported products was more likely than indigenous consumption to propagate mosquito-borne diseases. Even when the poorer members of communities had the opportunity to collect discarded bottles and tins for reuse as storage containers in their own households, they remained safer than wealthier households: "The natives here are not rich and consequently have very little rubbish about their houses and also very few water casks," reported Logan Taylor of a trading village in the Sherbro District of Sierra Leone, "the result being that I hardly saw a culex or shegonyia [sic] larva in the place."[74] These examples were not simply confined to rural communities lacking exposure to overcrowded cities and global trade. In 1956, a mosquito survey at Ikeja, Lagos, by the government entomologist identified the cause of a surprising lack of *Anopheles* larvae in one part of an otherwise infested stream at Iregun: "There was a lack of larvae in parts of the stream used by African women doing their washing, this presumably is due to the larvicidal properties of the soap."[75] The villages surrounding the GRA also "seemed to be clear of breeding, although there was much open water in the vicinity," but it was in such constant use that larvae were absent.[76] The same could not be said of Ikeja Police Station beside the GRA itself: this municipal building "proved to be the main source of breeding" for diverse insects and vermin. "The general condition of the sanitation of the station was exceedingly bad," with "dirt and debris" everywhere and un-cleared "rubbish heaps" harboring maggots, and "open water butts and tin cans" all around.[77]

Several scholars have pointed out that colonial infrastructure had the potential to produce, rather than to solve, the conditions under which "filth diseases" thrived.[78] Institutional buildings such as magistrates' courts, asylums, police buildings and prisons, schools, hospitals, and sometimes even the governors' own residences, were sources of mosquito larvae and vermin. Perhaps the most incriminating example of this imperial institutional culpability in the early twentieth century was the discovery of mosquitoes "in large numbers under the Medical Officer's quarters" in Axim in 1912.[79]

Governor Hugh Clifford of colonial Ghana was the unlikely mouthpiece for attempting to persuade ministers in London of their blindness toward the sources of contagion.[80] What might seem like an "unsightly collection of mud houses" in "inconvenient proximity to one another" in local villages and towns should be seen afresh, he argued, for "the precincts are carefully and regularly swept and those of the interiors which I visited were in excellent order."[81] While Sir Richard James Wilkinson, governor of Sierra Leone (1916–21; 1921–22), criticized the "squalid appearance" of West Africa's expanding towns, caused by the "obstructive and unsightly buildings" erected by local builders, Clifford cleverly reused the aesthetic category of the "ugly" to expose and critique racialized colonial town planning discourse. He suggested that an aesthetic response to African dwellings lay at the heart of the Colonial Office's most radical town-planning initiative, racial segregation, rather than a demonstrable lack of hygiene in locally constructed dwellings.[82] Clifford corrected his colleagues' misperception of the health impact of local buildings made from mud, wood, and thatch: West African buildings are "curiously ugly," he stated, "but what they lack of picturesque attractions they undoubtedly make up for by a notable degree of cleanliness and regard for sanitary requirements."[83] In this way, Clifford repositioned locally constructed buildings as aesthetically inferior to the architectural tastes of British observers, but showed how the policy of racial segregation, which offered the most extreme form of removal of "native" dirt from the vicinity of Europeans, ultimately stemmed from a category error whereby ugliness was mistaken for filth.

While African residents' voices and explanations are absent from colonial reports, one can identify in the archives a range of logics adopted by urban citizens seeking to survive in crowded cities. If there was widespread reluctance among local communities to change their sanitary behavior, then residents' open refusal to abide by colonial rules may have reflected and commented on the lack of resources and personnel for the implementation of public health measures, as well as the mass adoption of healthier alternatives. In particular, when local practices were sustained in the face of punitive consequences including the confiscation of goods and livestock, or the prosecution of householders, one can regard them as part of a collective, deliberate politics of noncompliance in colonial cities. In some cases, in the face of threats of prosecution and the visible—if sparse—presence of local sanitary enforcers, the unwillingness of individual urban dwellers to adopt "modern" methods of personal and social hygiene and sanitation may actually have helped to preserve public health in contexts where European-style latrines and building materials exacerbated the spread of disease among the urban population.

These local modes of reasonable urban behavior are not connected to the colonial state, nor do they necessarily recognize its authority; nor do they revolve around or invest in British messages about an improved future for modern African subjects. While one cannot simply delete the imperialist tone from the colonial public health archives, or glue together unmediated examples of African urban practice, it is possible to read quite literally "against the drain" in official documents and treat the many instances of supposed local prejudice as examples of African nonconformity with European sanitary measures, marking the persistence both of recalcitrance toward government and of established alternatives to the colonial state that were regarded by their agents as more practical and healthier than those described in the rules.

2

Malaria:
Lines in the Dirt

The man who shall successfully . . . find a cure for the fevers depleting our colonies and dependencies in many tropical countries, and shall make the tropics livable for a white man, who shall reduce the risk of disease to something like the ordinary average, that man will do more for the world, more for the British Empire than the man who adds a new province to the wide dominions of the Queen.
—JOSEPH CHAMBERLAIN

Improvement in the health of Europeans is absolutely the first desideratum for general improvement in these colonies.
—RONALD ROSS

Circling above the sanitary-minded governments of British West Africa in the early twentieth century was a scientific discovery that reduced many European colonial officials to a state of dread about the daily practices of locals in the vicinity of their residences. Developing on the work of Giovanni Battista Grassi and the germ theorists of the late nineteenth century, in 1898 Ronald Ross announced his discovery that the *Anopheles* mosquito transmitted the malaria parasite into human blood.[1] The noxious mists and vapors of nineteenth-century tropical disease theory did not, however, evaporate with this discovery: rather, they coagulated in human form. In place of the morbid landscape that characterized Western imaginings of West African nature and its characterization as the "white man's grave," colonial officials found more than the mosquito as the transmitter of deadly fevers to white people. In the decade after Ross's discovery, Europeans identified a singular human entity as the actual source of malaria, freely circulating in cosmopolitan urban spaces and transmitting the parasites to the mosquitoes that went on to infect the white population.[2]

Without gender, social status, ethnicity, religion, or rank, "the native" came to stand in for the mosquito as the visible signifier of West Africa's biggest killer. From people's cooking and house-cleaning practices to their bathing, toilet, and refuse-disposal habits, everything ordinary in African daily life came to be regarded as potentially deadly to Europeans because of local people's capacity, first, to house *Anopheles* mosquitoes and larvae in and around their dwellings, and second, more unnervingly, to host the malaria parasite asymptomatically in their blood.[3] Interracial sociality, including the proximity of Africans as neighbors, coworkers, service users, and servants, started to be regarded as an extreme example of contaminating behavior as this fear of Africans started to spread, especially in medical provision where rooms previously "used indiscriminately for the medical examination of European and native patients" were suddenly deemed to be potentially deadly, and where the "good, airy rooms" occupied by European patients in the hospital were rendered toxic by the "native wards practically adjoin[ing] them."[4]

This chapter examines the alarming speed at which advances in tropical epidemiology attracted racist ideology as European doctors and government officials attempted to find practical applications for breakthroughs in tropical health science and to imagine dirt-free municipalities without the sources of contagion. Europeans' fear of death became racialized through the etiology of malaria. "The native population act as the reservoir of the infection, and infect the successive swarms of mosquitoes hatched throughout the year," wrote J. Balfour-Kirk, one-time director of medical services in the Gold Coast, in one of his pamphlets for general circulation in Africa.[5] "This is the reason why the dwellings of Europeans should be located as far as possible from native settlements."[6]

The displacement of malaria from the mosquito into the colonial subject's blood can be seen as one of British imperialism's most far-reaching misapplications of science, with significant social and political consequences because the racialization of malaria led directly to proposals for the compulsory removal of Africans—on grounds of health—from the vicinity of Europeans.[7] If mosquitoes could not be eradicated in urban areas, the argument ran, then the local hosts of malarial parasites, with their bad blood, should be placed at a safe distance from Europeans. "Incomplete segregation, like incomplete mosquito-proofing, gives false security, and is only a little less dangerous than none at all," warned Francis Gethin Hopkins, principal medical officer of Accra in 1913.[8]

From an epidemiological perspective, while any African who had survived malaria became a carrier of the malaria parasite, often asymptomatically, so too did any European who had suffered from malarial fever.[9] As Sir Hugh Clifford observed in rejecting proposals for the racial segregation of Europeans from Africans, "Any one of these Europeans may introduce infection into any area inhabited exclusively by other Europeans, no matter how carefully it may be segregated from the buildings used as native dwellings."[10] Larger numbers of Africans than Europeans carried the malaria parasite with protective immunity simply because there were larger numbers of Africans in colonial West Africa, but any community with low transmission levels would have a higher vulnerability to infection.[11] The notion that Africans had a greater capacity than Europeans to incubate the malaria parasite in their blood exacerbated the rapidity with which racial politics were distilled into Ross's discovery, producing a homogeneous and bad-blooded "native" in the minds of colonial health officials that directly affected town planning in West Africa and exemplified the "crass lumping of colonial subjects by an imperial power" identified by Mary Sutphen and Bridie Andrews in their introduction to *Medicine and Colonial Identity*.[12]

In spite of his claims to scientific objectivity, Nobel laureate Ross was no more innocent of the imperialist racial prejudice that attached to early twentieth-century epidemiology than other colonial medics and their scientifically untrained peers in colonial government and administration. In his memoirs of 1922, Ross lightheartedly described how, in order to demonstrate the practical advantages of insect netting to a fellow white official, he deliberately exposed his Nigerian servant to malarial infection one night in Ibadan: "To test [Dr] Strachan's theory [that there are many mosquitoes in Ibadan] I put one of our servants for the night into an old net with many holes in it. Next morning, sure enough, there were five or six gorged *Anopheles* within his net. If we had slept unprotected we might have been bitten by scores of them. This makes a good kind of mosquito-trap for testing the real frequency of *Anopheles* anywhere."[13] Narrating it as an amusing anecdote, Ross did not consider the ethical implications of his experiment because his "guinea pig" was both an African and a servant.

To many white residents, the danger lay not simply in insect-borne diseases where the installation of insect mesh in European houses and the use of mosquito netting at night would help to rectify the problem.[14] Many Europeans, including doctors, identified health hazards in the very smells emanating from African settlements in the vicinity of their quarters, and mistook their own olfactory reactions for clinical truths. "The quarters for the officials are . . . either surrounded by natives or natives are in the immediate proximity. The odours arising from the native quarters are anything but conducive to the good health of the Europeans," reported Dr. Matthew Logan Taylor from Cape Coast in 1902.[15] Tropical miasmas had not lost their notorious potency in the racial discourse of the early twentieth century, but, as with tropical fevers, they had been attached to a new human source. "The noise, dirt, and stenches" of West African cities such as Lagos made them quite unsuitable as habitats for European officials, in the view of Dr. Henry Strachan, chief medical officer of Lagos, for whom racial segregation was imperative as a remedy. Europeans required state protection, in his view, from township "air filled with floating particles of excrement" and from "the dirt, odours, and noise, due to the presence of large bodies of natives in close proximity."[16] These suspicions of contagion morphed into popular opinions and were aired with as much conviction as medical truths. "The natives live in a very densely-populated part of the town, in mud huts and timber houses (though they cannot be called houses)," a Manchester trader and long-term Lagos resident, John Walkden, explained during the deputation of British produce traders to Joseph Chamberlain, secretary of state, on March 15, 1901, to request sanitary improvements. Walkden added, "I am sure that a good deal of the evil comes from that direction."[17] The term "proximity" attracted adjectives, and these were never favorable. "Dangerously close proximity" was how Gold Coast governor Sir Hugh Clifford described the location of the proposed new European hospital in relation to the "lunatic asylum, which is, of course, exclusively inhabited by natives."[18]

The constant use of the word "proximity" about the people whose lands they occupied, whose labor they employed, and whose habits and lifestyles they sought to remodel, captures the contradictions of a colonial system that claimed to respect African customs and traditions, and to preserve "native" political authority through the system of Indirect Rule and its precursors, while regarding African health and hygiene as universally dirty, and seeking to transform the most intimate areas of people's daily lives into recognizably British patterns.[19] Indeed, the word "proximity" recurs so often in official reports about disease and public health from the early twentieth century that it demands investigation, not least for its communication of a set of racialized visceral responses to multicultural urban cohabitation.

"Proximity" is the term that marks and maps the bodily presence of the unknown other in the form of a query about spaces and quantities: how near is the foreign body, how far away, how many are there, and for how long will they be in the vicinity of the pen-holding European who seeks to monitor their presence? More than a marker simply of external space, proximity also records the moment when strangers become neighbors through their sensory presence. Living "cheek by jowl" with Europeans, visible, odoriferous, and audible, the proximate other was too close not to be in sensory contact with the colonial observer.[20]

Anxious Europeans felt they were being forced literally to absorb the unknown other through their physical membranes and pores, breathing the other's air. In reaction, racist fears of bodily contamination were abundant in their descriptions of Lagos.[21] "There are many evil-smelling towns in this country," reported Governor Sir William MacGregor on a tour of the Lagos Protectorate in 1900, "yet the inhabitants do not seem to object" to the "fetid" atmosphere.[22] Of particular concern to one chief medical officer were the "offensive effluvia" given off by "the very rapid decomposition of the vegetable matter that accumulates even in a day" in the surface drains leading from African residences toward, but not always into, the Lagoon.[23] If in Britain, "people prefer, if they can, to live away from their work and away from the neighbourhood of the poorer class of dwelling," then "when the inhabitants of the poorer quarters are natives of West Africa, the desire is naturally intensified. The noise, smell, and dirt of a native quarter are not calculated to smooth tempers already tried by hard work in an uncongenial climate."[24]

Where Mary Douglas and her successors defined dirt as a particular type of intrusive matter that must be taken out of circulation for society to function, racist colonial discourse displaced dirt onto the proximate "native," regarding the latter as the source of contamination requiring removal, in the manner of waste, in order for white residents to achieve peace of mind. Subjects replaced objects in this anthropomorphic, racially homogenizing discourse.[25] In one spectacular example of this displacement from pollutant to person, at the sanitation conference of 1903 one produce trader informed the governor of Lagos, "I think some alteration might be made in the system of allowing the natives to carry away 'night soil,'" explaining that "I am quite sure deaths among Europeans have been caused by this alone."[26] This trader's outrageous misunderstanding of the source of "filth diseases" located the cause of death in the stigmatized figure of the African night-soil worker rather than in the European excreta the worker carried away to be dumped, and, in the process, starkly revealed the ways in which racist fantasies came to displace the etiology of disease.[27]

The work of introducing the "three Cs" of Civilization, Commerce, and Christianity to the four corners of the world involved spatial proximity to culturally distant indigenes. Unlike the concept of disgust in the traders' narratives examined in the introductory chapter, which often involved descriptions and lists in an effort to achieve full transparency for the cultural other, proximity describes a state of intercultural relationality in which the nearness of the body and commodities of the other are perceived with suspicion about what they hide beneath their surfaces. This "other" is not allowed to come inside in the form of hospitality, empathy, desire, or shared consumption. Unlike the sheer physicality of traders' experiences as they traveled through diverse host cultures handling local products and absorbing the other's smells and tastes, proximity conveys the problematic truth that the European is neither at home nor a traveler in the colonial setting, but a foreign body standing out noticeably in the midst of a multiplicity of locals.[28] As an expression of urban relationality in multicultural settings, therefore, proximity describes multicultural urban spaces of residential cohabitation where nobody is fully other and none is fully known to the other, and where, moreover, foreign bodies are porous rather than sealed.

Running freely through the dwellings of all classes and cultural groups in colonial West African cities, playing havoc with government health controls, children came to be regarded by the authorities as a significant public health hazard. "The malarialised infant population forms one of the constant sources of infection," Dr. Strachan warned in a paper for the African Trade Section of the Liverpool Chamber of Commerce in January 1901.[29] These unprosecutable nonadults were "insanitary nuisances" of the first order in that they could not simply be expelled from towns like other "nuisances" such as alleged prostitutes.[30] Children were, in the view of early twentieth-century medical officials, more dangerous than mosquitoes, circulating freely in large numbers with their contaminated blood, passing malaria and yellow fever to the mosquitoes that subsequently infected Europeans. In the busy railway suburb of Ebute Metta, Lagos, the general manager of the Railway Headquarters wrote an emergency circular to all staff: "Yellow Fever and Malaria are endemic in a number of Africans."[31] As a consequence, he stated, a number of rules were to be enforced with immediate effect, including the prohibition of Africans from the "European Compound" between 6:00 p.m. and 6:00 a.m., and the exclusion at all times of the day of Africans not in possession of a "compound permit"; most importantly, "African children from now on are not permitted to stay in any European compound at any hour, day or night."[32]

Medically, children are neither more nor less likely to transmit the malaria parasite to mosquitoes than adults, and, until the age of seven or eight, with the development of partial immunity, they are much more likely to die from the disease.[33] The fact that infants were more vulnerable than adults to mortality from malaria was ignored by these commentators, who instead feared the heavily parasitized condition of children and its impact on the European population's own health.[34] The secretary of state for the colonies, Viscount Lewis Harcourt, had no doubt about the scientific validity of his medical experts' view when he stated, in 1913, that "native children . . . are recognised as the chief 'reservoirs' of malarial infection, playing a far more important part than the adult native."[35] Arising directly from this vision of the contaminated West African child, Harcourt's proposed policy of formal racial segregation had "the advantage," in his view, of "placing between the sleeping place of the European and that of the native child a space of land quite unattractive to the mosquito and too wide for it to fly over."[36] In these examples of the need for exclusion and removal, a racial optic provided the means for colonial policymakers to bypass Victorian bourgeois beliefs about the innocence and vulnerability of children and the necessity for adults or the state to protect them, and to avoid sentimentalized views about impoverished "waifs" and "street urchins," popularized in melodramatic literature and ephemera such as jigsaw puzzles and biscuit tin lids.[37]

The powerful association of malaria with the blood of "the native" between 1900 and the 1920s was pivotal to a medical—or "haemo-political"—turn in imperialist rhetoric, adding an incendiary ingredient to the "mixed blood" fantasies that shaped metropolitan understandings of intercultural exchange in colonial societies and led medical officers to advocate full racial segregation in the 1910s.[38] Epidemiological evidence seemed to justify racial discrimination, in the view of colonial health officers. "It is sometimes argued that segregation involves the creation of offensive caste distinctions between natives and Europeans," wrote Accra's senior sanitary officer, Thomas E. Rice, but, he explained, the rationale for it is exclusively epidemiological: "Were the immune and non-immune populations subject to equal risks there would be some grounds for the objection, but since that is not so, there can be no justification for such a contention."[39]

Segregation was first proposed in the report of a "malaria expedition" to West Africa from the Liverpool School of Tropical Diseases in 1899, and again in 1901 in the report of the Malaria Committee of the Royal Society after the tour of Dr. S. R. Christophers and Dr. J. W. Stephens in 1900.[40] The idea of a "protective zone for the European quarter" was introduced by Professor William J. Simpson, whose influential report "Sanitary Matters in Various West African Colonies" was commissioned by the Colonial Office after an outbreak of bubonic plague in the Gold Coast in 1908.[41] The Colonial Office in London approved the principle of "protective zones"; with this approval, imperialist visions of tropical public health became permeated with racial prejudice. The arrival of Viscount Harcourt as secretary of state for the colonies in 1910 accelerated the principle into draft policy.[42] Following Simpson's recommendations, and the recommendations of the Principal Medical Officers' Conference in Lagos, held in November 1912, Harcourt authorized the senior sanitary officer of each West African colony to refuse permission to local public works departments for the erection of any new buildings for European residence unless they were at least 440 yards (a quarter of a mile) from the nearest African settlement.[43] In doing so, he empowered local medical departments to operate independently of West African governors and councils, setting senior medics on a collision course with politicians who were answerable, at least via the African press, to local taxpayers and educated elites. In confidential dispatches in 1912 and 1913 to the governors of West Africa, Harcourt proposed the formal implementation of this quarter-mile rule, enclosing maps drawn up by the sanitary inspectorate showing each governor which areas of cities had been identified for exclusive European residency, and sought their comments on the implementation of racial segregation in future town planning.

Harcourt's infamous "Memorandum on the 'Segregation Principle' in West Africa" of June 10, 1913, combines an epidemiological (mis)understanding of disease transmission with racist statements about the "natural" inferiority of Africans and exasperation at "native" recalcitrance in the face of colonial public health policies. A high proportion of Europeans was necessary for the administration of West Africa, he began, because "the indigenous element is very slow to produce the type which in other places . . . is available for filling minor administrative posts and the rank and file of the technical appointments."[44] However, "the principle of segregation admittedly presents the appearance of racial injustice," he confessed, "inasmuch as it forbids natives of West Africa to live in or near a certain part of town. It is not based, however, upon distinction of race, but on relative immunity to certain diseases, and on the inability of natives to appreciate the advantages of hygienic surroundings."[45] Yet again, Africans were held to blame: their inability to appreciate European standards of hygiene meant that segregation, albeit at "great expense," was the sole solution for the governing classes.[46]

Harcourt's solution to the public health crisis in West African towns was an attempt to materialize the antihumanist ideology that underwrote British imperialism by applying the false science of racial types through which particular ethnic groups were regarded as "backward" and "contagious." At the end of each working day, European residents would, the segregationists imagined, return through the new cordons sanitaires to clean spaces devoid of contact with a contaminated local world.[47] The quarter-mile rule was the logical outcome of a new imperialism that would shatter if it acknowledged or accommodated African alternatives to its own public health creed.

Unsurprisingly, African-owned newspapers of all political orientations spoke out against racial segregation in West Africa, with many editors accusing the British government of using epidemiological arguments to rationalize and veil an overtly racist policy.[48] Only one senior official in colonial government opposed the quarter-mile rule. As indicated above, Sir Hugh Clifford, governor of the Gold Coast from 1912 to 1919 (and subsequently of Nigeria from 1919 to 1925), argued that the policy was draconian, costly, ineffective, and politically incendiary, using African taxpayers' money without benefiting them materially. Clifford listed multiple reasons why segregation would fail:

> Even if complete segregation of European habitations on the Gold Coast could be effected at moderate cost, the European dwelling in them would not thereby be rendered immune even from mosquito-borne disease. No European in this country can exist without his staff of native servants, who cannot live at a distance of at least a quarter of a mile from his house. Few Europeans are not required by the exigencies of their public duty to come into daily contact with natives of all ages, and most Europeans have from time to time to make tours through the country, during which anything resembling segregation from the native population is a sheer impossibility.[49]

Clifford was the sole British official speaking for African urban dwellers at this time, offering sustained opposition to the quarter-mile rule.[50] Meanwhile, significant tracts of land were acquired throughout British West Africa "strictly for Europeans" to reside on. From 1900 onward, local people were routinely removed, or entire villages were relocated—sometimes more than once in less than a decade—to make way for European-only dwellings.[51] Out of these, the Government Reserved (or Residential) Areas (GRAs) emerged in subsequent decades to buffer white civil servants from African urban populations.[52]

Full-scale racial segregation of the type institutionalized in South Africa was constrained in West Africa, however, by the lack of finances, personnel, and political will for major urban restructuring projects involving complex arrangements for the purchase of land from local rulers and the relocation of urban populations elsewhere for the sake of relatively small numbers of Europeans. Nevertheless, the British argument for segregation on grounds of health persisted well into the 1930s as colonial medics attempted to explain the difference between their own ideas about segregation on grounds of health and the emerging policy of institutionalized racial discrimination in South Africa.

The official blindness to the systemic and global causes of urban disease and environmental pollution, and the British misinterpretation of local domestic practices that differed from their own, can be explained in part by a combination of scientific racism and the operation of a discourse about race and dirt in colonial institutions. The category of dirt facilitated an ideological displacement onto individual bodies, shifting responsibility from political systems onto the most vulnerable and exploited people.[53] But, paradoxically, the individual described in colonial public health reports in West Africa was so generalized as to be unrepresentative of any identifiable local person. In constructing "the native" as anathema to urban cleanliness, European medical officials not only failed to acknowledge the constructed nature of their subject as a dirty by-product of imperialist ideology; they also failed to describe the subjects (colonial or otherwise) who carried on their urban lives all around them. Put simply, "the native" was such a thoroughly constructed assembly of parts as to be unavailable to government for individualized address.

In West Africa as in colonial East and Central Africa, "many officials, both medical and administrative, understood that the real causes of epidemics lay in the major economic changes taking place" in and around the sites of epidemics, affecting people's decisions about when and where to travel, how to store food surpluses prior to sale, and what to purchase with their cash incomes.[54] While this deep-rooted awareness of the role played by colonialism and by the increasingly rapid globalization of trade in the exacerbation of infectious diseases in tropical towns did not prevent the development of European-only GRAs, the racial segregationists largely failed in their attempt to remove what they regarded as the human sources of contamination and dirt in West Africa.

The residue that officials left behind in the public health archives of the Colonial Office, in the face of this failure, is evidence of this sustained, decades-long European obsession with African bodies as "dirty" in a discourse that excluded African voices. Unwilling and unable to understand colonial subjects' rationales for diverse local healing and hygiene practices, or local epistemologies and economies, British health personnel patrolled the minutiae of everyday physical life, attempting to transform people's bodily practices all the way from ingestion to excretion, from consumption to waste.

The public health archives display a half century of British desires for, and failures in, the bodily control of Africans. How the African-owned press addressed the olfactory fantasies examined in this and the previous chapter, in which contamination flowed on invisible, unidirectional currents from Africans toward Europeans, is the topic of the next chapter, for, when it came to town planning and urban sanitation, Nigerian newspapers and their readers in the early twentieth century had to negotiate many complex ideological boundaries put in place by the racial logic of colonial epidemiology.

3

African Newspapers, the "Great Unofficial Public," and Plague in Colonial Lagos

For many pro-imperial liberals in Britain, the right to criticize government through independent newspapers was evidence of the democratic legitimacy of the British Empire in contrast to its European rivals, where freedom of the press was curtailed.[1] Government officials "on the ground" in British West Africa were often less liberal-minded than supporters of empire in the metropolis: for them, African newspapers served a useful, if irksome, purpose. Given that, in the absence of political representation, educated Africans' chief mode of public expression was the press, any anti-colonial views could be closely and easily monitored by reading their newspapers: criticisms could be countered and court cases brought against "libelous" or "seditious" editors and contributors.[2]

Some colonial governors would probably have preferred to curb the so-called native press altogether, but their views on this matter demonstrated that they, too, were avid readers of African-owned newspapers. In a report to the Yellow Fever Commission of West Africa in 1913, for example, the governor of the Southern Nigeria Protectorate, Lord Frederick Lugard, described the influential role of the Lagos press in mediating—and undermining—

colonial public health messages and noted its wide field of influence, reaching out from Lagos to the educated population of Abeokuta and beyond. His comments illuminate a colonial bureaucrat's interpretation of how European public health policy was interpreted in politically unpalatable ways in the anticolonial press. "Its 'educated' section," he commented sarcastically of Abeokuta, "is dominated by a fear of the Lagos Press, and I find opinions expressed in that Press to the effect that yellow fever is a disease to which Europeans are liable, but to which natives are immune, and that, if Europeans find that by residing in an African community they are liable to contract yellow fever, the remedy is that they should betake themselves elsewhere."[3] Lugard's comments react to the manner in which the Lagos press unanimously rejected the principle of racial segregation in African cities as a mode of protecting European officials from insect-born and "filth diseases" in the 1910s. As the previous chapter suggested, such a policy, under serious consideration by 1913, made little or no provision for African sanitary welfare in the expanding towns and cities of British West Africa.

In Sierra Leone, Lugard's counterpart, Sir Edward Marsh Merewether, was so concerned to correct liberal public opinion in Britain, which appeared to be siding with African doctors' newspaper articles and petitions asking for corrections to racial disparities in employment, that, with a symptomatic lack of insight into who spoke for whom (and to whom) in imperial contexts, he informed the Colonial Office: "The native medical practitioners on the West Coast of Africa are mostly 'Creoles,' and the newspapers which ventilate the alleged grievance of native doctors, and are constantly harping on the alleged demand of the natives to be attended by men of their own race, are owned and edited and entirely written by 'Creoles.'"[4] The educated migrant elites who made up the medical profession were not authentic Africans in his opinion, and should not be allowed to speak on behalf of genuine "natives."

More than a century of West African slavery, displacement, emancipation, migration, and resettlement is collapsed into these complaints against the diaspora of African professionals living and working along the littoral.[5] From the perspective of these hardline governors, independent media outlets run by local professional elites posed a threat to imperialist ideology per se. Simply by existing as vehicles to carry colonial subjects' commentaries on government to the rest of the world, African newspapers had the potential to erode colonialism using the language of the dominant power.[6]

In spite of their bile, Lugard's and Merewether's complaints against the African-owned press confirm the international impact of Anglophone

West African newspapers in the early twentieth century, which circulated as far afield as London and the United States through imperial, pan-African, and anticolonial networks.[7] Alongside their capacity to criticize colonial policy through the press, from the 1880s onward educated West Africans made extensive use of newspapers to complain about the "filth" of their urban environments and to call on municipal authorities to improve public health. As early as the 1860s, according to Bigon, Saro elites used African American and diaspora newspapers such as the *Anglo-African Magazine* to call for improvements to the infrastructure of Lagos while praising the colony's British rulers for any "evidence of the determination to introduce civilised improvements into the town."[8] Without newspapers of their own at this time, Lagosian elites inserted their voices into the print media of the African diaspora to applaud the civic authorities for local infrastructural work, and to express gratitude for the transformation of their neighborhoods.[9]

By the 1910s and 1920s, a flourishing local newspaper culture served Lagosians in Yoruba and English alongside the regular influx of broadsheets from Britain and the colonies.[10] This politically diverse array of newspapers reported on public lectures on town planning and sanitation, and, in their early days, reprinted entire government debates and ordinances over many weekly installments.[11] Editors encouraged readers to send in letters on all aspects of urban policy. The newspapers hosted their own enquiries into urban hygiene and sanitation, creating space for editors' views on legislation and readers' reactions, and, in the process, generating a discursive arena for African argument that stood in stark contrast with the silencing of African opinion in official documents. Editors used the press to try to influence the political systems from which they were largely, although not completely, excluded until the 1940s.[12] They continuously defined the newspaper as a medium to generate public opinion, and many saw their role as one of creating new reading publics that could engage in intelligent, even combative, discussions with one another about the topics of the day.[13] Indeed, Nigeria's longest-standing daily, the Nigerian *Daily Times*, was established in 1926 as a government-backed moderate newspaper with African and European contributors, designed to intervene in public debates, to counter the anticolonial press, and to provide newspaper readers with information and explanations about government policy in the face of an increasingly radical anticolonial press.[14]

Were it not for these myriad newspapers, the absence of African voices from the colonial public health archive would pose major problems for historians seeking local perspectives on colonial policy in the early twentieth century. As it is, the "official sphere" of government communications that formed the core of the discussion in chapters 1 and 2 found lively, politically diverse interlocutors in the "native press." African newspapers were publicly circulating, "unofficial" texts that paralleled, rivaled, and commented on the official sphere of government reports and gazettes, speaking for the "great unofficial public," as the *Nigerian Pioneer* described the African population with no direct connection to the colonial state through work or education.[15] From the 1880s onward in newspapers such as the *Lagos Observer*, the *Lagos Times*, the *Lagos Weekly Record*, and the *Nigerian Pioneer*, an African public sphere was continuously and consciously being shaped by editors who attempted to produce "public opinion" for circulation in the public sphere of print, often in hostile competition with one another and with editors in other West African colonies.

For Kitoyi Ajasa, the conservative, ultra-loyalist editor of the *Nigerian Pioneer*, however, this apparently democratic vision of the public sphere was anything but open to all contributors. While he agreed that "opinion" was rife among the masses in Nigeria, he believed that "mass-ignorance" prevented the emergence of intelligent public opinion. Indeed, in much the same tone as British censors in the 1920s, he described the uneducated masses as vulnerable to exploitation by "dishonest demagogues" who used the authority of print, especially Yoruba-language print, to convince them of the validity of their pronouncements on local political crises.[16] Nigeria "is wanting what is known in civilised countries as public opinion," he stated in a condemnation of his newspaper's rival, the bilingual *Lagos Weekly Record*, which had been praising home rule in India and thereby stirring up the "mob."[17]

Showing a bias toward British imperialists, Ajasa believed that "the opinion of the majority is neither sane nor healthy," and that the responsibility of newspapers was to educate, lead, and uplift this "unthinking populace," to transform the "mob" into a "public" through the intelligent dissemination of messages and facts designed for their betterment.[18] By contrast, in fueling "the passions of the mob" and creating a "mobocracy," anticolonial newspapermen such as Thomas Horatio Jackson and his allies in the new Nigerian National Democratic Party (established 1923) were using their party mouthpiece, the *Lagos Weekly Record*, to exploit "gullible" readers who believed everything they saw in print, putting them into "a frantic and frenzied state," and violating the "sacred vocation" of the editor to maintain order, calm, and intelligent reflection.[19]

African-owned newspapers in British West Africa participated whole-heartedly in debates about public health and sanitation in the early colonial period, giving visibility to African health professionals such as doctors and sanitary staff, and, in the process, providing an important archive for historians of public health. Newspapers functioned like a shadow cabinet for the discussion of colonial policy and expenditure. Whereas the conservative newspapers gently chided governments for their failures to improve sanitation at an adequate pace, and emphasized the necessity for filth to be removed through increased government expenditure, politically confrontational newspapers such as the *Lagos Standard* and the *Lagos Weekly Record* held colonial governments to account for failures to protect African public health in the cities, using sanitation as a platform to expose colonialism's lack of legitimacy.

This vibrant newspaper culture comes with its own health warning, however: researchers wishing to retrieve nonelite Africans' perspectives from the press in the early twentieth century cannot be satisfied by the Anglophone newspaper archive alone, for editors almost unwaveringly adopted the public health and town-planning perspectives of colonial and municipal authorities. Their commentaries were so firmly government-oriented—whether fiercely critical or politely encouraging—as to omit the views and values of broader urban populations for whom mud and thatch houses with small (or no) windows, always labeled "slums" in the African press, may have been the dwellings of choice with their outdoor cooking spaces and interiors that were considerably cooler than those of concrete and iron structures.[20] For this urban majority, as the previous chapter argued, defecation in the bush, or in domestic pit latrines, may have been preferable to using shared public facilities. The Anglophone press in Lagos often regarded these populations' standards of hygiene and cleanliness as lower than those of educated Africans in European-style buildings. Especially in the eyes of conservative editors, the "inmates of the bamboo huts live under conditions most deplorable with respect to their health."[21] As one African medical officer put it at the start of the annual Health Week in November 1926, "the faulty hygiene" and "the faulty habit of living of some of our people" was causing the spread of infectious diseases as well as inducing anxiety, alcohol dependency, immorality, and other social evils.[22]

A distinction between Anglophone and Afrophone newspapers is necessary at this point, because Yoruba and bilingual Yoruba-English newspapers such *Eko Akete* (est. 1922), edited by Adeoye Deniga, who described it in one editorial as "The People's Paper," often passionately defended African building styles in the face of officials' unfair condemnations of pre-colonial urban architecture.[23] In a furious response to the governor's address of welcome to the Prince of Wales on his visit to Nigeria in April 1925, for example, one pseudonymous correspondent used the columns of *Eko Akete* to reject the contrast drawn in the speech between Lagos before and after the Treaty of Cession in 1861. Before the Treaty, Sir Hugh Clifford told the Prince of Wales in a carefully tailored speech that contradicted and reversed his hitherto accommodating stance toward Lagosian architecture and hygiene, "the people dwelt in squalid huts and were steeped in heathenism and ignorance," whereas in Lagos under the British Crown, "comfort and sanitation have taken the place of wretchedness and squalor."[24] Such a "perversion of the truth," Atari Ajanaku (pseud.) declared, was incorrect and unacceptable, for prior to the treaty "natives dwelt not in squalid huts but in big compounds usually too spacious for their accommodations; their politeness, civility, and hospitable disposition to all the European Merchants and African strangers within their gates long, long before the Cession 'in those unregenerate days' were beyond dispute."[25] Atari Ajanaku's line-by-line response to the speech, published over two editions, highlights the vital function of newspapers in the colonial period to serve as correctives and to answer back to official representations of precolonial Africa.

One of the crowning ironies of British officials' rejection of African professional elites and the Lagos press in the early twentieth century was that, whatever their views about precolonial Lagos, local editors generally supported and reiterated British sanitary principles about the sources of the "filth diseases" in the quarters of nonelite urban residents, and called for intensive town planning as well as "education" of the people in matters of hygiene and sanitation. While the ratio of coaxing to critique varied enormously according to the political persuasion of editors, the press did not question European public health paradigms for urban "improvement." Adeoye Deniga, the editor of *Eko Akete*, wrote in 1925 that the "filthy and miry state" of Griffith Street, as a consequence of "the dumping of foul water thereon without proper drainage," necessitated the intervention of the town warden: this is, the headline read, "A Street Crying for Help. Mr Town Warden, Will You Help?"[26] Even the anticolonial staff at the *Lagos Weekly Record*, during its long existence from 1890 to 1930, adopted the language of filth and dirt to describe the poorest communities in Lagos, although they stopped short of using the word "civilized" to describe public health initiatives that came in the wake of colonialism. For the *Lagos*

Weekly Record, with its continuous exposure of cracks in government policy, as much as for the *Nigerian Pioneer*, with its effusive pronouncements of loyalty to the British Crown, questions of sanitation and public health in Lagos were central to their assessments of the efficacy of government. Poorer urban residents propagated disease in their "slums," they agreed, but where they differed was in the tone of their calls for the mass provision of free public latrines, along with the staff to clean them, and in the tone of their critique of sanitary provisions.

The elephant in the newsroom was the "native" of colonial public health discourse. While they may have shared British sanitary and public health goals, newspaper editors never invoked the homogenized African of colonial public health discourse. In deciding who to blame for the ubiquitous dirt of Lagos, editors of all political persuasions refused to blame Africans as a group or a racial type. Even Ajasa placed the blame for urban dirt and disease firmly with the government. "The tropics must be made healthy for the natives themselves," he wrote in a 1924 editorial, reiterating views he first expressed in the early 1900s, and leaving no doubt about who was responsible for the introduction as well as the cure of "filth diseases": "Making healthy the natives consists mainly in curing those diseases which the advent of civilisation has brought in its wake."[27]

Ajasa remained supportive of the "three Cs" throughout his lifetime, proud to advocate British ideas about public health, sanitation, progress, education, trade, and "civilisation." "Our people must be helped in spite of themselves," he insisted.[28] As mentioned above, his elitist approach to urban development shared features with the views of influential members of the European community from previous decades: his paternalistic views about the uneducated masses in the 1920s, while carefully devoid of racial markers, reiterated the opinions of earlier public figures such as Herbert Tugwell (1854–1936), bishop of Western Equatorial Africa and bishop of the Diocese on the Niger from 1894 to 1921, for whom Lagosians' sanitary slackness required coercive intervention in the early 1900s.[29] Ajasa had been present at the inaugural meeting of the Lagos Literary Institute in 1901, at which Tugwell articulated his views. The Institute chose "sanitation" as its first debating topic, and boasted influential members of the European and African community on its executive committee, including Governor Sir William MacGregor and pro-imperial Africans such as the Right Reverend Bishop I. Oluwole and the Honorable C. A. Sapara-Williams, the latter a nominated member of the Legislative Council and supporter of the policy of indirect rule rather than English civil law.

Ajasa's elitist, pro-imperial conservatism may be unpalatable today, but his scrupulous repositioning of African urban residents in relation to colonial public health policy was more complicated and critical than allowed for by a dismissive view of him as a colonial stooge, and deserves examination for the ways in which it transforms the discourse of dirt from racialized into socioeconomic terms. While publishing frequent declarations of loyalty to the British Crown, Ajasa and the other African professionals who remained in colonial service also challenged and modified the imperialist representation of urban Africans as a homogenous group. In particular, they rejected racial segregation as a principle for public health while condemning the "evil" of "impetuous settlement" by incomers to the "poor section" of the city.[30] In doing so, they asserted their own high environmental and sanitary standards as a property-owning, rate-paying African minority over and against the uneducated masses of "poor and ignorant [people who . . .] are those to be quieted and brought into the ring on the side of Sanitation."[31] Social "quieting" replaced racial "pacification." While the *Nigerian Pioneer*'s anticolonial peers blamed the colonial state for failures in sanitation and disease prevention, reprimanded individual officials in open letters, and attacked the pervasive policy of racial segregation in the 1910s and 1920s, Ajasa continued—well into the early 1930s—to expand on the view he first promoted in the early 1900s, that certain *classes* of Lagosian needed help from the state to change their unhygienic local practices, and to adopt the rational alternatives on offer in their place.[32]

With the outbreak of bubonic plague in Lagos in 1924, the *Nigerian Pioneer*'s top-down view of town planning in Lagos led to such draconian proposals for the removal of dirt that it provides a case study in the ways conservative African elites made use of print media to attempt self-preservation as a class in a colonial context where the racialization of dirt permeated policy decisions at the state level, and where social class remained largely absent as a vector for government understandings of public health and the urban environment.[33] How Ajasa asserted his status as a spokesman on public health during the plague epidemic in Lagos offers an example of the capacity of print to be put to the service of local elites at times of crisis, while sweeping the "dirt" directly onto the doorsteps of others.

The *Nigerian Pioneer* and the Bubonic Plague Epidemic of 1924–1931

Lagos was a bustling commercial town by the mid-1920s, with trade networks connecting its harbor with ports throughout the world. The city enjoyed a postwar boom in exports, with constant flows of people and goods moving in and out of the country by sea, river, road, and rail.[34] The pages of the city's Anglophone and Yoruba-English newspapers were packed with advertisements for cinemas, bookshops, and retailers with "fancy goods" available for purchase. On a single page of *Eko Akete* readers could see advertisements for ladies' crepe de chine hats, georgette silk hats, lace panamas, silk stockings, gloves, gentlemen's raincoats, Tussar silk accessories, and patent medicines for a number of ailments.[35] As was true of global entrepôts elsewhere, its economic success made Lagos more susceptible than other West African cities to the entry of contagious diseases through international shipping and cross-border trade.

The Lagos plague is iconic for historians of African public health because, in spite of overcrowding and the infamous lack of sanitary infrastructure in Lagos, a total of under 1,000 fatalities was recorded out of a population of 126,000.[36] Its management and containment were exceptionally well documented by the city's medical and sanitary staff, leaving a rich archive for scholars in the Nigerian National Archives at Ibadan. Bubonic plague is said to have entered the city from Kumasi via the maritime kola nut trade with colonial Ghana.[37] The government reaction was swift, and medical staff immediately implemented the rules for quarantine laid out in the Infectious Diseases Ordinances of the 1900s and 1910s.[38] Lagos Island was divided into sections, with the affected areas placed under quarantine. At the harbor, passengers and cargo were subject to rigorous disinfection and fumigation regimes determined by the race and class of passengers.[39] Meanwhile, travelers by road and water were sprayed with kerosene and required to show evidence of inoculation.[40] Financial incentives were offered for the extermination of rats, with 2d paid for each rat corpse delivered to the authorities. Controversially, the private goods and property of people suspected of being infected with plague could be placed at the disposal of sanitary inspectors for disinfection or even destruction, and suspected cases could be compulsorily removed to the infectious diseases hospital.

Given this flurry of medical and clerical activity, it is perhaps curious that at the outset of the epidemic in July 1924, the editor of the *Nigerian Pioneer* was unable to print the word "plague" in connection with Lagos. For several weeks, Ajasa avoided referring to its presence in town. In his first editorial after the announcement of the outbreak, he mentions "the recent epidemic in town" without naming or describing it.[41] Rather, he uses the editorial to criticize the insanitary state of indigenous buildings erected in the "old days" in Lagos, before the arrival of imported construction materials from Europe.[42] Subsequent references to "the epidemic" are buried in editorials under titles such as "Rambling Notes and News: War on Rats" and "Lagos, The Liverpool of West Africa."[43] Plague was the unmentionable visitor to Lagos: its removal from the printed page fulfilled Ajasa's wish for its absence from the city.

Ajasa had every reason to downplay the epidemic. First, on behalf of his class, he feared the significant negative economic impact of quarantine on trade, with restrictions to imports and exports as well as stringent disinfection and clearance procedures for people and goods passing through the port.[44] Second, the epidemic erupted shortly before the greatly anticipated visit of the Prince of Wales to West Africa in April 1925. On April 12, anticolonial and rival newspapers as well as the international press publicized a Reuters telegram from the Gold Coast announcing that the royal visit to Nigeria had been canceled. The *Nigerian Pioneer*—a weekly—did not go to press with this information.[45] On April 17, 1925, Ajasa made his own announcement. Claiming to have been "taken into confidence" by a top government official, the editor mocked his rivals with the news that the first Reuters telegram had been "pulled" and the visit would go ahead as planned.[46]

For many years, the *Pioneer* had argued that Nigeria was economically superior to the Gold Coast: it was the "jewel in the Crown" of Britain's West African empire because of the country's "economic importance, her wealth, her population and her high-strung and almost unbounded loyalty to the throne and to the Imperial Self behind that Throne."[47] In the weeks before the prince's visit, the *Pioneer* boasted that it was "only right that the Prince of Wales should make a longer stay in Nigeria than in any other British West African colonies."[48] The idea that the royal visit would include Nigeria's chief rival—the Gold Coast—alongside lesser sister colonies, was perhaps too unpalatable for Ajasa to transfer into print.[49]

One month in, as the reality of the epidemic became unavoidable, Ajasa's editorials moved from denial into a tone of presidential authority: he offered public health leadership to the people, as well as advice to the government, and reminded officials of his own sanitary warnings to them at the turn of the twentieth century. "Uneducated" Lagosians required behavioral modification as well as sustained reeducation, in his view, and while the African newspapers could play a major role in mediating public health messages, the largest portion of responsibility fell to government at this time: "The people . . . turn their eyes to the Government to prepare a programme of Sanitary Improvements of the town."[50] Without dramatic social engineering led by the state, he believed, urban improvements would come slowly, if at all. "Drastic treatment at the hands of Government" was necessary, he reiterated in weekly editorials throughout the remainder of the epidemic, because the inhabitants of the "slums" at the epicenter of the plague had placed trade as well as municipal ratepayers' lives in jeopardy and were incapable of voluntarily observing rules that were never enforced by the authorities.[51] His proposals for the obliteration of informal settlements included the forcible relocation of residents to purpose-built government housing schemes outside the commercial center of the city, funded by the municipality.[52] "Our people must be helped in spite of themselves," he repeated;[53] "the people seldom know what is for their good."[54]

Ajasa's proposals for the relocation of new urban subjects and the removal of indigenous dwellings "from the municipal map of Lagos" are evidence of the ideological and discursive resettling of dirt-related concepts from earlier decades.[55] His proposals adopt key aspects of the segregation debate from the 1910s, in which compulsory removals of "the native" were necessary for the successful implementation of the quarter-mile rule: these are reattached by Ajasa to the poorest urban classes. In doing so, he repositioned the colonial racialization of dirt by pressing for investment in urban infrastructure, all the while maintaining strict social boundaries on grounds of class.[56] Through this displacement of race onto social class, the *Nigerian Pioneer* remediated the "contagious native" discourse promulgated by colonial medics by carefully avoiding racial classifications and offering, instead, a socially oriented palette of urban proposals that took account of Africans' role in global trade. Such a resettlement of colonial discourse produced its own blind spots, not least in Ajasa's failure to appreciate the implications of his own fleeting acknowledgment that the "extraordinarily low" daily death toll from plague in Lagos was a consequence of the people's "love [for] soap and water," no matter what type of dwelling they inhabited.[57] Rather than celebrating indigenous soap manufacture as a result of this observation, he used it as a platform to promote local consumption of Lifebuoy Soap, manufactured by the global giant, Lever Brothers, for which a large advertisement is included below his editorial.[58]

The important point about Ajasa's discourse is that ethnic displacements onto other urban groups were completely absent from the *Pioneer's* discussions of the connections between filth and the spread of plague. While colonial medics did not hesitate to ethnically classify Africans into more or less dirty types, Ajasa and his peers steadfastly refused to deploy the language of ethnicity and maintained instead a consistent focus on the responsibilities to townspeople of local and colonial government.[59] Off the printed page, a wide range of sociocultural stereotypes about particular people's levels of hygiene and cleanliness would have circulated in Lagos in the early twentieth century, as they do today.[60] Then, as now, people's jokes and commentaries about dirt would have drawn attention to the (in)sanitary behavior of other ethnic groups in food preparation, bathing, eating, defecation, child-rearing, and home life (see chapters 7 and 8). But the particular public space represented by the newspaper—with its commitment to verifiable news and educated opinion—meant that contagion and sanitation were treated politically, socially, and economically by editors in Lagos, and never biologically or ethnically.[61]

Unlike the anticolonial press with its investment in ideals of pan-African racial unity and burgeoning interest in communist forms of anticolonialism, Ajasa and his conservative peers were among the earliest media professionals to wholly reject racial categories, whether used for empowerment or prejudice, in favor of social class. This aversion to race did not prevent him from deploying the colonial category of "primitive," however, or from endorsing the idea that the uneducated masses were incapable of development—sanitary, economic, or otherwise—without colonial management. "The tendency . . . of the primitive man," he wrote categorically, is "towards and for things bad."[62] But two decades before class replaced race among colonial public health officials, his categories contained the potential for nonracial modes of urban differentiation on the part of one section of the educated elite. The class-conscious editorials of the *Nigerian Pioneer* exposed precisely how and where the loyalist elite of Lagos "buttered their bread" by asserting their status as a pro-British minority at the apex of African society. Ajasa remained unwavering in his gradualist and pro-British approach to self-government, insisting that *"we have to serve like other nations our apprenticeship."*[63]

Given the recent upsurge of scholarly interest in the topic of class in Africa, the *Pioneer's* elitist pronouncements on who should lead public opinion, and who should be removed from town, are important for what they reveal about the attitudes of a self-identified upper class, and the way in which it shifted colonial racial prejudice onto lower-class urban populations.[64] In his paternalistic tone, Ajasa borrowed from colonial discourse while stripping it of racial attachments. The outbreak of bubonic plague in Lagos reinforced conservative elites' slum-clearing, people-moving mentality. It marked the consolidation of a class consciousness that existed in tension with the racial logic of colonial discourse without altering the Eurocentric vision of public health in colonial cities.

CHAPTER THREE

Flickering in the margins of the Anglophone press are editors' infrequent efforts to understand local health cultures in which infectious diseases were understood, prevented, and sometimes deliberately spread. Groups such as the Sopono cult that worshipped the god of smallpox, and inspired awe and dread among Yoruba residents with their ability to deliberately infect a person by scratching them with infected material, were condemned outright in the newspapers even though their methods closely mimicked those of a medical vaccinator.[65] Convictions under the "Juju and Witchcraft Ordinance," amended in 1909 to accommodate Sapara's findings, were heralded under headlines such as "Six Months' Hard Labour for a Small Pox Worshipper," without any explanation of the rationale or motivations of members, or how they accessed their targets.[66]

Likewise, the Anglophone newspapers insisted on the wholesale destruction of rodents in people's dwellings during the plague epidemic with no attempt to understand why rats were tolerated with indifference—even affection—by many Lagosians, for whom Yoruba sayings such as "if you eat *enu eku* (food nibbled by a rat), you will have wisdom" contained reactions from a period before the era of global trade and the rodent-borne diseases that came in its wake.[67] These and other maxims indicate toleration for the ubiquitous rat and its lessons for humans. One popular Yoruba jibe holds that the absence of rats from a dwelling serves as a comment on the occupier's low socioeconomic status: "if there is no rat in the house, it is so . . . like the person is like a pauper. Rat[s] will only be in a place where they can see something to eat."[68] A middle-aged Yoruba man, interviewed in 2018, told of how "my grandma used to tell me that '*ahh*, you know you are going to school. This prepared pap, so rat touched it last night, but [you must] eat it.' We too, then, we will be dancing '*ahhh a á je é*' (We will eat it). So as how Yorùbá believe that if one is eating the fish head you won't know book in school, but Yorùbá believe that *tí eku bá je . . . eni bá jenu eku orí e máa pé* (Anyone that eats food nibbled by a rat will be smart). So that is their belief in the olden days."[69]

These beliefs and sayings fill the gaps of incomprehension in Anglophone newspaper reports, which, in turn, drew their behavioral prescriptions from colonial health officials' condemnations of local living conditions. As one white medical officer stated in 1925, "Even in Lagos after eighteen months of plague many of the inhabitants do not understand or believe the connection between the rat and plague. They say 'The rats have always lived in our houses with us yet we only have had plague since last year.'"[70]

At other times, Anglophone editors offered fleeting commentaries on local health traditions, often presented in terms of the need to leave indigenous malpractices behind. Even though these popular beliefs are framed by the press as arising from ignorance or the need for education, through them it is possible to glean some information about public opinion concerning the spaces of contagion in the city. In an item on the new Infectious Diseases Hospital (IDH) that was opened in Lagos in 1930, for example, the Nigerian *Daily Times* criticized uneducated urban residents because "the doctrine of, or necessity for, prompt isolation or removal to an Infectious Disease Hospital is usually the last thing to be thought of or appreciated" in homes experiencing contagious disease among family members.[71] As Karin Barber notes, however, the Yoruba press from the 1920s and early 1930s contains a wealth of information about the old and new IDHs, revealing that, rather than being remote from people's minds at times of disease at home, the IDH was regarded as a place of contagion and certain death, rather than a place for recovery and cure, a place that loved ones should be hidden away from at all costs if they were to stand any chance of recovery.[72] This view was undoubtedly based on empirical evidence, for when the very sick were forcibly removed by health officials to the IDH, their health was often beyond repair.

Global epidemics find meaning in local, culturally specific contexts, where the etiologies of disease are often reinterpreted and attached to sources that differ from official explanations. People weigh whatever evidence is in circulation locally, including the clinical, and make up their own minds about how to respond practically to the public health messaging that comes from official as well as unofficial media. Given that the field of public opinion comprises an infinitely wider range of explanations and interpretations than the discipline of public health, and an infinitely broader set of narratives than those shaped by mass media such as newspapers, popular explanations for health and hygiene can be a great deal more persuasive and multidimensional than public health messaging from official channels, especially when those channels are regarded with mistrust as having ulterior motives, such as revenue raising, or the removal of shanty towns to make way for elite housing.

Nonelite Lagosians' interpretations of the etiology of plague and other contagious diseases remain largely absent from African newspaper records of the 1920s and 1930s. When present, the views of the "great unofficial public" are so thoroughly mediated by the elite's desire for public health transformations that they are continuously filtered through a language of behavioral transformation, removal, reeducation, and "improvement," albeit from strongly anticolonial political platforms. The next two chapters confront the methodological challenges posed by these archives in an attempt to draw nonelite Africans' perspectives out of textual resources from the colonial era, before the book moves in its final three chapters toward other types of archive, including oral histories and interviews with contemporary urban residents, producing a new and different set of methodological problems with their own ramifications for locally grounded histories of dirt.

4

Screening Dirt:
Public Health Movies
in Colonial Nigeria
and Rural Spectatorship
in the 1930s and 1940s

This film . . . has one lesson to teach and one point to make,
that to be healthy you must be clean.
—WILLIAM SELLERS

This chapter considers the range of methods available for cultural historians to identify and reassemble valuable data about African audiences' responses to colonial educational films from written archives that are saturated with racist assumptions. From one perspective, exemplified by the work of Mahmood Mamdani, the written colonial archives contain identical types of unfavorable knowledge—or ignorance—about "natives," whether they are represented as media consumers, as (un)clean bodies, or as (un)governable subjects. Such negative knowledge, generated by and for British officialdom, circulated around the imperial archives until the early 1950s, gaining credibility with each iteration and demonstrating Edward Said's observation, now a truism, that imperial ideology operated discursively through a process of constant repetition, re-inscription, and conditioning, transforming officials' perceptions and prejudices into banks of knowledge that informed the actions of colonial personnel in their daily working contexts.[1] From this perspective, colonial film productions for the health education of Africans contributed to an existing archive in which intended audiences were represented as ignorant and inherently filthy.

From another perspective, however, while very few traces of African filmgoers' interpretations can be found in the paperwork that resulted from these processes of knowledge-production, and no oral histories of West African film spectatorship seem to have survived from the 1930s and 1940s apart from occasional African voices transcribed in the colonial records, spectators were not only essential to each screening as the target of colonial health propaganda; they were also visible and vocal in colonial cinema spaces alongside the large number of African intermediaries who participated in the making and exhibition of films. As will become clear in this chapter, vital and noisy streams of audience commentary accompanied the screening of colonial health and hygiene films. Target audiences did not sit or stand quietly during film displays. As officials acknowledged repeatedly, often in annoyance, spectators provided running commentaries throughout each movie, filling the breaks between reels with noisy discussions, reacting to scenes with exclamations, applause, laughter, conversation, debate, judgment, and speculation, and directly addressing commentators about the behavior of individual characters on screen. With few exceptions, target audiences responded to local-language film commentaries "by shouting questions at the interpreter, by loud adverse comment, and by a hubbub of conversation in their own tongue to each other, trying to make out amongst themselves what is on the screen."[2] Audience members reacted to other audience members, as well as to the material on screen, actively negotiating the messages and meanings of scenes with one another. Colonial health movies were accompanied by these vibrant, noisy parallel discussions among spectators, demonstrating the intensely dialogical character of the cultures in which the films circulated, as well as gender (and other) divisions in the interpretation of particular scenes. As one official reported, the audience "chatters, ululates, interrupts, hisses, anticipates the embrace of the heroine by the hero," or simply vacates the cinema if a film does not meet its standards.[3] But colonial health officials showed little interest in the local tastes and values expressed in viewers' noisy communications, even when audience reactions became so loud and unrestrained that they "made commenting very difficult even with the amplifier working at full capacity."[4] The presence of these spectators and intermediaries takes many verbal and nonverbal forms in the written colonial archives, highlighting the complexity of local populations' responses to the simple ideological formula of British health propaganda material.[5]

The Colonial Film Unit in West Africa

The Colonial Film Unit (CFU) was established by the Ministry of Information in 1939 after considerable debate about the value for money of such an expensive initiative. It was yoked immediately to "information and news" about the "British Way and Purpose" in the wake of the outbreak of the Second World War, but it was subsequently expanded for general educational propaganda.[6] Films were one of the key attractions of colonial health events, providing one particular type of public space in the wider program of activities organized by the Health Propaganda Unit (HPU) in which local community leaders—including chiefs, council members, teachers, and other educated individuals—were recruited to model good practice in housekeeping and domestic hygiene.[7] The medium of film was harnessed to wider colonial public messages about cleanliness and dirt. Lectures and practical demonstrations were given to members of the community before and after film screenings, and designated "clean-up days" and "dry pot days" were introduced alongside "school health displays," "healthy baby" competitions, "clean house" competitions, and cake-making competitions for which teachers and elders were recruited as judges, with score charts and certificates provided by the HPU (fig. 4.1).[8]

By the time the CFU began its work in earnest in the early 1940s, commercial cinemas and private cinema vans were commonplace throughout Africa, providing low-cost mass entertainment to wage-earners from all social groups in urban and rural areas.[9] In British West Africa, early commercial cinemas and film distribution channels were controlled by British, Lebanese, and Syrian traders, but increasing numbers of African entrepreneurs entered the market in the late 1930s. In 1939, for example, a local company, Entertainments West Africa Ltd., bought old 1920s equipment from a European filmmaker, H. M. Lomas, and set up an "attractive" cinema in Lagos;[10] in the Gold Coast by the early 1940s, the local Ocansey family controlled ten cinemas, having expanded their entertainment businesses in the 1920s and 1930s.[11] Their films were supplied by the Lebanese Barakat brothers, who established the West African Picture Company along with a Syrian, S. Khalil, in 1937, and who, by 1942, controlled seventeen cinemas throughout Nigeria and two in the Gold Coast, featuring ninety movies per year with a total annual attendance of 600,000.[12] All of

FIGURE 4.1. "Apapa Tidy Street Photo." *African Morning Post*, May 11, 1964, 9.
Author's collection.

the Picture Company's British material was more than two years old, having been subject to double censorship for colonial audiences, but they secured a steady flow of up-to-date American movies directly from the producers, triggering concerns in Britain about the negative moral influence of Hollywood movies on supposedly gullible African audiences.[13]

The doyen of colonial educational films for Africans was the sanitary superintendent William Sellers, whose passion for amateur filming in Nigeria between the late 1920s and early 1950s was combined with his work to promote European ideas about health and hygiene in films like *Plague* (1926; reedited as *Anti-Plague Operations in Lagos*, 1937) and *Lagos Health and Baby Week* (1933), and in other movies focusing on the need for urban sanitation.[14] Sellers's HPU traveled regularly to rural areas of Nigeria to screen general educational films for "backward" audiences with titles such as *The Construction of Bored-Hole Latrines, Modern Slaughter House Practice, Slum Clearance and Town Planning in Lagos,* and *Anti-Malaria Field Work* (fig. 4.2).[15] These films were powerfully described by their makers and pro-

FIGURE 4.2. Mobile Cinema van in Ghana, early 1950s. Photo screenshot
from Tom Rice, "British Empire's Forgotten Propaganda Tool for 'Primitive
Peoples': Mobile Cinema." https://delectant.com/british-empires-forgotten
-propaganda-tool-primitive-peoples-mobile-cinema/.

moters as "documents of the future" for British imperial subjects, teaching
them not only how to be free from dirt, but also how to be modern participants in the global economy.[16] For Sellers and his numerous supporters in the Colonial Office, government films, inspections, demonstrations,
competitions, and exhibitions all enabled sanitary officials access to otherwise closed African domestic spaces "to study the habits and home life" of
residents and to conceive further schemes for transforming "dirty" homes
into "modern" habitations.[17]

Sellers had detractors from the outset of his mission, not least among
colonialists for whom African audiences possessed equal capacities for film
comprehension as Europeans and were too sophisticated for simplistic propaganda movies.[18] As many media historians have observed, and as his own
lectures and publications confirm, however, Sellers asserted himself, and
was widely recognized in official circles, as *the* authority on African filmgoers' aesthetic tastes and sanitary values at least until the late 1940s.[19] From
his position "on the ground" in Nigeria, he worked assiduously to promote
European beliefs about public and personal cleanliness. To achieve these
goals, for the duration of his career Sellers insisted that "points to be rig-
idly avoided" in films for non-European audiences included "affairs of the

heart, transition by suggestion and camera tricks of any description except, of course, the change of camera speed."[20]

Sellers's approach set an aesthetic in place that governed colonial notions of African film literacy for at least fifteen years, driven by the understanding that "films featuring familiar scenes of home life are particularly popular," and, "providing the tempo of the action is slow enough, lessons taught in this way get home."[21] The new medium was enormously popular with target audiences, with each six- to twelve-week tour of the mobile health unit attracting tens of thousands of people. Two hundred people were considered "a small audience."[22] Some films attracted larger crowds, and audiences became "so noisy and uncomfortable that the film had to be stopped while they rearranged themselves."[23] Even in these situations, however, rather than consulting audiences directly and noting their comments, "official log books" were maintained by colonial regimes to record British officials' observations of African responses to films screened by the Health Propaganda Unit: these log books were used to adjust scripts to suit different local settings.[24] As was symptomatic of imperialism, African audience members' opinions and interpretations were completely excluded from the record.

After 1931, when he obtained filmmaking equipment under the Colonial Development Fund and pioneered the filming technique believed to reach the hearts and minds of "primitive" audiences through simple shots and singular lessons, Sellers used all of his "spare time for producing and projecting local documentary and instructional films."[25] A government truck was converted into a mobile cinema and propaganda vehicle during the Lagos Health Week of 1935; from it Sellers oversaw the production and distribution of numerous short information films and educational parables.[26] By 1936 a special section of the Medical Health Service had become the dedicated HPU, and by 1940 Sellers had been joined in his work by the moviemaker George Pearson, famous for his silent films.[27]

The Colonial Film Unit operated on completely different principles from local commercial cinemas in West Africa. It drew techniques and themes from the recently concluded Bantu Educational Kinema Experiment (BEKE) in the southern African copperbelt in the mid-1930s, as well as from Christian missionary films aimed at transforming moral and physical practices in African communities, where photographs and other educational materials were used in conjunction with movies to impart colonial health messages about the avoidance of "filth diseases" and the "modernization" of African consumption patterns. Thus, the CFU was preoccupied with imparting Eurocentric public health messages to African spectators in films in which any potentially disreputable conduct was carefully framed for intended audiences in plots that emphasized the necessity for behavioral reform.[28]

Bodily reform was the tangible counterpart to moral reform in CFU movies. From the inception of Sellers's work in West Africa, dirt and the cinema were closely connected. His first film for public display to Nigerian audiences, *Plague*, responded to the epidemic of bubonic plague discussed in chapter 3. It opened with close-ups of rats scrabbling in waste heaps in the alleyways of Lagos, while infants played in the dirt and women prepared food in nearby doorways, oblivious to—or, more accurately, exhibiting no revulsion toward—the proximity of the rodents and the rubbish.[29] Described as the "first motion picture created specifically for a colonial audience," *Plague* established a theme and an interpretative framework for subsequent colonial moviemaking in Africa.[30] As the epigraph to this chapter makes clear, *Plague* and its successors were intended to communicate health messages without any possibility of opacity for spectators.[31] Sellers's educational parables were designed to stimulate transformations of Africans' social and domestic lives by placing public health and personal hygiene at the forefront of narratives. Behind these transformations was a firm belief, visualized in numerous films, that modernity in hygiene was exemplified by the purchase and consumption of imported British manufactures such as soap and toothpaste.[32]

In film after film shown throughout Africa by colonial health and information officers between the late 1920s and early 1950s, cleanliness was associated with European cultural practices such as the use of soap-washed knives, forks, and tableware; medical and maternity treatment in hospitals away from home; the cremation of corpses rather than their burial; the removal of refuse from the vicinity of homes; the use of mass-produced, imported British soap products in place of locally manufactured equivalents; the removal of livestock beyond home and village boundaries; defecation in enclosed pit latrines rather than in the bush or on the beach; a willingness to have vaccinations; and the wearing of footwear to prevent parasites from entering the bloodstream. Meanwhile, local and traditional medical, culinary, beauty, and hygienic practices were all represented in these films as dangerous to human health, especially to that of infants. These dangers were incarnated in numerous movies in the figure of the male herbalist, or traditional doctor, always represented as a wild-eyed and filthy individual, living in a windowless, dirty hut and charging extortionate fees for chanting useless incantations over the bodies of the sick and dying.[33]

One particular film, *Machi Gaba* (1939; Hausa: *The Village That Crept Ahead*), was Sellers's pride and joy. He was especially pleased with the film's use of Muslim amateur actors recruited from the Hausa area of northern Nigeria where it was filmed and set. To him, this film was a perfect example of what had come to be known throughout the British colonial film-world as "the Sellers technique," being "a simple [story . . .] full of human interest" that "show[s] how filth and dirty habits bring misery, poverty and sickness and then follows enlightenment, self-help, improved general health and prosperity."[34] The film opens with scenes of a typical northern Nigerian town, designed to be familiar to spectators. Close-ups then reveal the truth about spectators' reality, with "heaps of refuse lying about the streets, untidiness and dirt," and, as the local commentator is scripted to explain, "there is a great deal of sickness in the town."[35] At this point in African screenings, the local interpreter was required to interact directly with the audience: "'Here is a very dirty house. Who is that man?'"[36] The technique, Sellers explained in a demonstration at the Royal Society of Arts, London, "is to get the audience to answer questions. We say 'what is the matter with him?' and back comes the answer 'he is sick.'"[37] The interpreter is required by the script to reply: "'Yes. Sick people cannot work properly.'" The audience is then asked, "'Are you sorry for that man?' Back comes the answer 'Yes, we are very sorry for him.'"[38] To and fro go the questions and answers, with colonial information about the connections between dirt and sickness repeated back to audiences in the form of a vernacular lesson containing explanations for the scenes of distress. "Yes . . . He is very sick," runs the script. "That man's sickness, it is more than likely, is caused by all this filth and dirt that you see lying about his house, and a great deal of the sickness in the town is caused by the filth and dirt that the people allow to lie about all over the town."[39]

Sellers's script takes the form of a pantomime rather than a Socratic or genuinely dialogical exchange, allowing only one correct answer to each question. As he insisted in his general guidelines for the vernacular commentaries accompanying the screening of all such educational films, "Often it will assist if it contains a few questions involving short and obvious answers for the audience to shout out."[40] Thus, as the "dirty" and "foolish" protagonist of *Machi Gaba* lies down in sickness and the audience is asked, "'Are you sorry for this man?'. . . back comes the answer in a roar, in a revision of their opening expression of pity, 'No! we are not sorry for him.'"[41]

"'Why are you not sorry for him?' and back comes the answer 'Because he is a dirty man and lives in a dirty house.'"[42]

Later scenes in *Machi Gaba* show "the people busy and, acting upon the advice given them by their new District Head and his council, they clean up their homes and all useless water pots are broken."[43] In this manner, the happy-ever-after ending of the colonial script is played out in what the media historian Brian Larkin compellingly describes as a "futuristic urban fantasy of colonial rule."[44] As in fairytales, the final scene of *Machi Gaba* shows a land of health and wealth, with "plenty of corn and cloth, [while] the children play and dance and prosperity reigns." At this point, the audience is asked, "'Do *you* want to keep fit and strong? . . . Are *you* going to keep your town clean and free from sickness?' to which the reply is 'Yes.'"[45] How difficult could the effective communication of such a stark colonial health message be?

Each time Sellers's favorite film was shown in rural Zambia, *Machi Gaba* reduced its audiences to helpless laughter. Reporting back on this reaction in 1943, a bemused and "surprised" British information officer, who had placed Sellers's exemplary film at the top of his bill, tried to fathom the causes of his audience's mirth. The information officer could not understand where the problem lay. Perhaps, he speculated, "the type of native character is so foreign to the Northern Rhodesian native that he finds Mohammedan dress amusing and instead of being taught that clean village life makes for healthier living, he is left with the idea that the Nigerians are funny people."[46] As a consequence of this failure of its intended message, the information officer judged *Machi Gaba* to be "the least popular film so far" of all the CFU productions circulating in southern Africa.[47] Based on the audience reaction, however, one could equally conclude that the film was a triumph with local filmgoers. Unsuccessful in its direct educational messaging rather than unpopular as a movie, the film had simply failed to remain anchored to the genre intended for it by the CFU. Southern African audiences seemed to regard it as a type of anthropological comedy rather than an educational parable. Indeed, the officer in Zambia admitted that "*Machi Gaba* as an educational travelogue would have been successful," acknowledging the failure of the creators' intentions and generic categories rather than a failure of the film per se.[48]

Nearly a decade later, on the other side of the continent in the Hausa-speaking village of Soba, Nigeria, a Ghanaian infant nutrition film, *Amenu's Child* (1950) was screened in 1952. Believing they are acting in the best interests of their baby, who has dysentery, malnutrition, or another curable disease, the parents in the film take their infant to an expensive traditional healer rather than following the advice of a Western-educated urban character who tells them to take it to the European hospital for treatment. The scene with the healer shows an obvious charlatan in a filthy hut, surrounded by heaps of unidentifiable and grotesque "fetish" objects, waving a fly whisk over the baby in an exaggerated way.[49] The film cuts to the parents' return home with the baby who is found to have died on the journey. In Soba, there was a most unexpected response: "The whole audience was hilarious when they heard of the death of the child."[50]

In the summer of 1951, a young British anthropologist was seconded by the Colonial Office to undertake "systematic research" into the success or failure of officially sponsored films among rural cinema audiences in Nigeria.[51] By the time Peter Morton-Williams received his portfolio from the Colonial Office, "research into the causes of laughter" was deemed not only pressing but essential.[52] Why, the Colonial Office needed to know, did African spectators laugh at such inappropriate moments in educational movies? Given the logic underlying the making of CFU films, the Colonial Office wished Morton-Williams to find out why their blatant health messages had failed to transform intended audiences' attitudes and behavior over the course of two decades, for, as the director and producer George Pearson commented dejectedly about his work for the CFU, "many a film deemed successful in its showing has been revealed as futile through subsequent close questioning of the audience."[53] Perplexed about the impact of all his hard work in the previous decade, Pearson continued, "We have got to know far more than we at present know about how much our audiences really appreciate—and far more important, what they fail to appreciate, and WHY?"[54]

"Inappropriate" laughter was such a problem for the Colonial Office, who funded the expensive CFU movies with their basic messages, that in a survey of the impact of "cinema propaganda" in the colonies in 1943, the CO included a request that officials should "give a few examples of typical sequences that make people laugh."[55] This survey, and subsequent ones through the 1940s and early 1950s, form the problematic archive out of which this chapter is constructed.

With the support of a British film technician, a Nigerian projectionist, a full-time commentator, and a temporary local commentator whose combined linguistic skills enabled communication across diverse Nigerian language groups, Morton-Williams set out from the Lagos headquarters of the CFU early in 1952 equipped with a mobile cinema van and a selection of films, with the aim of gauging audiences' reactions to British colonial productions. While traveling through Yoruba-, Igbo-, Hausa-, and Berom-speaking villages around the country, the newly constituted Audience Research Unit screened CFU productions on a range of topics relating to health and hygiene in Africa. The program included short health documentaries such as *Dysentery* (1950, Uganda, 12 mins.), *Tapeworm* (ca. 1944, Northern Nigeria, 11 mins.), *Mosquito* (ca. 1937), and *Clean Cooking* (1951, Nigeria, 11 mins.), as well as short dramatizations such as *Mr Wise and Mr Foolish Go to Town* (reedited 1944, South Africa, 23 mins.), *Daybreak in Udi* (1949, Nigeria, 42 mins.), *Smallpox* (1950, Nigeria, 24 mins.), and *Amenu's Child* (1950, Gold Coast, 36 mins.).[56]

British officials frequently explained what they regarded as the failure of a film's educational messaging as a consequence of the flawed reactions of audiences to techniques of naturalism designed to elicit identification rather than alienation. Countless filmmakers expressed concerns that "even slight misrepresentations of native life and customs can change the most serious film into comedy."[57] A journalist writing for *United Empire* in 1940 described how, during the screening in Nigeria of a scene showing close-ups of hookworm, in which "the object . . . was to impress upon people the tragedy which results from dirt and disease," to the great surprise of CFU personnel, the audience "found it highly amusing," reacting with "unsympathetic laughter and ribald remarks . . . they roared their delighted appreciation!"[58] At other times, "moments of great pathos in a film . . . cause[d] considerable laughter."[59] Partly entangled with colonialism, but not defined by it, these late colonial film audiences exhibited a cultural distinction that colonial officials interpreted as a sign of parochialism and the presence of "closed systems of thought."[60] Whether regarded as closed and parochial, or as refreshingly remote from the behavioral prescriptions of British culture, the fact remained that "not all African peoples [were] prepared to acknowledge the superiority of all European practice to their own."[61]

Naturalistic acting and settings were a prerequisite of the CFU's educational parables, intended to increase the impact of the didactic script, but colonial officials expressed repeated concerns that African audiences would transform both documentary and narrative non-entertainment films—with their serious messages designed "to act as a stimulant towards social and material progress"—into "first-rate comedy."[62] People laughed at the most unexpected material. Among the replies to the 1943 Colonial Office survey question about what elicited laughter, for example, came the following selection of seemingly unamusing scenes: "Mr English being handed his attaché case by his wife as she bids him goodbye with a kiss (quite foreign to natives);"[63] "Simple things of everyday life, e.g., a white man eating a meal;"[64] "Indian children eating out of bowls on the ground in *Children of the Empire*. The little girl skipping and dancing in *Mr English at Home*."[65]

By 1952, when Morton-Williams commenced his screenings in Nigeria, this colonial aesthetic of simple naturalism for Africans had become immovable, in spite of ongoing critiques from liberal commentators and the "failures" of numerous educational films. Yet, as Morton-Williams discovered, rural Yoruba audiences watching *Amenu's Child* (1950) were perfectly aware of the film's status as a drama acted by performers, a parabolic story offering examples for commentary and comparison rather than a documentary about real-life people. Yoruba audience reactions during the movie, and people's reflections and recollections afterward, showed both a desire to understand the anthropological reality of the foreign society portrayed in the film, and the operation of established, local aesthetic conventions governing storytelling and spectatorship, including conventions relating to appropriate moments for laughter and other nonverbal responses. In the Yoruba village of Ilaro, Morton-Williams reported, "after watching quietly the opening shots, the audience soon became more observably responsive, becoming absorbed in the film," saying "Aa!" at a shot of a boy jumping on a lorry, with "indulgent laughs and cheers from children in the audience at Saewa's elder child helping the younger to eat."[66] In the scene where "the party was visiting the Diviner, there were exclamations of 'A!' and some laughter when the Diviner appeared. Everyone was intently quiet while he brushed the child with his fly switch; a few gasped."[67] As Amenu pays the diviner his exorbitant fee, "someone jokingly compared the prices with those charged by a body of witch-finders who had visited Ilaro the previous year, and whose prices were considered extortionate."[68] Different groups of spectators absorbed different messages from the film, demonstrating their preexisting biases, their differential immersion in the narrative, and their judgments of recognizable behavior on-screen, rather than simply showing a blanket acceptance of the colonial educational parable as if it were a nonfictional documentary.

Numerous members of Morton-Williams's audiences—young people, married and unmarried people, mature women and men, Muslims and Christians, people from all of the language groups included in his study—laughed at the scene in the Ghanaian film *Amenu's Child*, when the baby is found to have died after its expensive trip to a traditional healer.[69] The infant's death caused such havoc in the Berom village of Dashit in May 1952 that "the film had to be stopped during this scene, to re-order the audience."[70] Some of the colonial officers described above would undoubtedly have become apoplectic at this point and concluded that these audiences were laughing barbarically at the dead baby and its sobbing mother. In his own comments on their laughter, however, Morton-Williams suggested that it was "an appropriate reaction" in the context of "the social norms and values of the audiences. Laughter, whether of approval and enjoyment, or of ridicule, is a form of social control, a sanction for behaviour."[71] While he did not explain what type of social control was being exercised, or by whom over whom and for what reason, Morton-Williams carefully avoided concluding that audiences agreed with the film's health message about not taking infants to traditional healers.[72]

The unanimous Nigerian reaction to *Amenu's Child* demonstrates the operation of local notions of appropriate and foolish behavior. If the CFU's intended messages about hygiene passed audiences by, the film's moral messages about foolish behavior were understood loudly and clearly by audiences. The death of the baby clearly showed Amenu and his wife to have made a poor decision. Audience members in Soba were overheard to say, "It's just what they deserved" and "If they haven't any sense, they must put up with it; why all the fuss?"[73] This does not necessarily show acceptance of the film's message about Western medicine, although this might have been the case among some spectators; rather, people's laughter seems to have been aimed at the "stupid" parents for visiting an incompetent healer. They laughed in reaction to being proven correct by the narrative trajectory of the film, having successfully predicted the narrative outcome suggested at the start of the film. Their reaction confirmed the public vindication, in the film, of the accuracy of their assumptions, and running commentaries throughout, about the foolishness of the parents for consulting this particular doctor.

In this manner, the CFU's educational parable was successfully "parabolized" by Nigerian audiences, but in a different shape to the one intended by its British makers, with meaning accorded to details deemed irrelevant by officials. As Morton-Williams commented of Yoruba audiences, *Amenu's Child* was "ineffectual" in its message because its lengthy sermon on child nutrition was overlooked by audiences, and the parents' folly was inflected with local explanations and beliefs about infant mortality stemming from spiritual rather than medical beliefs.[74] Spectators' laughter exhibited a confident capacity to cross-reference film material with an existing corpus of moral and spiritual narratives. In general, for viewers of *Amenu's Child*, with its numerous lessons about infant cleanliness and nutrition, "traditional practices about child care [were . . .] too well sanctioned to be readily altered by the simple assertion that one kind of food is better than another."[75] Films were thus incorporated into local intertexts and contexts, and in the process their propagandist power was diluted or neutralized altogether.

Interestingly, Morton-Williams's inquiries into Yoruba laughter at the baby's death also raised technical factors relating to filmmaking and poor acting above cultural, spiritual, or sociological explanations for people's mirth. After the screening in the villages of Egan and Ilaro, people commented that, first, "there was a note of false sorrow on the screen, through inadequate acting";[76] second, the mother was "foolish" in the view of many spectators for refusing to take her child to hospital, so "many jeered at her folly";[77] third, "the sudden cut from Amenu and his mother walking away from the Diviner with the living child to their arrival home, carrying the dead child, was startling," triggering laughter.[78] These audiences recognized the medium's forced naturalism, applied the principles of existing narrative genres in which foolishness is jeered at rather than pitied, and reacted to editing techniques in the studio. Contrary to filmmakers' constructions of African village dwellers as naïve, gullible, and susceptible to the propaganda power of naturalism, Morton-Williams's rural audiences recognized and commented on filmic technique and genre; they rendered the medium equally visible to the message; and they critiqued the structure of films. In doing so, they comprehensively overturned the "truth" or "reality" claimed for the medium by filmmakers.[79]

In other CFU "contrast" films—or "before-and-after" films[80]—that juxtaposed the success of European medicine with the failure of traditional remedies, audiences experienced similar types of pleasure at the fulfillment of their interpretative projections. Among Igbo audiences watching *Smallpox*, for example, "there were claps, laughs and cheers when Alabi left hospital," free of infection, with members of the audience "saying a prayer of thanks to God."[81] As with *Amenu's Child*, the narrative trajectory—or destiny—established at the start of the film was confirmed by its ending, allowing audiences to experience pleasure at the fulfillment of their interpretative projections, which predicted the fall of a character who clearly tempted fate by not agreeing to be inoculated against smallpox. Spectators' laughter expressed pleasure at their proficiency in interpreting the moral formula of CFU educational parables. The health messages of *Smallpox* and *Amenu's Child* may have taken a back seat to this affirmation of success in the judgment of character.

From an official perspective, extraneous ethnographic details about other cultures were often "so obtrusive that many failed to understand" the films' lessons about hygiene, disease prevention, agricultural improvements, and infant nutrition.[82] Thus, for Yoruba audiences of a Zimbabwean film, *Wives of Nendi* (1949), which focused on the necessity for women to remove domestic waste from the vicinity of their homes to prevent the spread of diseases, the "main interest seems to have been in seeing a strange place and people."[83] Indeed, Yoruba audiences became so absorbed in what, for information officers, were the inconsequential details of scenes designed to establish verisimilitude and to enhance audience identification with the story, that they failed to realize the film's simple message was intended for themselves. *Wives of Nendi* generated so much moralizing among Yoruba audiences about the need for perseverance in the face of life's obstacles that "no one felt it had other lessons for them."[84]

Within the cinema spaces created by mobile health units across Africa, spectators processed images and values through their own aesthetic, spiritual, moral, economic, and political value systems. Even when filmed locally in familiar settings, however, naturalism did not yield behavioral transformations among viewers. Yoruba audiences watched the Yoruba film *Smallpox* (1950) "with noticeable horror" for the way the film "attracted attention to the disease" by depicting it realistically on screen, and, according to Morton-Williams, they were not persuaded that vaccinations were anything more than a potent "charm" to ward off an essentially spiritual affliction.[85] Indeed, *Smallpox* aroused more terror, fascination, and laughter in Nigerian audiences than any other film shown by Morton-Williams's research team in 1952. Audience members remembered the plot "vividly and in detail" when interviewed afterward about their impressions.[86] Again and again, Yoruba and Berom audiences expressed reluctance to see this film a second time when Morton-Williams toured with it in the early 1950s. "To people who are so afraid of smallpox that they never mention it by its proper name for fear the spirits may overhear and visit them," he explained, "the portrayal of the disease on screen seems very dangerous."[87] In his interpretation, the audience's proximity to the infected characters on the screen would invite the disease into viewers' own homes, and when finally persuaded to watch the film, people conveyed with laughter their shock at the vivid representation of the infectious skin lesions.

Whether or not one agrees with Morton-Williams's interpretation of Yoruba and Berom viewers' responses, what becomes clear is that no matter how stark the colonial health parable, no matter how naturalistic the technique, and no matter how binary and simplistic the oppositions between cleanliness (wisdom) and dirt (foolishness) depicted in films, existing beliefs about infectious diseases were not supplanted by colonial propaganda movies in the rural communities visited by the Audience Research Unit.[88] Unlike elite African media producers in the colonial period, who engaged directly with colonial policy and demanded European-style town-planning and sanitation systems, and unlike those Africans whose working lives were likely to involve direct experiences of colonial racial hierarchies, what emerges in Morton-Williams's numerous detailed summaries and translations of audience responses is most people's lack of concern with the direct, unmediated communication of British colonial ideology. Thus, Berom audiences "looked at the scenery and did not try to discover a message to be learnt" in the health film *Dysentery*, with its explicit lesson about how to avoid fly-borne diseases, because "they had a well-entrenched belief about the supernatural in this disease."[89] Likewise, for viewers of *Amenu's Child*, the film's health message was refracted through people's beliefs about infant nutrition.[90] Indeed, given the size of crowds at screenings and the open air cinema environment served by the loudspeaker (or microphone and amplifier), communication would often have been cracked and muffled, if not inaudible to sections of the audience, leaving people to interpret the film's message among themselves.

Morton-Williams's audiences seem to have regarded a character's behavior on-screen not so much as a message to their community to accept new health and hygiene regimes from abroad, but as evidence of an individual character's wisdom, poor judgment, failure to conform to spiritual and social norms, foolishness or outright wickedness as a person. At this particular moment of Nigerian media consumption in the early 1950s, many spectators—at least in rural areas of the south and southeast—simply refused to extrapolate from the CFU's naturalistic representations and to apply the health parables to themselves. From the errors and prejudices of the incompetent community leader in *Daybreak in Udi*, to the ineffectual medicines and extortionate prices of the native doctor in *Amenu's Child*, and the assertiveness of the heroine in *Wives of Nendi*, who withstands bullying and ostracism by her neighbors to implement a new European regime of household cleanliness, audiences focused on the extraordinary behavior of the individuals portrayed in films above the generic lessons such behavior conveyed. In short, during the screening of movies, they neither recognized nor rejected "dirty" local practices as bad. The simple binary framework of CFU productions for Africans, blatant to the point of condescension, seems to have held far less importance for audiences than the behavior of individual characters. In spite of repeated screenings of the same film to some audiences, heroes and heroines remained individuals in the eyes of respondents, exemplary or deplorable, but largely irrelevant to the viewer's own life.

Seen outside the thematic categories imposed by colonial information officers—for whom health, sanitation, cleanliness, and hygiene provided the rationale for screenings—the widespread fascination with other cultures among the Nigerian filmgoers that made up Morton-Williams's audiences offers an important jigsaw piece in the history of the reception of transnational media genres on the continent. These responses were not confined to rural areas less "touched" than urban areas by the colonial encounter. While Sellers and his cohort of British imperial filmmakers continued to insist that simply made, naturalistic story-films filled with contrasts and overt messages were the only forms suitable for "illiterate" Africans' comprehension, the evidence furnished by attendance figures at commercial cinemas in African towns in the 1930s and 1940s, and by the types of film that proved most popular in these venues, contradicts their robust notions of African aesthetic values and preferences.[91] For example, the ongoing popularity in urban African-owned cinemas of de-sequenced, out-of-date films suggests the operation of interpretive priorities other than naturalism and narrative linearity among audiences. In the commercial open-air cinemas at Alli Street and Oshodi Street, Lagos, "for prices of admission of one penny and threepence, non-critical audiences view films of great antiquity which in the course of time have lost their beginnings, their ends and a great deal of their sequence."[92] While some viewers of these dis-ordered and deteriorated films might have pieced together an original storyline from their memories of previous screenings, stretching back months or years, the ongoing popularity of these clipped and jumbled films suggests the operation of another aesthetic altogether, through which fragmented scenes and deconstructed plots made sense to local spectators without any need for "the slow tempo [and . . .] continuity of movement" required for CFU movies by the "Sellers technique."[93]

Additionally, African audiences were a great deal more resistant to the reality effects of mimetic representation than indicated by officials. In 1943, when audiences in Orlu, southeast Nigeria, were shown a CFU documentary about a mongoose and a python, entitled *Killing the Killer*, a perplexed

British information officer reported that "the audience regarded the film as symbolic, representing the battle between Britain and Germany, personified in Mr Churchill and Hitler."[94] "The propaganda value was much more subtle," he reflected, "than (presumably) the authors intended it to be."[95] The audience in this case had collectively translated an informational wildlife documentary into their own framework of animal symbolism, demonstrating, in the process, a subtlety of interpretation of world news far exceeding the expectations of filmmakers operating within the black-and-white optic of Sellers's method. Other information officers commented on the symbolic potential of *Killing the Killer* for audiences in British colonial Africa: in response to the request for ideas of "suitable subjects for films," for example, one Gold Coast information officer suggested a "fictional film on the basis of *Killing the Killer*, showing the victory of good over evil."[96]

People's unscripted laughter was not only unfathomable but offensive to some British officials, further obstructing their efforts to interpret local filmgoers' responses to material intended for social and physical improvement. Wishing for empathy and emulation, shocked colonial officials often identified cruelty and an absence of refined sensibilities above other causes of the apparent failures of identification that resulted in laughter. As a consequence, they cautioned, cinema in Africa required rigorous control, or else "ridicule results."[97] "It is unfortunate that films such as *Air Raid Warden* and *Heroic Malta* fail to rouse the sympathy and admiration for the courage displayed that they do in European audiences," one tight-lipped Kenyan information officer commented in the Colonial Office audience survey of 1943. He went on to say, "The laughter provoked by the wounded being rescued and treated, in spite of the most careful preliminary explanation, I found so upsetting that I show them but seldom, and have cut out some portions."[98]

The failure of African audiences to be aroused by wartime propaganda designed to stimulate empathy between imperial citizens and to strengthen support for the Allied war effort clearly offended and angered imperial officers, and their racism increased in direct proportion to the volume of African laughter. The Kenyan official concluded, "The Kenya [*sic*] natives have not reached a stage in which they are capable of feelings for others. They laugh at a man being wounded or killed as they do Charlie Chaplin slipping on a banana skin."[99] As he warmed to his catalogue of African interpretive failures, other familiar complaints about the "native" came to the surface. "Scenery again leaves them unmoved," he added. "They seem to be unaware of the beauties of nature which surround them. The attitude is summed up in 'Whats [*sic*] the use of growing flowers, you can't eat them!'"[100]

In one of the few full-length scholarly studies of laughter as a popular response, Simon Dickie describes "the guiltless, intoxicating pleasure of tormenting the disabled" in early modern culture.[101] In accepting people's "cruelty" and "malice" as authentic feelings, Dickie seeks to explain these reactions as fearful responses arising from the proximity of affliction to their own lives.[102] As demonstrated by the Kenyan information officer's reaction, however, if applied to colonial African audiences as consumers of transnational mass media, the attribution of cruelty and malice serves to reinforce colonialist stereotypes of African savagery. The Kenyan officer's report draws from a corpus of prior colonial representations rather than an effort to understand the audience's response. Like the CFU archive in which it is situated, the report offers historically specific information about the *producers* of colonial knowledge, but it does not help media historians to understand African cinemagoers' laughter because its way of seeing is determined by the British imperialist ideology.

A host of cognitive failures is encapsulated in these accounts of the responses of African audiences. British officials—charged with reporting back on filmgoers' aesthetic experiences—failed to recognize the presence of local interpretative conventions that took precedence over the intended educational messages of imported propaganda films.[103] In particular, in attributing African laughter to unrefined "cruelty," callousness, and the desire for crude entertainment, white officials precluded the possibility of a politics of ridicule among audiences. The laughter of audiences may rather have expressed deliberate, deliberative contempt for the patriotic messages of pro-imperial wartime propaganda, or a general refusal of colonial educational messaging.[104] The "banana skin" antics identified by the Kenyan information officer as the source of African amusement take on a different, more political hue in the context of colonial discourse and power. As one information officer in Nigeria noted, "Chaplin and other similar slapstick films in which the little man is up against it and wins through" were more popular with audiences than educational documentaries on CFU programs.[105]

Chaplin's portrayals of the resilience and cunning of powerless "little" people in the face of authority may have generated empathy and recognition among colonial audiences, responses that were often absent from films depicting African empowerment through the adoption of British health and hygiene practices. Understanding Chaplin from the perspective of a "common person" subject to local and colonial political hierarchies, as well as to complex power relations involving gender, seniority, marriage, and wealth, gives us a better sense of why audiences laughed at other scenes in the supposedly "serious" CFU films. For instance, in one Yoruba village visited by Morton-Williams and his team in 1952, when the traditional healer in *Smallpox* (1950) runs away with his patient at the arrival of the vaccination team, "everybody laughed" and one man "roared with laughter"; similarly, "there was general laughter" as the health team entered the escapee's recently vacated hut and found it empty.[106] Echoing a pleasurable thread in folktales, the "little" person cunningly defeats—in this case, temporarily— the powerful authority figure who comes looking for him. The spectacle of a barefooted old man and a smallpox victim outwitting colonial officials by running into the bush aroused laughter among every audience to whom *Smallpox* was shown in Nigeria in 1952, including the generally quieter Hausa viewers. While the commentator was scripted to emphasize the foolishness of the smallpox victim for fleeing government health officials, and the foolishness of the traditional healer for failing to report the smallpox case as he was legally obliged to, audiences may have laughed out of empathy as well as pleasure at the slapstick potential, rather than shock or critical distance, at the sight of two villagers fleeing from an ambulance and government officials in uniform. In an Igbo village visited by the Audience Research Unit, as "one man remarked to another, if it had been in their own village, many would have run away (from vaccination)."[107] Indeed, Morton-Williams observed, "I have been in a village when vaccinators arrived and seen most of the population vanish into the bush."[108]

By the early 1950s, in the wake of postwar transformations to British colonial policy, even Sellers's own totalizing and reductive views about what he continuously termed "primitive" people started to be tinged with doubts and revisions. "It is often thought that any film will be above the head of a primitive audience," he wrote in a memorandum to the Colonial Office in 1951. "This is undoubtedly true of a great many of the films which are made for more sophisticated Western audiences but it does not seem to be necessarily true of all films."[109] Sellers's comments capture the revisionist tone among veteran pro-colonial film personnel in the early 1950s as they struggled to catch up with the new imperial rhetoric of postwar Britain. As R. O. H. Porch of Nigeria wrote to a civil servant in London in October 1950, "I believe that we have assumed rather too readily that because an audience is composed of semi-literate to illiterate persons that one has to present a film to them as if one was showing it to four-year-olds in England."[110] "It may be a mistake to over-emphasise the primitiveness of Colonial audiences," he confessed: "They will probably be found quick to learn the tricks of the trade in the same way as Western audiences have done."[111]

From the vantage point of the Nigerian audiences with whom Morton-Williams and his team worked, spectators showed cultural self-confidence in their consumption of the new global medium, absorbing films into their own discursive frameworks, and as Charles Ambler found in his study of African spectatorship in the Zambian Copperbelt in the 1940s and 1950s, viewers would "weav[e] their own practices . . . into discussions of the meanings of particular sequences."[112] One point is clear. Whether it was in Nigeria or in Zambia, colonial film producers' public health messages frequently failed to achieve their objective among the intended audiences of these expensive films. For that reason, as will be discussed in the next chapter, cultural historians and media scholars should not refer, in an abstract, ahistorical manner, to "the reader" or "the audience" (or "readers" or "audiences") or to "the message" of media texts as if these were singular, extractable entities.

5

Methods, Unsound Methods,
No Methods at All?

"Do you," said I, looking at the shore, "call it 'unsound method'?"
"Without doubt," he exclaimed hotly. "Don't you?" . . .
"No method at all," I murmured after a while.
—JOSEPH CONRAD

Chapter 4 questioned the extent to which the responses of audiences in Nigeria, as preserved in colonial documentary archives, can be used by historians to gather information about local aesthetic values, or to glean clues about African health and hygiene practices that have fallen off the written historical radar. Midcentury film spectators' responses are present in the archives, but they take the form of untranslated and untranscribed commentaries and opinions—including disagreements and debates between different sections of the audience, such as men and women, and married and unmarried women[1]—as well as laughter and other types of nonverbal communication. Taken together, these indicate flexible and heterogeneous interpretations of Colonial Film Unit (CFU) movies far beyond the public health messaging that formed the rationale for film production.[2]

Scholars interested in the reception of transnational media and methods for researching media histories in global contexts face the challenge of how to retrieve, let alone interpret, this record of historical spectators' responses where even the presence of translators was represented by officials as an obstacle, introducing misinterpretations and frustrating the desire for cross-cultural transparency. Norman F. Spurr's report on his film shoot for *Trees Are Cash* in eastern Uganda typifies the attitude towards African translators. Language presented "a serious difficulty. . . . I had to tell the Forest Officer what I wanted in English, whereupon he translated it into Swahili for the benefit of the chief, and the chief translated it into Eteso for the benefit of the actors. . . . It was more than disconcerting to find upon starting a scene, your principal character, instead of coming to the camera, mounting a bicycle and setting off in the opposite direction!"[3]

A small but revealing indication of the lack of trust in African translators as interpreters of scripts can be found in a report by William Sellers on a Health Propaganda Unit (HPU) tour of the Southern provinces of Nigeria in March and April 1937. "It was found essential to check all interpretations" by the local narrators who provided commentaries and voiceovers, Sellers wrote, "and this was done by going amongst the audience and asking an English-speaking African to retranslate what was coming through the loud-speakers."[4] In this manner, film screenings were marked by the surveillance of translators and interpreters rather than by curiosity about the ways in which these mediating figures localized film messages to achieve impact and stimulate discussion among spectators.

A methodological dilemma persists beyond the end of the preceding chapters and reinforces the gulf separating the colonial archives from the "living archive" of urban residents to which this book turns in the remaining chapters. The official archives on which this book has depended until now whited-out and wrote over local people's opinions and perspectives. The barely concealed repugnance for indigenous health and hygiene practices underpinning so much of the archive presents major challenges for historians with an interest in African audiences' responses to the circulation of global mass media and propaganda. Yet the same archive clearly also reveals that local audiences' responses conveyed aesthetic values and interpretations far beyond the imaginations of the colonial producers who reported back on the success or failure of health propaganda campaigns. If there is more in the colonial archives than a simple reflection of British ideology, how can media historians access and approach the knowledge produced by the linguistically diverse audiences who attended CFU screenings and consumed other media materials in the colonial era, for whom even the most prescriptive, educational story contained potential for alternative interpretations? What kind of publics were constituted by and in the colonial media spaces analyzed in previous chapters? What methods help us to understand the polyphonic "chatter" overheard by CFU staff working in diverse African territories?

For Michael Warner in his influential book *Publics and Counterpublics*, the circulation of texts in the Global North stimulates the formation of otherwise discontinuous publics.[5] Publics, Warner argues, are a "space of discourse organized by nothing other than discourse itself"; they exist "*by virtue of being addressed*," and "cease to exist when attention is no longer predicated."[6] In contexts of colonial rule, however, as Brian Larkin suggests, the "logic of governmentality" shaped colonial media spaces and organized the publics therein.[7] Organizations such as the CFU undertook far more than the screening of movies. Larkin shows that the impact of British propaganda on colonial subjects' cultural lives, aesthetic values, and self-confidence as interpreters of mass media texts was far greater than the convening of villagers as publics for occasional educational films. Rather, screenings were an element in the physical regulation of bodies according to the dictates of colonial authority.[8]

The organization and structure of CFU performances meant that spectators were present as a particular configuration of publics, as state-controlled citizens in receipt of a "political education" and a training in "new forms of perception and attention," rather than simply as freely consenting consumers of global cultural commodities.[9] "What they were attending was first of all a political event" directly connected to political rule, Larkin insists.[10] Colonial power was exercised alongside, as well as within, the textual content of British propaganda films, rendering "the mode of exchange between image and spectator . . . one governed more by politics than by the commodity."[11] No matter how rural, CFU audiences were bound into a Foucauldian-style panopticon, not least as a result of the physical presence of local chiefs, literate elites, and other political authority figures at screenings, including in the form of giant silhouette figures on the screen as they positioned themselves in the glare of the projector to publicly endorse the CFU's health messages at the end of film shows.[12] The entire colonial apparatus and political agenda that buttressed health officials' visits was therefore on display at CFU performances.[13]

Any discussion of the media spaces in which colonial African publics were convened—including the African-owned newspapers discussed in chapter 3—must include this exoskeleton of colonial power. Present as a "pre-given framework," it denied audiences access to Warner's definition of "public" spaces in the contemporary Global North, which is vitally dependent on individual autonomy from the state and other institutions.[14] In

Larkin's view, the CFU's African film publics were recruited and assembled by, rather than simply attracted to, the discursive space of the cinema, and as a consequence they were put on display much like the products they consumed.[15] For health propaganda officers, individual films were one important element in an elaborate, wider spectacle of colonial rule, contributing to and reinforcing the colonial framework through which African audiences were observed and understood by the regime. In this manner, as John Hartley suggests for television audiences in 1980s Europe, the discourse that organized these publics was also an expression of institutional power. "Audiences are not just constructs," Hartley writes. "They are the invisible fictions that are produced institutionally in order for various institutions to take charge of the mechanisms of their own survival. Audiences may be imagined empirically, theoretically or politically, but in all cases the product is a fiction that serves the needs of the imagining institution. In no case is the audience "real," or external to its discursive construction. There is no "actual" audience that lies beyond its production as a category."[16]

Larkin's and Hartley's persuasive models of institutional hegemony, intentionality, and ideological power help to explain the perspectives and presence of two out of three vital mediators in the colonial film dynamic: British filmmakers and government officials. But they do not fully explain the third element at the core of this study: the audiences that flummoxed and offended colonialists over the years with their unpredictable responses to educational films and other media materials. Here, Warner's model of publics (and counterpublics) might be reengaged in colonial African contexts. Colonial West African audiences—like media consumers worldwide—had multifaceted reasons for attending film screenings, including a desire for entertainment, peer pressure, political coercion, the wish to be seen by others, a desire to learn about strangers and about neighboring ethnic groups, the wish to sell foodstuffs and other goods at screenings, curiosity about the content of films, sociability, time away from domestic chores, and, enveloped within these other motivations, an interest in or resistance to colonial educational messaging. In conjunction with the colonial state apparatus that made CFU screenings possible, the arrival of the mobile cinema, as Larkin writes, "disrupted the steady flow of everyday life. . . . Children got to stay up late; people congregated in public spaces; friends got to chat and hang out; and the entertainment provided an excuse for larger groups to gather."[17]

If film shows were more than mere screenings, they were also more than spectacles of political domination. Peter Morton-Williams's Audience Research Unit was one of the few initiatives to capture responses that are missing from other reports on African audiences in the colonial period and that are largely absent from subsequent research into postcolonial audiences and readerships.[18] Exclamations and running commentaries recurred among almost every audience during Morton-Williams's screenings, to the extent that he noted how Hausa spectators' silence was exceptional compared with Igbo, Berom, and Yoruba audiences. (The infrequent laughter of Hausa audiences, he explained, generally occurred during scenes depicting the emulation of European customs by Africans, which they regarded as "farce." Their own cultural pride prevented any "desire to ape the domestic customs of Europeans," so they laughed at their fellows' adoption of Western ways.)[19] Except for Morton-Williams's report, however, the colonial film archives contain no sustained acknowledgment of West African audiences as *critical* spectators, that is, to borrow from bell hooks's work on black female spectatorship, as individuals who "resist[ed] the imposition of dominant ways of knowing and looking," and who neither entirely accepted nor entirely rejected the intended messages of colonial filmmakers.[20]

There is a need for considerable further research into the history of film spectatorship and media consumption in colonial Africa, and oral history work is helpful for this task. Many senior Nigerians remember the arrival of mobile cinema units in their villages in the 1940s and 1950s, and how, as children, they flocked excitedly to open-air cinemas where they sat on the ground at the front, craning their necks at the screen. These retrospective accounts usefully highlight the child's-eye-view of colonial propaganda; but as Glenn Reynolds comments in his outstanding study of the impact of mining and transnational labor migration on African spectatorship in southern Africa, one cannot draw too many conclusions from people's reminiscences about the old days of colonial film screenings because "memories fade and stories change for those few [people living today] who actually helped to swell colonial-era audiences before the 1960s."[21] A child's-eye-view is not representative of the plural, vociferous crowd.

Morton-Williams's open-ended and unglamorous conclusion was that rural Nigerian audiences were unlikely simply to adopt and apply the health messages of educational parables without reference to their own aesthetic and behavioral rules. Such an obvious conclusion has far-reaching implications for how we think about "the spectator" or "the reader" in transnational media contexts. People's opinions, perceptions, prejudices, self-understandings, aesthetic preferences, memories of the past, and dreams for the future prevent direct "educational" media messaging from reaching its targets: whether analyzed by a colonial information officer in the 1950s, or by a media historian today attempting to mine the archives for evidence of local responses to colonial propaganda films, African audiences escape sociological, or ethnographic, or formalist, methods of research into the impact of colonial public health and hygiene work, rendering academic constructions of "how spectators are manipulated" by films erroneous.[22] No matter how anticolonial or postcolonial a media historian's perspective may be, no one can simply recuperate local audiences' voices and responses, nor can such information be easily extrapolated simply by viewing the films themselves. Content analysis alone is insufficient for anybody wishing to fathom the impact and reception of transnational texts.

The Last Laugh

A quarter century of colonial "theorizing" about Africans was challenged by the laughter of African audiences.[23] As chapter 4 argued, even the most starkly racialized parable of African backwardness was capable of eliciting the "wrong" reaction among audiences who rarely, if ever, regarded themselves through the same ideological lens as the filmmakers. People's laughter reverberates through colonial accounts of film spectatorship like a form of dirt that cannot be removed from its host. Almost always identified as "inappropriate," laughter was a spillover, or a waste product, produced by the film itself; it was a form of "matter out of place" according to the standards of those in positions of power.[24] As an intensely local response preserved in the archives, laughter offers an interpretive starting point, if not a "method," to postcolonial researchers wishing to highlight African agency in colonial records. Local audiences' laughter explodes unpredictably and uncontrollably, and it sticks to colonial officials who, as report-writing bodies, find themselves incapable of removing it from their scene of power. Laughter suspends relations of power and, albeit temporarily, confuses confident assertions of British colonial legitimacy.

At the very least, people's laughter can be regarded as a form of recalcitrance about the explicit didacticism of CFU films from communities familiar with more sophisticated performance genres than the pantomime morality of public health movies. Laughter was a form of collective film commentary among audiences, arising from diverse sources and motivations, conveying the spirit of individuals and crowds on the night of a particular screening as well as the core cultural and aesthetic values spectators brought to bear on movies. The purveyors of colonial health propaganda did not see that local audiences' responses provided insights into local interpretative practices, and that these practices, in turn, could teach them a great deal about the effectiveness of their messages.

The media consumers who hooted at *Machi Gaba* and found the dead baby "hilarious" in *Amenu's Child* were rather different entities from the African colonial subjects who were welded into colonial power structures as taxpayers and government employees, or as newspaper readers and citizens of colonial municipalities. Literate and Christianized, these "modern" entities were exemplified by the African professional elites discussed in previous chapters. As suggested in chapter 3, African urban elites may sometimes have been closer to colonial officials in their opinions about sanitation and hygiene than to the rural filmgoers at the center of CFU propaganda. Among audiences of a film about syphilis, *Mr Wise and Mr Foolish Go to Town*, screened in Yoruba villages and depicting a visit to prostitutes, Morton-Williams noted that "several of the most educated men in the audience were offended by the public showing of this film," whereas other spectators found the content highly entertaining.[25] The educated men, who had spent time in Nigerian towns, considered the scenes showing a visit to prostitutes, and the subsequent portrayal of symptoms of sexually transmitted diseases, "unsuitable for such a group of spectators, which included several hundred children."[26] The same category of urbanized "young men" were "facetious" about documentary films such as *Making Books*; they preferred films addressing "matters of direct concern" and material that offered "obvious entertainment."[27]

The reaction of these new elites to the inappropriate morality of the STD film demonstrates the successful impact of mainstream Christian and colonial standards of propriety about suitable content for children, the covering up of nakedness, and the portrayal of sexual immorality. These urbanized spectators, who were often also newspaper readers, can be found in the archives as visible, recognizable colonial subjects. Their presence facilitated the realization among British officials that "there will of course be many audiences in the Colonial Empire who can by no means be classed as primitive. For them the films made for Western audiences would probably be perfectly suitable."[28]

From an urban, educated, Christian, clothed, and vaccinated perspective, villagers' unpredictable responses to the binary aesthetic of CFU movies might be regarded as "illiteracy" in film spectatorship and, more broadly, as "backwardness" in standards of cleanliness, hygiene, modernity, and civilization. From the vantage point of the audiences with whom Morton-Williams and his team worked, however, such a vision of film literacy does not account for the cultural self-confidence with which people absorbed the new medium into their own discursive frameworks. Audiences' responses are available in the archives in the form of chatter, laughter, curiosity, disgust, disavowal, and other types of untranslatable commentary well beyond the colonial binary of dirt and cleanliness that formed the rationale for film production and circulation. The majority of film audiences for CFU productions were at several removes from urban elites in their "subaltern" status on the outskirts of colonial knowledge and ideology.[29] They are, as a consequence, considerably more difficult to retrieve from historical records or to identify using conventional archival research methods.

Additionally, Anglophone researchers' own linguistic limitations can help to produce representations and interpretations dominated by Eurocentric conceptual frameworks inherited from the very imperial cultural histories that are under scrutiny.[30] Wendy Willems persuasively argues that the dearth of African-language material in colonial archives contributes to ongoing Eurocentrism in cultural history research.[31] Her search for African-language material highlights a major methodological problem faced by media historians. Introverted and circular, the colonial film archives contain a sustained reiteration of the values and beliefs—about health, dirt, cleanliness, (il)literacy, Christianity, marriage, morality, and "native" cognition—that underwrote British assertions of the colonial right to rule. Like other media historians, Willems turns to African-owned newspapers for historical sources of local opinion.[32] While her sources are Africanized in the process, they remain largely Anglophone and elite, however, in tension with her call for Afrophone material to challenge the "hegemony of English in the public domain."[33]

In relation to CFU productions in Nigeria, the absence of African-language transcripts of the material provided by Morton-Williams's participants leaves Willems's question insistently in place. African audiences' complex and often unfathomable responses to films generate a new kind of archival presence, different from and more productive than the positivist vision of the "native" to be found in 1940s and 1950s audience research surveys, in which local people's attitudes and behavior were confidently described and evaluated by foreigners. Outside colonial hegemonies of representation, yet contained in and by colonial paperwork, the critical sounds of African audiences demand careful and deliberative retrieval techniques from cultural historians, not least because this submerged record of nonverbal responses provides clues about late colonial audiences' reactions to representations of their own and other cultures in globally circulating media, out of which some limited information can be gleaned about the social and aesthetic values through which particular films were filtered by different audiences.

The variety of nonverbal expressions is captured in Morton-Williams's report using various configurations of Anglophone vowels, which strain to cover the heterogeneous array of expressions and judgments articulated by audiences. This untranslatable soundscape gives an important sense of audience members' emotional reactions during screenings, helping to partially reconstitute their responses in an archive otherwise saturated with colonial logic. Unusually, Morton-Williams attempted to capture the timbre of these expressions in his transcriptions. In the screenings of *Smallpox*, for example, Yoruba audiences exclaimed "Aa!" (translated as "expectations fulfilled"), "A-a!" (at the sight of a long queue), "Aaa!" and "A-a-a!" ("sympathy"), "Aa!" ("relief"), "A! . . . a!" (surprise, shock), "E!" (shock, alarm, concern), "U-u-u!" and "A-a-!" (absorption in scene), "Ah!" (confirmation of interpretation), "A!" (negative judgment). In *Amenu's Child*, Yoruba women and some men "sighed 'E-e-e!'" at the sight of the sick baby lying on a mat, while some men laughed, and "some of the men exclaimed in envy 'A-a-a-a!' at the sight of so many imported shot guns" in the Yam Festival scene at the end of the movie.[34] Except for Morton-Williams's report, these participatory modes of film interpretation are absent from the archives. The exception demonstrates the wealth of interpretative material that is lost from the records, untranscribed by the very colonial officials who were charged with ensuring the successful local impact of media materials.

Judging from the evidence presented in chapter 4, Nigerian spectators of colonial educational movies can be said to have been keen to compare themselves with others, highly entertained by cultural differences, and fascinated by the habits of strangers on screen. They exhibited an ethnographic curiosity that was anything but a manifestation of the "disembodied eye floating through a foreign landscape" identified by Jennifer Lynn Peterson as typical of American audiences of early travel films.[35] Yet their reactions to films convey interpretations so far beyond the imaginations of the colonial filmmakers who reported back on the success or failure of screenings that they remain largely irretrievable, except in untranslated, untranslatable, and nonverbal forms. People's laughter at the protagonist's infection in *Smallpox*, for example, which the English script insists should be described in the voice-over as a consequence of his "foolishness," appears to have expressed far more than derision. As Morton-Williams pointed out, "The Yoruba expression for a person who is in peril or in trouble is fixed by convention as one of sympathy, not admonition."[36] In this fleeting comment, an entire library of colonial parables is thrown into question, for "foolish" behavior was a central requirement in the binary structure of "before-and-after" educational films. From films that insisted on the wisdom of choosing Western medicine over traditional healing (*Amenu's Child*, 1950; *Mr Wise and Mr Foolish Go to Town*, 1944) to parables of good versus poor agricultural practice (*Two Farmers*, 1948), the word "foolish" recurred in voice-over scripts to describe characters who followed "native" customs above "wise" Western alternatives. If a character's apparent foolishness aroused sympathy rather than admonition from spectators, and if fate and destiny were seen to shape a character's success or failure rather than his or her individual life choices, then the simple CFU message that behavioral change will bring prosperity would have had little traction with audiences.

The intended messages of films were unmoored and displaced by sociological commentary and speculation about the cultural practices of strangers. Curiosity about other people's clothing, cooking methods, architectural styles, hair and makeup, gender, religious festivals, and general social habits was so strong among many audiences that spectators' attention became diverted from the educational messages of films whenever such naturalistic details were used to establish the background for a health parable. Personal identification with the story lessons on-screen was blocked by this fascination with the minutiae of other people's lives, and, in the view of officials, local spectatorship *failed* when the cultural differences displayed on-screen became too great for processes of recognition and empathetic identification with health messages to occur. Audiences' "parochialism" obstructed the effectiveness of films, causing information officers to call for more local content, and to intensify initiatives such as the Raw Stock scheme for the provision of local material that producers in London could splice into each educational parable before sending it back into particular localities.[37]

But what if the presence of local tastes represents a significant third space of mediation and historicity alongside film content, on the one hand, and filmmakers' intentions, on the other? Can Nigerian media consumers in the past offer present-day researchers an alternative model for the interpretation of the circulation and impact of transnational texts without being dismissed as "parochial"? Yielding few African speaking subjects, no overt anticolonial political articulations, and no unmediated access into what people were saying about CFU productions, the colonial archives neverthe-less offer important insights into the history of naturalism, documentary realism, and other genres that were imported into Africa from the me-tropolis, as well as tantalizing hints about local aesthetic values in the late colonial period. With these histories and the impact of global media con-sumption in mind, we turn in the next three chapters to a "living archive" of urban residents in present-day Lagos to further examine the connections between mass media and local audiences while retaining an emphasis on the specificity and complexity of "public opinion."

The audiences that rose to the surface of the colonial public health archive in the first half of the twentieth century were protean and cultur-ally self-confident. They challenged preconceptions of African media con-sumers as available for political rescripting, and they resisted the simplistic ideology of colonial contrasts between dirt and cleanliness. The next three chapters ask if present-day urban dwellers exhibit the same interpretive au-tonomy as their precursors appeared to do in the early and mid-twentieth centuries, and what Nigeria's long history of global media consumption contributes to current debates about the homogenization of world cultures under an increasingly voracious global capitalism.[38]

6

Popular Perceptions of "Dirty" in Multicultural Lagos

Lagos is welcoming, but the crowd is out of this world, O!
It's no man's land. No discrimination. You can just come from nowhere
and start up anything and you are good to go.
—PHU-F-63, INTERVIEWED BY OLUTOYOSI TOKUN

In Enugu, anytime we go to church, you see people come up
when they say Thanksgiving Service. They say "I want to Thank God, O!
I went to Lagos!" People who come from Lagos, they go to their village,
they become kings and king makers!
—MISC-M-88, INTERVIEWED BY OLUTOYOSI TOKUN

The final three chapters make use of over 120 in-depth interviews with contemporary Lagosians conducted by the project team—Olutoyosi Tokun, John Uwa, and Jane Nebe, supervised by Patrick Oloko—to ask how people from different sectors of society describe dirt and cleanliness in an urban environment that city planners, media workers, and international agencies have termed a "global megalopolis," a hub of regional business and investment ripe for development, and that sensationalist commentators, largely located outside Lagos, have described as "the dirtiest city in Africa," a "mega-city of slums," and, simplistically, "one of the worst cities in the world."[1]

The written archival sources that formed the backbone for previous chapters indicated that in the past, African media consumers' local value systems often exceeded government officials' understandings of them and defied assimilation into Eurocentric categories of dirt. In what ways, this final part of the book asks, do contemporary Lagosians continue to reinterpret and reprocess official interventions in urban health and hygiene practices? How do people's tastes and values affect their responses to questions about dirt, public health, and the environment, especially as these relate to government and mass media messages? What attitudes and topics, if any, show continuity with earlier twentieth-century discourses among urban residents and media producers? Is "dirty" as replete with negative connotations in African languages as it is in the Anglophone commentaries examined in previous chapters?

In an attempt to capture local people's perceptions and interpretations of daily life in the city, the chapters that follow present the opinions of residents of diverse ages, language groups, and social backgrounds in relation to media reports about Lagos, government initiatives in waste management and urban infrastructure, and popular accounts of hygiene, sanitation, (mis)behavior, and (im)morality in the urban environment. This emphasis on grassroots African opinion is designed to complement quantitative studies of the city and to continue the methodological experiments started by "new imperial historians" such as Ann Laura Stoler and Antoinette Burton and by Africanist cultural scholars such as Glenn Reynolds and Ato Quayson, who have refused to place official archives at the center of their historical research and have sought alternative methods and sources—including ephemera and oral history—to compile cultural histories of (post)colonial countries.[2]

Participants were not chosen randomly for this study. Volunteers came forward in response to the circulation of information about the project around schools and health centers, and in the vicinity of waste management sites.[3] The presence of the researchers—Jane Nebe, Olutoyosi Tokun, and John Uwa from the University of Lagos—had a balloon effect in most neighborhoods, attracting additional participants whose socioeconomic status ranged from, on the lower end, street hawkers, carpenters, janitors, mechanics, tailors, and seamstresses living in neighborhoods with limited access to electricity, water, and drainage through to, on the higher end, salaried and self-employed people who identified as "middle income" and lived in rented housing with access to generators when "NEPA" failed.[4]

The small number of participants who self-identified in the high-income bracket included a female "business tycoon" with property on Lagos Island and a retired university professor. By far the largest portion of participants were urban residents on low to middle incomes with no influence over policy or the shaping of official discourse. Indeed, on several occasions interviewees appealed to members of the research team to convey messages upward to people in positions of power, especially about the need for the regularization of refuse collection by "PSPs" and the clearing of blocked gutters to prevent neighborhoods from flooding in the rainy season.[5]

Most of the interviews were held in institutional settings: focus group discussions were generally held in the project's offices at the University of Lagos and run by John Uwa, although several were held in venues near participants' neighborhoods when transport or other exigencies prevented travel to campus; one-to-one interviews were held in a wide variety of private rooms such as health-center side rooms and school sick bays, or in temporarily vacant spaces such as disused buildings. In spite of assurances of anonymity, this type of privacy did little to neutralize the institutional contexts of meetings where the outside world constantly made itself known through the numerous interruptions and background sounds of phone calls, knocks at the door, conversations outside windows, and other distractions.

Alongside the interviewer and interviewee in one-on-one meetings, the audio recorder was an influential and tangible third presence in the room, rendering anonymity uncertain in the eyes of some interviewees. Participants frequently asked whether or not the recorder was switched on, and in so doing highlighted their consciousness of its capacity to fix and transmit their voices to external auditors at the University of Lagos and farther afield. Educational, gender, and generational differences also vitally affected participants' interactions with the researchers and the microphone. For the majority of educated Yoruba men aged over fifty, the recorder served as an amplifier for illuminating discourses about Lagosian history and the Yoruba language, as well as offering a platform for commentaries on contemporary social issues such as women's rights in marriage and homosexuality. At the other end of the scale, working in noisy school environments with young participants who were frequently overawed by their proximity to an inquisitive stranger, Jane Nebe frequently had to invite schoolchildren to "speak loud so that this thing will hear you," particularly in the first ten minutes of recordings.[6]

Numerous adult interviewees commented on the fact that their responses would be different were it not for the invisible audience represented by the recorder. In a report from the start-up period, Olutoyosi Tokun noted that "some of the participants . . . bluntly refused to state their views on certain issues discussed because it was being recorded."[7] "If you turn off this speaker I will tell you," one health worker joked during an interview that touched on popular perceptions of the hygiene of different ethnic groups in the low-income neighborhood where the participant worked.[8] Another health professional stopped mid-flow: "And another thing that I also believe is that . . . I think we should leave, let's leave that one [*laughs*]."[9] Unsurprisingly for this participant, as for the other professionals interviewed in their workplaces, people were conscious that their comments needed to be carefully self-regulated for the sake of our project, and in recognition of this obvious point our topic guides for media, health, and education professionals prioritized information gathering above questions about their personal opinions. Taking place in participants' offices, these interviews yielded a wealth of information about the recycling of solid waste and public relations campaigns to transform popular perceptions of people who work with refuse and sewage, as well as comments about the activities of traditional birth attendants, and uses of *agbo* (bitter herbs mixed in various combinations), in conjunction with prayer and visits to the doctor or hospital for fever, vomiting, diarrhea, malaria, and other ailments.

Even when people were not interviewed in their professional capacity, adult participants observed a social etiquette similar to the one expressed by the health worker cited above, clearly demarcating the boundaries between their civic principles as multicultural Lagosians in the presence of a microphone and researcher, and, if different, their own personal opinions on contentious topics such as the innate dirtiness or dirty behavior of other social groups in the city. When asked by John Uwa if there were any parts of Lagos where she would not wish to live, for example, one middle-income resident replied, "Emm, you know what, I am not going to answer your question because that's actually putting me on a very hot seat."[10] This divide between socially acceptable and individual opinions formed a recurring pattern that was impossible to regard simply, or solely, as a consequence of our particular research environment. Repeatedly in their responses to questions about sensitive subjects such as the domestic hygiene of other ethnic groups, or about their views on stigmatized types of labor such as sewage removal and so-called scavenging, participants self-consciously moved between the moral space of the civic (or civil) and the moral space of personal opinion.[11] "If I try to understand why some people would do certain things, you know, I might not necessarily consider it as being dirty. But for me it's very dirty," one health professional explained to Olutoyosi Tokun, adding, "I can't see things exactly from their own perspective, I don't know why they are doing it, so I might leave that to them. Maybe they are doing it for a particular reason I don't understand, so I would not judge them. I'm not indifferent. For me, it is dirty."[12] Another interviewee spoke in a similar vein: "Something that is dirty to you might not be dirty to me. It depends on our morals, it depends on our background. It depends on how you are raised."[13]

In the presence of the microphone, which can be seen to stand in for the other as an unknown yet proximate auditor, participants elaborated a civic consciousness in which the toleration of strangers' and neighbors' domestic practices took priority over their own individual views, and the latter, no matter how widely shared among their own social group, and no matter how visceral the negative responses they evoked, were bracketed off in a separate sphere from the "public." "My faith might be different from whoever is going to listen to this recording, okay?" one interviewee stated at the beginning of John Uwa's recording.[14] A public health worker said to Olutoyosi Tokun,

> I'm actually going to give you my own opinion, O, but basically I don't think there is any dirty tribe in Nigeria. It has to do with you as a person, do you understand? Some people would say that the Hausas are dirty. Why? Because they live in clusters if you see them. And there's no how that environment won't be compromised. Now some people would tell you that Igbos are very dirty. Now that's a common thing that you would hear from landlords. You give them an apartment they mess the apartment up. To me as a person I feel this has to do with the person himself or herself not actually the tribe now, so to say. Because I mean that's, erm, ethnocentrism.[15]

Paradoxically, this refusal to make generalizations about people's behavior arose from an awareness, on the part of many interviewees, that their own attitudes, ideas, and interpretations arose from their generalizable cultural backgrounds and religious beliefs. "If I see somebody that is just wee-weeing and is not using water to clean it, I see that person as being dirty because of my [Islamic] religious background. And to some people it doesn't really mean anything. It's just like, 'ha, it is a natural thing, I should do it!'"[16] One elderly man in an all-Yoruba focus group convened by John Uwa described Nigerians' different palates in similarly relativistic terms:

"There is a food that the Igbos call *abacha* [with grated cassava and fish]. Yorùbá cannot eat that food with them. Mere looking at the food alone you will wonder how it was prepared. You will say to yourself, 'what are these people eating?' But then, we Yorùbá also have some foods that the Igbos will not be interested in eating."[17] The other participants agreed. One Yoruba interviewee pointed out that the Igbos eat raw vegetables, which is "unacceptable to us. . . . We will boil our vegetables, mix with sauce, and it becomes delicious. To eat fresh vegetables without boiling is unacceptable to me."[18] In this and other interviews, food provided a constant reference point for comments about the cultural relativity of dirt: "If you are an Igbo man you consider *amala*, because it is black, you consider it as being dirty. It is black, it looks like it's got particles in it and all that, but I tell you, it is one of the best foods that you ever have ventured."[19]

Numerous interviewees emphasized that their own cultural conditioning, rather than the inherent dirtiness or immorality of particular persons or behaviors, structured their perceptions of other social and ethnic groups. As one man stated tactfully to Olutoyosi Tokun, "I think dirtiness or cleanliness has to do with upbringing and individual perspective and individual environment and the kind of parents that brought you up. And maybe sometimes the religious aspect of people."[20] "It has to do with the personal conviction of the person to be dirty or not to be, really."[21] "You have to understand the cultural perspectives of these people, speak the local language, you know, not judge them when they say certain things."[22] These carefully articulated, self-aware comments exemplified the grassroots multiculturalism of Lagosians in praxis. With the notable exception of homosexuality, discussed in chapter 8, people emphasized the priority of tolerating others' behavior, no matter how "dirty" or "disgusting" it might appear when judged from their own personal standpoints. "For me I just think you have no right to question another person's way of living," said one man who could not otherwise be described as liberal, judging by his sexually conservative comments that women who dressed in a "dirty" manner openly invited sexual harassment in public places.[23]

Participants' sensitivities to being on record as part of our research project provide important information about the Lagosian public sphere. The putative "other"—whether the microphone, the interviewer, or the proximate urban stranger—acts as a forceful mediating presence in contexts where urban civility involves the careful awareness of the presence of neighbors and their protection from overhearing offensive or inflammatory speech. "You have Igbo, you have Yorùbá, everybody is staying in Lagos," commented one participant in a focus group comprising participants from six different Nigerian states. "Lagos is multidimensional."[24]

While interviewees were unwilling to contemplate adapting or changing their own behavior in response to others' disapproval, they nevertheless recognized their own perceptions of others as being culturally conditioned and subject to external scrutiny. Commenting on the use of a potty during nighttime in the households of certain Yoruba sub-ethnic groups, for example, one non-Yoruba man told Olutoyosi Tokun, "In my own tradition, sleeping with urine in the house, you will be considered as being dirty; you will be called a dirty person."[25] This caused him to reflect on how Nigerian cultures operate according to vastly different defecatory practices: "Muslims, what they practice is that when they poo they use water to wash their self, but for a Tiv man using your bare hand to wash yourself is even dirty. They will prefer that you should use a material, either a leaf or paper."[26] In comments such as these, interviewees recognized that they operated according to the category of taste—a culturally specific and socially conditioned mode of judgment that is subject to change—rather than according to unequivocal or universalist moral categories such as truth or virtue or dirt.

There was a tendency among some participants, however, to essentialize the category of culture, and for it to become fixed onto particular ethnicities. Many interviewees generalized about the dirtiness of Fulani (Hausas) and Muslims, whether as fruit sellers or waste collectors. "The Malam sees it [poor hygiene] as their culture," one of John Uwa's focus groups agreed. This group, comprising five elderly Yorubas, became fixated with the dirtiness of Muslim fruit sellers from the north of the country, and discussed the topic at length.[27] For many participants, Igbo traders also featured as figures of suspicion and blame for selling shoddy goods and for duping customers.[28] In one interview held by John Uwa, an educated woman tried to equalize the ethnic distribution of blame: "As you have a dubious Igbo man, you have a dubious Yoruba man, you have a dubious Hausa man. It comes in all tribes and shapes and colours," she began.[29] As she expanded this point, however, a number of fixed ethnic characteristics came to the fore:

> I am an advocate for "Oh, everyone can be different, don't lump people together," and all that. But when it comes to Nigeria sometimes, hem, so this should be like a caveat. Not all Igbos are entrepreneurial or go-getters, but it's almost like it is coded in the Igbo man's DNA to be self-

dependent, to strive for the best, and sometimes even to the extreme, that people say *"Ha! Igbo, wón máa gbá ẹ ni o"* (Yoruba: Ha! An Igbo! They will dupe you!), that you have to keep your eyes open when you are dealing with an Igbo man. If you are dealing with the Hausa man, the Hausa man is more straightforward: if it is A, it will A; if it is B, it will B.[30]

Another interviewee also attributed dubious business practices to the ethnic makeup of Igbos, stating that "the Igbo have very disappointing trading practice towards their customers. First of all, the Igbo are very stubborn. They have *agídí* (stubbornness): they cannot be trusted. When you get there to buy an item, it is the bad one they will bring out and sell to you."[31] On this occasion, the other interviewee in the discussion reacted vehemently to dilute his companion's statements: "I have been doing business with the Igbos. Some of them are good and some of them are bad. It is both ways. It is like that among the Yorùbá. There are people among Yorùbá that are not sincere, and there are those who are sincere."[32] Throughout this statement, the first participant laughed loudly and sarcastically in an unusually open display of skepticism at the second participant's sincerity. Meanwhile, many people agreed that people from Calabar are inherently clean, which explained why so many of them became domestic workers in Lagos. All of these ways of marking the multiculturalism of Lagos contained flash points of absolute difference alongside a recognition of the other's cultural differences.

On (Not) Being Overheard by Others

On one occasion, the careful self-moderation by participants in the presence of visible or invisible others broke down during a focus group discussion facilitated by John Uwa involving four men and one woman, held in downtown Lagos. At the center of their disagreement was the question of who could be identified as a true Lagosian. This topic emerged in response to a discussion about the status of "strangers" in the city. An argument erupted between two of the men about the relative legitimacy of *"Ará Èkó"* (non-Lagos-born people living in Lagos) and *"Ará Òkè"* (uplanders, sometimes used to connote "uncivilized" people) compared with *"Ọmọ Èkó"* (Lagos-born indigenes, lit. a child of Lagos Island). "The true Lagosian cannot come and destroy his father's land. It is those who come from uptown [other Yoruba-speaking states such as Kwara and Oyó] those who have nothing to lose. Will someone like me who is Lagosian, who have no other home, want to destroy the place?"[33] In a view commonly expressed by Lagos-born indigenes about incomers to Lagos, this participant accused immigrants to the city of dirtying the environment with litter and pollution, and exploiting its resources only to disappear back to their home towns when they had accumulated sufficient wealth to leave.

The ensuing disagreement erased the mediating presence of the microphone and produced an environment of unmoderated individual opinion. The argument escalated rapidly, and John Uwa terminated the session. The expression of metropolitan pluralism that characterized our other interviews collapsed, in this focus group, into a politics of identity fueled by the first man's evident frustration with conditions in the city. Clearly, these men's experiences of the pressures for survival in the overcrowded city overrode any collective identity as Yoruba-speaking Nigerians, causing those for whom Lagos was their birthplace to insist on ancient forms of legitimacy based on an antagonistic notion of civic purity.[34]

Except for one significant category—girls and young women in low-income neighborhoods, discussed below—the vast majority of interviewees delighted in describing the wealth of opportunities and choices available in Lagos for quick-thinking individuals to harness and enjoy. But indigenes were defensive about their city. "In Lagos at the moment it is *irú wá ògìrì wá*," one old man stated.[35] "People, they throw dirt in the streets, they throw dirt in the gutter and it gets clustered. It's smelly. Because they feel they have no stake there, they only come to make money and go back."[36] "What they are doing here, they cannot do it back home."[37] One old man, an *Ọmọ Èkó*, complained bitterly in a Yoruba-language interview that "Lagos has now become overpopulated with *àlejò* who are less concerned with taking care of gutters and drainages, so long as they have tidied their homes. The result is our homes are flooded."[38]

Reflecting on the differences in content between English-language and Yoruba-language interviews, John Uwa remarked, "When you begin to speak other languages, you see all the discriminations. All the sentiments begin to play out. African language is a very wonderful thing!"[39] In particular, he noted the number of "stereotypes and abusive jokes about Yorùbá domestic hygiene" among Lagosians from different Yoruba-speaking regions, complicating assumptions about a homogeneous Yoruba-Nigerian ethnic identity. In one unrecorded interview, for example, an elderly Yoruba woman insisted that the Ijẹbu (Yoruba from Ogun State, bordering Lagos State) make use of night-soil potties as food bowls for *gari* during the day. This, she explained, was the reason why Ijẹbu are called, abusively,

"*Ìjẹ̀bú olóòórùn*" (fragrant or smelly Ijẹbu). Unsurprisingly, this woman's popular ethno-regional stereotype about the "*póò*" was vehemently denied when a Lagosian of Ijẹbu origin heard of it during a focus group discussion: "Of course I have heard that [*laughing*]. It is a snide remark at the Ìjẹ̀bú. There is no iota of truth in it. The truth is that the Ìjẹ̀bú drink gari a lot, okay . . . and eh . . . of course it is not true that they use potty to drink gari, okay? Contrary to that assertion, I think when you line up the Yorùbá . . . you will find the Ìjẹ̀bú ranked among the neatest, okay?"[40] On another occasion, while at a car mechanic's, John Uwa requested that an apprentice dispose of his engine oil in a container rather than on the ground, attracting the attention of the Urhobo garage manager. "Is he not a Yorùbá boy?" the manager said within earshot of the employee. "That is how Yorùbá people behave! Yorùbá people can live with shit in their house, eat where there is shit, and even eat with the same plate they use for shit, so I am not surprised at his stupidity."[41]

Similar references to the poor defecatory hygiene of people from certain Yoruba subethnicities recurred in numerous recorded interviews. These comments represent a fascinating commentary on sanitary practices introduced in the colonial era, offering an insight into the adoption in western Nigeria, particularly Lagos, of the colonial *pôt de chambre*, or potty, in Yoruba households, where the "*póò*," a loanword from English, is still used as an alternative to going out of the house at night to use the external toilet with all the disruption to sleep that entails. As one Yoruba oral historian—also a landlord—put it unsympathetically, dirty people in his compound will use an improvised potty in their single-room residence instead of going outdoors to the toilet, especially late at night. The Igbos will always go outdoors to the communal toilet, but his Yoruba tenants "are comfortable with doing it in their room as if standing up from the bed and going into the toilet will make them miss something!"[42] In his preferred toilet system, the (rural) pit latrine, by contrast, "shit all becomes sand. And we can cultivate that piece of land for farming or as garden in the future; it will still serve us as a fertilizer."[43] The strong reactions of non-*póò*-users against the presence of this indoor toilet, and the urban myths surrounding uses of the *póò* as an eating bowl among Ijẹbu, reverse the direction of disgust from colonial discourse by identifying the most insanitary local defecatory practices with apparatus introduced by the British. "We the Yorùbás have been 'brainwashed' by the colonial master into using '*póò*,'" stated one oral historian: "I want you to know that shit carrying started with the '*póò*' system. When the colonial master first came, it was the '*póò*' he first started using.

Practice make perfect. '*Pòò*' is primary and the carrying of shit in buckets by night-soil men is secondary."[44] "It is not proper to keep shit in the house and inhale the smell," another old man commented. "This potty we are talking about are usually improvised paint plastic containers with cover; they use it and dispose the content at dawn."[45]

These examples from twenty-first-century Lagosian public discourse challenge the category of "dirty people" offered by British travelers, traders, and administrators in their written accounts of West Africa a century earlier, and introduce historicity and relativism into our understanding of disgust as a universal human reaction to dirt. Epidemiologists of dirt, such as Valerie Curtis, have argued that disgust originates in the biological realm: it is evolution's way of preserving the human species and crosses diverse cultures and histories as our species' instinctive reaction to potential contaminants.[46] Whether or not dirt is experienced in relation to objects, environments, or people, Curtis argues, the impulse to withdraw from it or remove it altogether arises from nonrational genetic wiring in our brains in reaction to external sense stimuli; she calls this "uncleaning" the "other."[47] For epidemiologists such as Curtis, the global public health challenge is to persuade people to be more, rather than less, disgusted by the presence of dirt, and less, rather than more, tolerant of other people's (in)sanitary behavior.[48] In handwashing campaigns and other public health initiatives designed for tropical settings, public health workers try to further hone people's instinctive reactions to visible dangers through information campaigns aimed at mapping disgust onto the array of microbial contaminants—bacteria, parasites, viruses—spread by poor domestic practices such as incorrect handwashing after defecation or the use of unclean water for drinking and food preparation.[49]

This epidemiological understanding of dirt strips cultures of diversity in favor of biological explanations and offers dirt as an objective substance, available for recognition and rejection worldwide, albeit through public health interventions to strengthen and orient the senses and emotions. While this model might work for dirty objects, and to some extent for dirty environments, in the vast majority of cases in which people are labeled using categories of dirt, there is no scientific evidence to justify their removal from society, nor, except in extreme situations of social breakdown, is their removal sanctioned by the media or public opinion.

Throughout this book, I have argued that the relationship between revulsion and the removal of a perceived human contaminant is mediated by taste, politics, and power. For colonial-era newcomers to West Africa from Europe, the somatic experience of revulsion at the sight and smell of the other was too corporeal to be perceived as merely subjective by the body experiencing it. Colonial-era commentators' embodied experience of disgust was treated as evidence in itself of its empirical validity, and, consequently, the observers' reactions were generalized into inherent characteristics of the other. Out of reactions such as this, as the opening chapters of this book suggested, came a raft of colonial policies aimed at educating and improving the unhappy "native" and enhancing his or her environment.

In contrast to these historical examples where the category of dirt functioned to transform subjective responses into objective "truths," for the twenty-first-century Lagosians we spoke to, feelings of disgust about "dirty" Yoruba defecatory behavior or unhygienic Igbo cooking utensils or Igbo prostitutes and "419-ers" (scammers) or the prevalence of Hausa beggars in Lagos or problems with Hausa hygiene in low-income settlements were, in most cases, separated off by interviewees into the realm of personal opinion rather than universal judgments. This is not to say people did not experience revulsion at the idea of others' dirty behavior. "I can still remember the look of disgust on the faces of the interviewees as we talked about these [dirty personal hygiene] habits," Olutoyosi Tokun recalled of her interviews.[50] But the sheer multiculturalism of the city prevented individuals from extrapolating general principles from the evidence of their eyes. In Lagos, one interviewee explained, "everybody is just the same: Hausa, Igbo, Yorùbá, everybody. So nobody will ask you questions and you are free to dress anyhow you like. Not that they will restrict you and all that."[51] "I like to assess people individually," another interviewee said. "I don't want to look at it from that general point of view that every Hausa is dirty, every Yorùbá is dirty."[52] People were sensitive and deliberative in their efforts not to appear biased. "If I should buy from only the person I know and is performing my religion," one fifteen-year-old Muslim girl explained, "it may cause some kind of conflict between them [market women], and I won't want to let this happen. So if I want to buy large number of things I buy from different people."[53]

This Lagosian civic consciousness could not be further from colonial conceptualizations of "dirty" local bodies. Our interviewees effectively eclipsed a century of colonial and epidemiological objectifications by articulating a relativistic understanding of dirt that acknowledged the bias inherent in their own sense perceptions alongside how their own behavior appeared in the eyes of other urban residents. While the category of "dirty people" was always associated with other households, never one's own, in the public space represented by the interviewer, the microphone, and our project on dirt, time and again participants blamed themselves for the experience of disgust. One health worker went so far as to describe herself as having "OCDs" in order to avoid casting judgment on the sanitary habits of other groups: "Some people, the way they live their lives, you know, they feel if the toilet is not dirty then you don't have to wash it," she explained, but "I'm very finicky. I pay so much attention to details. In fact, it's actually more of OCD."[54] Other interviewees described how they strategically and quietly chose to shun shared facilities such as toilets, bathrooms, and kitchens in compounds that were perceived to be too filthy for use, and reverted to classic avoidance tactics from the twentieth century, such as the use of potties and "shot-put" defecation into drains and other waterways.[55]

Schoolchildren's Perceptions of the Urban Environment

In asking Jane Nebe to gather children's and young people's comments about health, sanitation, recycling, and the urban environment, I hoped to compare their accounts of metropolitan life with the views of adult interviewees. Would children's more concentrated exposure, in the schoolroom, to public health messaging about waste disposal and environmental sanitation differentiate their responses from adults' comments about living in Lagos, especially in the aftermath of the Ebola epidemic? Children absorb and reflect on currents of opinion in their communities, often making sense of what they hear through the exchange of knowledge and stories at school.[56] I was especially interested in whether, and how, public health messages featured in schoolchildren's perceptions of the urban environment. On one side was the loudspeaker of public health: in schoolchildren we had a constituency with heightened exposure to official channels of public health education through school assemblies and formal classes on hygiene and sanitation. On the other side was the dampener of inferiority: children and young people are often considered secondary to adults, and in Nigeria few children expect to be asked for their opinions or interpretations about social matters. Jane Nebe commented on the novelty of the space opened up by her presence in schools: "It's very uncommon to do this research where you allow these young people to say their mind: it's not a normal thing, especially in our context. It's not common to have them say their mind about issues. It was quite interesting to get them to *speak*, you know, speak through interviews and focus group discussions, without fear, in a safe space for them to say their mind, as they felt. That was my experience in the field."[57]

For one nine-year-old girl attending an elementary school situated in a low-income settlement where the majority of residents had no electricity and restricted access to water, the experience of sitting alone in a room under the gaze of an unknown researcher produced a description of Lagos that exceeded adult belief and reason, and, in the process, added an important layer of meaning to our project. Released from the classroom into what was an atypical and bizarre situation in which an adult asked for her opinions about the environment, and listened in all earnestness with reassurances of confidentiality, this girl reacted by weaving all kinds of fabrications into her descriptions of urban life. Our topic guides for interviews with children and young people were composed with such positivist zeal—including, for the seven-to-nine-year-olds, pictures of markets, waste disposal trucks, rubbish heaps, and traffic, in order to encourage them to talk about external matters—that we failed to factor in the centrality of the imagination to children's experiences of life in the city, and the forceful role played by fantasy in children's exercise of personal agency in their efforts to understand proximate adults. But this girl was a magnet for extreme versions of reality, and the world she described, rather than clouding her account, clarified the fears and experiences of many other girls we interviewed.

"When I'm small they used to beat me. My mummy have left. My daddy have left. My mummy and daddy have . . . my mummy and my daddy have die. And it's only my sister that is at home. They will be beating me to wash my cloth," she began.[58] In a story rich with attempted kidnappings, imprisonments, violence, deaths, and bombings, the girl described the terrifying environment in which she lived: "They [mother and father] die on Tuesday. Armed robbers come to our house, they are finding for me. When I'm running, they are finding for . . . they now throw bomb in our house. Our house just bomb like that. My mummy, my daddy and my mummy now die."[59] Nobody was exempt from this nightmare vision of the neighborhood in which the most trusted adults were the most likely to cause harm. Beginning with a description of the cruel behavior of her parents, the girl's account had grown into a picture of a monstrous world where real harm was done to children by adults. As her truth-claims escalated and collided with one another, Jane Nebe intervened: "I did not hear of any bomb in Lagos. So that means you are telling me lies. You should tell me the truth. Do you want to stop this thing [the digital recorder]?" "They are lies," confessed the girl, "because of I didn't like my mummy and my daddy."[60]

While this girl did not witness the violent scenes she described, the figures in her stories incarnated her worst fears about her physical vulnerability, alienation from her parents, and lack of control over her home environment. Her fear of armed robbers and kidnappers—based, it turned out, on a schoolmate's encounter with a man with a knife—meant that she took alternate routes home to avoid people and places regarded as dangerous by the other children. Fixated with the perils of movement across ordinary urban spaces, she vividly narrated a scene allegedly witnessed by her mother, involving a man arrested at a police checkpoint with a pocket full of excised, but still wagging, human tongues. The man's "pocket is now shaking, shaking. The police . . . now look at the pocket. They see five tongue. They beat the man."[61]

Similar stories of kidnappings and the excision of organs in ritual murders were repeated by other schoolgirls, albeit in diluted forms compared to this storyteller.[62] Describing what she was afraid of in her neighborhood, one eight-year-old girl told Jane Nebe, "They [kidnappers] will be hiding. I will now be seeing them. I will now run away. . . . They will wear something like *ojuju*.[63] They will now tell small child to come. 'Come, come and take sweet.' They will just put something in your nose like this, or in your eye. They will carry you and go. They will go and cut your head. They will do you money."[64]

While the source of the threat remained shadowy for this girl, who identified the kidnapper with either Boko Haram or a religious cult, she—like the first girl—used the interview to actively process what she had heard in her school and neighborhood about national news stories and local events, incorporating others' speculations with her own to produce a vivid, real threat to her personal security. In this manner, lessons from guardians and school gatekeepers combined with news stories and their own interpretations of the grim consequences of mingling too closely with urban strangers to shape schoolgirls' perceptions of the immediate environment.

Boko Haram featured prominently in the anxieties of several girls. The movement's presence in their imaginations, epitomized by the figure of the kidnapper, shows how intimately they identified with the Chibok schoolgirls kidnapped in Borno State in April 2014 and other more recent kidnappings of girls by Boko Haram, and how carefully they projected themselves into national news stories featuring children of their age and gender. One girl whose new stepfather had insisted she convert from Islam to Christianity narrated how a Christian schoolgirl was kidnapped, and then "the Boko Haram dug a ground, buried her alive with only her head above the ground, and they stoned her to death."[65] Another girl from a Muslim neighborhood described how, "all that school girls, Borno girls, they take all our girls and go. And they . . . all that girl, they are dying there and I want them to come back from there. They should come outside from that Boko Haram place."[66]

If Lagos is described by adult residents as a city of opportunities and prospects waiting to be harnessed by enterprising individuals, as indicated in the epigraphs to this chapter and the buzz of enthusiasm expressed by adults when we asked them to describe urban life, the schoolgirls who participated in our project revealed numerous anxieties about an environment filled with pollution, noise, and the uncertain motives of neighbors and strangers. While these were not always gendered in terms of the sexual vulnerability of women and girls, the younger girls' imaginations mixed potent threats out of the ingredients around them, particularly in the vicinity of their homes where they performed domestic tasks.[67]

The majority of children and young people Jane Nebe spoke to lived in compounds in low-income neighborhoods with limited or unusable—because insanitary or controlled by adults—shared toilets. They generally resorted to the classic "shot-put" method of sewage disposal. Whether fetching water for household laundry or visiting the shared toilet or bathroom—all sites of power imbalances in compounds where children occupy the lowest rung of the social ladder—the younger girls imagined risks that multiplied and reverberated all along the topography of the compound. Caught up in local micro-economies of water distribution and control, they undertook the daily tasks expected of them by their families, but they often did so with heads full of vivid scenarios in which the risks of the worlds in which they moved were played out and embellished as terrifying stories.[68]

These accounts of acute local hazards help to explain the reactions to environmental "dirty" of one Muslim schoolgirl, aged fifteen, who lived with her single mother in a one-room dwelling. This girl hid from everybody in the compound. "I just don't go out. I prefer to stay at home," she stated, when Jane Nebe asked about her neighborhood.[69] She neither visited the communal toilet and washroom nor interacted with any neighbors, preferring to use a potty indoors at all times of day and night, and then dispose of the fecal waste in the drains. She avoided all shared facilities, including the kitchen, on grounds of their filth; she fetched water for cooking, bathing, and laundry reluctantly and hurriedly, on grounds of the filthy environment; she cooked out of doors, on the other side of the building from its inhabitants, rather than in the kitchen area; and she hung the laundry to dry by the roadside rather than using the communal clothesline. In response to every question, this girl rationalized her reclusive behavior as a reaction to the dirtiness of the compound. What became clear during the interview, however, was that her hypersensitivity toward "dirty" enveloped a plethora of other apprehensions about the threats posed by neighbors and strangers in her crowded environment. In response to questions about why she didn't use communal facilities, she repeated, "We don't know the type of disease each and every one has."[70] For her, the dangers posed by other people at every level of daily life were enveloped and explained by the discourse of public health and hygiene. The catchall term "dirty" described the residue these adults left in the environment without her risking the insolence of naming her neighbors.

Threatening adults stepped in and out of the imaginations of numerous schoolgirls, demonstrating what Filip de Boeck and Marie-Françoise Plissart describe, in their powerful account of children's witchcraft confessions in Kinshasa, as the coexistence of submerged, invisible realities and surface realities, or the simultaneity of "the image of the thing and the imaged thing."[71] Listening to boys and girls as young as five disclosing their thefts of adults' souls, and marriages in the underworld, de Boeck and Plissart explain how these narratives carry explanatory force and truth for the child confessors, distilling their experiences of mental disturbance, the voices and interpretations of their behavior by adults, and their attempts to understand primary carers' rejections of them, into potent self-condemnations that gave some agency back to the child in the form of crisis and social disjunction.[72] The children de Boeck and Plissart worked with in Kinshasa believed they were possessed and manipulated by Satan, as did the adults around them. While considerably less traumatic, the powerfully imagined scenarios about abduction and contamination described by the schoolgirls interviewed for our project in Lagos carried a similar potency, conveying the terrifying double reality produced by their imaginations in contexts where children and young people have little or no control over their environments.

In contrast to the nervousness and distrust of the younger girls, several of the older schoolgirls Jane Nebe interviewed from low-income settlements confidently described an array of guardians with whom they lodged and worked while maintaining their school attendance. One fifteen-year-old girl listed such a dizzying array of guardians that she had to be stopped repeatedly for clarification.[73] Similarly, boys did not vocalize threats in the same way as the younger girls, although they frequently mentioned gang violence in their neighborhoods. While boys also participated in tasks such as doing the laundry, hawking produce after school, and fetching drinking water and *baff* (Nigerian Pidgin: bath) water for the household, unlike the girls they did not reveal fears for their personal safety during these activities. Time and again, however, they recounted the disruption to schooling and family life caused by evictions from rented accommodation. Underlying the stories of many children from low-income households was this continuous threat of sudden evictions by landlords. Indeed, eviction featured prominently in the recent past of all except one of the children Jane Nebe interviewed from low-income areas, placing the prospect of sudden homelessness at the forefront of their experience of community and settlement.

Translating Dirt: Dirt as a Comparative Category

In Nigerian Pidgin, "dirt" is not only a noun, and "dirty" is not always used as an adjective. A person will say "throw your dirty here," or, when the refuse workers arrive, "Mummy, dirty people are around, O."[74] In interviews, we used the Yoruba noun "*ìdọ̀tí*" and verb *dọ̀tí*, as well as the Nigerian Pidgin noun "dirty," and participants were asked to name words from their mother tongues connoting dirt in order to clarify the implications of their uses of "dirt" in different contexts. The wealth of words, phrases, and maxims differentiating among dirty people, objects, and environments is included in the appendix, illustrating the depth of Lagosian—particularly Yoruba—conceptualizations of dirt beyond the scope of English translation.

In an effort to find out how ideas about dirt shaped local people's perceptions of the urban environment, we asked participants to define what they understood by dirt, to recall particular local stories or media coverage in which dirt featured, and to think about whether there were objects, places, professions, people, or behaviors they associated with dirt and dirtiness. Answers ranged from the concrete to the metaphorical and moral as interviewees considered the multifarious entry points we offered, alongside which terms to use for the different levels at which dirt could be explored in Yoruba, Nigerian Pidgin, and English.[75] As we expected, a vast range of topics arose in interviews, including sexuality, food preparation, the domestic practices of neighbors from other ethnic groups, and a host of topics relating to living in rooms and compounds overseen by powerful landlords. While striking commonalities emerged in participants' definitions of "dirty" in relation to litter (or environmental dirt), household waste (or domestic dirt), and absolute dirt (stinking, rotting matter exemplified by feces), major differences emerged in how they described municipal workers responsible for the removal of discarded and unwanted matter and people whose manners or appearance they characterized as "dirty."

An obvious drawback of deploying an Anglophone term to support an ambitious multicultural investigation into diverse people's opinions and perceptions about urban experience was that, in a fieldwork context, "dirt" required immediate (dis)qualification in the polyglossic environment of a large city where communication was in Yoruba, Nigerian Pidgin, Hausa, and a multitude of other African and international languages. Our English category of "dirt" stimulated considerable commentary among project participants, but it also introduced confusion: indeed, it created sufficient confusion for people to wish to disentangle it and redefine it in locally meaningful terms.

For all our interviewees, physical waste was characterized as "materials or substances that to us or to me I consider no longer useful at the present, and I don't have need of them, so I dispose them."[76] Participants repeatedly described domestic waste in equivocal rather than in absolute terms, regarding nonorganic items as useless only to the person who throws them away. "Waste is something that is not useful. It doesn't fit the need. You can't find a place to use it, so you find it useless. You feel you cannot do anything, you know, reasonable with it again. It becomes a waste but for other people it might not really be a waste."[77] "Waste is just some un-useful things to me: because they are waste I can't use them to me."[78] According to this view, household "dirty" was always available for transformation into something else that might be useful, even valuable, to another person as one's own waste passed through human hands to potentially reenter the social and economic cycle. For this reason, it was regarded as *pàntí* (Yoruba: light dirt, litter or debris). "They know they will actually see some fancy things inside your dirt," one man commented of waste removal workers: "You know they probably say *'Àwọn báàgì yìí sì dáa o!* (Yoruba: These bags are still good!) I will take it, I will wash it, I will repair it.'"[79] He went on to explain, "waste is not just dirt. It can be something that is not useful to you. *'That thing na waste jare, make it just dey. I no dey wear am'* (That thing is waste. I'm throwing it away, I don't wear it any more). Waste can be anything generally. It is your perception."[80] As one private waste contractor put it, echoing international "waste-to-wealth" or "trash-to-treasure" slogans, "What is waste to you is a resource to another person."[81]

People politely accommodated our English category of dirt in order to differentiate between types of dirt using local criteria. Crucially, while sometimes the two terms converged, waste was not always seen as the same as dirt. In talking about their own waste materials as one type of dirt, for example, interviewees continuously imagined the progress of items out of their hands through chains of collection, sorting, recycling, and upcycling by enterprising waste workers. This type of dirt was never able to become "matter out of place." Discarded domestic material was regarded as matter out of use rather than absolute waste. One public health worker put this position clearly to Olutoyosi Tokun: "Waste is not waste until it gets so useless that you feel it cannot be used, it is not useful again."[82] This double consciousness about domestic waste—that it may be useless to oneself but not to another—rendered dirt a slippery category in relation to the objects people threw away. Dirt was not negative, but it was not positive either: a thing became a piece of "dirty" when it was no longer useful to the person discarding it, but it did not become true dirt until it was no longer useful to any person at all. For contemporary Lagosians, providing that an object remained in human hands—providing that matter still *mattered* to somebody—it could never become true dirt. "We actually don't see waste," a private waste contractor explained as she laid out her ambitions for zero landfill in Lagos by 2020: "We see wealth when we see waste. We see wealth because what people call waste can be used for so many things."[83]

Unlike organic waste and outdoor detritus creating a stench in streets and drains, which people regarded as dangerous and requiring immediate removal to the dump, almost without exception participants' own household waste was considered to be available for repurposing by others, even after it had reached the municipal dumpsite. As such, nonorganic waste was not disgusting to people in the manner of organic waste: some of it was debris or litter, homeless matter that was blown about until it was swept up and removed, and some of it was available for recuperation and reuse by others. Central to this perception of the usefulness of household waste was the new emphasis on recycling in Lagos, discussed in more detail in the next chapter. "I saw this one thing, people packing bottles, plastic especially, they were like turning it into something. I was like 'this is money!'" said one woman in amazement about discarded plastic water bottles, which were regarded by most people as a public nuisance, especially in the rainy season when, along with "nylons" (lightweight plastic bags), they caused blockages in the canals and partially covered drainage channels running through the city.[84] A public health worker explained to Olutoyosi Tokun, "They have now seen that there is a lot of potential in waste. You can recover a lot of materials from it, so it is a money spinning business. People are just seeing it now. It's no longer waste, it is now a raw material, so the way we do our things, the way people perceive waste right now is quite different from what it used to be."[85] For reasons that will be discussed in chapter 7, waste has acquired a new legitimacy in Lagos in this century, and most of our interviewees were alert to the recentness of this transformation.

As these careful explanations reveal, in attempting to clarify and translate the English word "dirt" for themselves, interviewees resorted to impromptu theorizations of different types of dirt. They pluralized our English category with a spectrum of local possibilities ranging from light dirt such as litter, easily swept from the house, to recyclable objects found in household trash, and, finally, to absolute dirt, irretrievably expelled from circulation. In this way, project participants translated our questions into locally meaningful terms and produced a framework for the reconceptualization of our project theme.

In talking about people and domestic environments, the opposite of physical dirt did not emerge as cleanliness per se. When asked to describe how they recognized a dirty person or a dirty environment, people repeatedly explained that something was dirty if it was not "neat." Neatness referred to a number of areas of personal and domestic hygiene, and it captured local attitudes toward a person's appearance in a single term. "You don't look neat. I consider that dirty," said one health professional of people's rumpled external appearances.[86] An unemployed man stated, "You don't need to be rich for you to be neat. You should be neat inside. You should be neat outside. Some people try to be neat outside but inside they are very dirty."[87] Another man said, "When you see a pretty lady, very neat. The hair and everything. The man will admire her. If you see dirty this thing, it would put you off."[88] A discussant in a focus group convened by John Uwa said, "You know, a lot of the physical aspect of dirt comes from the inside—from the way you talk, the way you dress, the way you address people, the way you see life, you know, so dirt is a perpetual expression coming from the inside and going outside."[89] "When people see you, they look at you externally when you are neat," a woman explained to Jane Nebe. "You take care of your teeth, every part of your body, the clothes you wear, everything is clean, that person is neat. . . . It is the physical appearance that will judge whether he is okay or not."[90]

Neat was the opposite of dirty for many interviewees, and the criteria for neatness stimulated extensive commentaries that dwelt on what was not neat. During a lengthy focus group discussion about neatness among low-income residents of "Face-me-I-face-you" accommodation, one woman in her sixties contrasted neat with dirty households in this way: "If you enter the house of a *tálíkà* (poor person), they will mess the whole place with water and make everywhere look *pọ́nṣọnpọ̀nṣọn* (disgusting) and *yámayàma* (filthy). . . . Even when you come out of the house, mosquitoes come out with you. The rich treat their house better than the *tálàkà*."[91] "To make sure they are always neat," explained a public health worker of the low-income families with whom she worked, "the surrounding should be clean, whatever they eat they should cook it very well, and they should make sure that when they go to toilet they clean their hands so those are the things we have been telling the public. We see that people are really complying with us."[92] In short, "a dirty person . . . err . . . oozes."[93]

By these accounts, neatness, as the opposite of dirtiness, involved substantially more than the superficial absence of blemishes. It was a principle of arrangement, a relationship with objects that was inextricable from a person's inner self. Neatness as a category referred to a well-ordered home, the presence of consumer goods, and the absence of litter, mosquitoes, overcrowding, shabbiness, clutter, creases, and dust. Behind these external signs, a particular attitude toward comportment and self-presentation showed an absence of inner (and spiritual) dirt. All of these visible features contributed to other people's recognition of a person as dirty or neat.

In recognizing neatness as the opposite of dirtiness, interviewees allowed for the fact that the majority of Lagosians live in cash-strapped households where goods and garments are rarely brand new. Neatness has deeper significance than newness: a person whose appearance is both washed *and* properly arranged is a person who has harnessed the environment and found the correct place for things. Perhaps this is where Lagosians came closest to Mary Douglas's classic definition of dirt in relation to spatiality and placement. For Douglas, dirt was culturally contingent rather than definitive. It signified people's need to withdraw from a habitus perceived to be dirty, and, in reaction against the negative encounter, to reassert their own interpretive boundaries.[94] As one focus group member stated, "If things are not properly placed, it is then you can say the place is dirty."[95] While domestic waste could be either useless or useful, as discussed above, and rarely entered the ontology of dirt, "it is the person that is dirty, that will be dirty, even if he or she is rich."[96] Regardless of the age of one's possessions, a self-respecting person keeps themselves and their environment under control: by maintaining neatness and putting things in their proper place, a person keeps disorder at bay. By contrast, "clean" requires newness and gloss, factory freshness in an urban environment where the majority of side roads are not tarred, and the coming and going of vehicles churns up films of dust that penetrate people's homes. For this reason, people often keep thick plastic covers on furniture so the items remain "clean" underneath.[97]

Public Opinion

In highlighting the perspectives of people targeted by, but often excluded from, official articulations of public health policy and environmental planning, this chapter has focused on people who, in describing their perceptions of the urban environment, contribute to public opinion and occupy a dynamic space of critical judgment without being wholly determined by official discourses about urban development, cleanliness, and dirt. If the pattern of mutual toleration identified above is more than an outcome of our particular research environment, then its recurrence across so many interviews might be regarded as constitutive of contemporary Lagosian "public opinion."

For our interviewees, multicultural toleration across mutually incomprehensible languages and behavioral practices took precedence over a liberal cosmopolitan desire for dialogue, translation, mutual understanding, persuasion, or rationalization, which are defining features of the public sphere in Western theorizations since Habermas. Where scholarly conceptualizations of publics and the public sphere in the Global North generally require mutual comprehension and the visibility of others through the presence of translators (if not national languages), the Lagosian public sphere described in this chapter shows hypersensitivity to inclusiveness without the demand for mutual transparency. One participant in a focus group facilitated by John Uwa summed up the multiculturalism of Lagos: "We have disparities in our culture. We don't see things from the same perspective, even though we are Nigerians. . . . There is this discrepancy, there is a break in connection."[98] As neighbors in the vicinity of strangers, Lagosians adopt a policy of live and let live, involving scrupulous attention to the behavior of others and an equally scrupulous avoidance of critical public engagement with it. "We are in Lagos and we have been living peacefully. We have not had any major fight between the Yorùbá, the Hausa and the Igbo. What we've had is a few instances in Mile 12 market between the Hausa and a few Yorùbá."[99]

Nobody—including the Yoruba oral historians we interviewed—wished to discuss the brutal civil war of 1967–70, in which ethnic tensions against Igbo migrants living in the north of the country turned into a nationwide bloodbath that led to the declaration of the secessionist Igbo state of Biafra. With such a trauma still present in living memory, and with the proximity of Boko Haram in the north with its murderously purist understanding of African authenticity, one can understand why Lagosians, when asked about the dirtiness of people, wished to avoid dehumanizing discourses that constructed others as incomprehensible to the point of disposability.[100]

In focusing on in-depth interview transcripts without filtering them through the gauze of economic and environmental interpretations, this chapter has attempted to open micro-spaces for the voices of contemporary Lagosians, and to suggest the presence of a living archive within and behind quantitative types of study. The extent to which our in-depth interviews can yield sufficient data to identify Lagosians as producers of, and participants in, a distinctive civic consciousness that prevents the sprawling, economically divided megalopolis from fragmenting into violence remains open to question. At the very least, however, these qualitative interviews help to supplement quantitative work on Lagos by highlighting the ways in which people's attitudes and imaginations are a vital and material part of the urban environment, shaped in part by politicians, churches, and the media, but drawing constantly from a clearly defined field of public opinion according to which their own behavior and that of others is judged to be socially acceptable or unacceptable. Again and again, participants stressed that, in the words of one senior man, "anything that is not your culture you will kind-of not like it. So what is dirty to somebody might be right to the other person, but for me, I will tell them, 'No, I don't want.' Some people likes it, some people don't like it, but of course for some people who don't like it they see it as being dirty."[101]

Whether looking down on the metropolis from the vantage point of the presidential helicopter, as Rem Koolhaas did in parts of *Lagos Wide and Close* (dir. Bregtje van der Haak, 2002), or avoiding individual opinion in favor of a statistical route through quantitative data, as Alhaji A. Aliyi and Lawal Amadu, David Mautin Oke and colleagues, and Felix Olorunfemi do in their work on Nigerian urbanization, Lagos takes on different hues depending on the discipline, methods, orientations, and cultural biases of analysts.[102] The multicultural toleration identified in this chapter as Lagosians' response to the crowded urban environment gives an idealistic hue to the city. Partly this is because the focus of this chapter has been physical dirt, literal waste rather than "dirty behavior" or dirty bodies. Even so, it would be impossible to assume that up to 21 million Lagosians share existential experiences with one another as urban citizens no matter their socioeconomic circumstances, or that ethnic tensions do not exist in the metropolis.[103] Nevertheless, at the level of thinking about domestic waste and waste management, our socially and economically mixed group of participants modeled a multicultural approach to urban living so persistently and consistently as to suggest a shared ethos for cohabiting in a city that they repeatedly described as "bubbling," "noisy," and "mixed up," where "everyone is on the road, on the rush, nobody is slowing down," where "the hospitality is high if you meet the right set of people, and it could be very, very brutal if you are unfortunate with the other side of people."[104] The people we spoke to were proud of the cohabitation of diverse cultural groups in Lagos, and their way to preserve multiculturalism was to insist on individuality above ethno-regional markers: "I don't assess people based on their size or their tribe or their colour, whatever. I just assess them individually."[105]

7

Remembering Waste

As a classification, waste has the unique capacity
to overflow its semantic limit, to conjure qualities of feeling that are more
fundamental, more expansive than the objects to which it refers.
—SHANNON JACKSON AND STEVEN ROBINS

Moving away from light dirt such as litter and domestic waste to focus on organic matter and its handlers, this chapter focuses on local and international media representations of dumpsites and waste workers in post-colonial Lagos, and includes a case study of the pictorial symbolism used in the presidential election campaign of 2015. The chapter examines how public relations campaigns since 2005, aimed at transforming people's perceptions of stigmatized forms of labor, have entered contemporary popular discourse in the form of new, or revised, interpretations of dirt. In an effort to gauge the gaps and overlaps between past and present, foreign and local, the chapter contrasts recent discourses about dirty bodies with historical conceptualizations of dumpsites and waste workers, on the one hand, and colonial and Eurocentric representations of dirt in Lagos, on the other.

Unwelcome in Lagos: Postcolonial Slum-Talk and the BBC

In April 2010, the BBC aired a major three-part documentary with the title *Welcome to Lagos* (prod. Will Anderson). Focusing on "the ghettos and slums" through the eyes of "strong characters who would let us into their lives," the BBC aimed to offer empathetic and informative entry-points to urban experience in Lagos via three liminal spaces: the dumpsite, the abattoir, and the shoreline.[1] For many Nigerians, however, the tone and substance of the voice-over, scripted to produce surprise in British audiences at the conditions under which impoverished classes survived in the city, exposed the BBC itself as condescending and judgmental in the manner of colonial discourse. The BBC appeared to ignore the fact that, as one Nigerian media worker put it, "the picture of Lagos as a very dirty city is changing very fast. So I think the [BBC's] description of Lagos as being one of the dirtiest cities in Africa has to do with the Eurocentric conception and perception."[2]

In positioning themselves on the side of the most impoverished people in the city, the makers of the documentary strove for a human connection with the individuals chosen for attention. One episode focused on Eric, an aspiring rap star secretly working in the stigmatized job of waste picker at the dump in order to finance the recording of his debut album. Another episode focused on Joseph, a waste picker and buyer of reclaimed metals, saving for his daughter's first birthday party and on the lookout for retrievable trash to recycle as gifts. A third episode focused on Esther, displaced from her shack in an informal settlement by Lagos State Government bulldozers, separated from her daughter and subsequently from her husband, living in a flimsy dwelling on the shoreline. Through this personalized attention, named individuals were carefully separated off from the crowd in order to create empathy among viewers for the millions of impoverished Lagosians.

What prevented transcendence of the "us versus them" dichotomy, however, was the ubiquitous presence of people's relationships with rubbish *as dirt*. Trash was not normalized in the documentary. Whenever the camera panned out from the stories of individuals to view the low-income communities en masse, the voice-over by British actor David Harewood took on the fascinated curiosity of a touristic outsider, reinforcing the cultural otherness of the people portrayed, even in the process of ostensibly forging empathetic connections between Western spectators and the Lagosian poor. A typical pattern of commentary described how Lagosians living in poverty "are resourceful, determined, and unbelievably resilient, and they are successfully adapting to the realities of modern city life in ways that *you*, in the so-called developed world, couldn't even imagine."[3] As the first episode explained, "Where *you* see filth and rubbish, the scavengers see a livelihood."[4] This was not helped by the producer's post on the BBC TV *Blog* designed to promote the series but containing a patronizing comment that did not escape the notice of the blogpost's many critics: "Yes, they may be terribly poor, but that doesn't stop them being human and, if the films have succeeded, then I hope they've succeeded in showing that."[5]

As with the colonial travelers and traders analyzed in the introductory chapter, in *Welcome to Lagos* the category of dirt functioned in a sensationalized form to signify disorder, inefficiency, borderline humanity, and extreme types of social otherness. Unlike the colonial archive, however, where ontologies of race surpassed class as explanatory tools, the BBC included injunctions to observers to take note of how clean the slum dwellers were, in spite of their squalid environments. Whereas, in the era of colonial town planning, the British category of dirt was used to convey irrational and often racist responses to local people's apparent lack of cleanliness, in *Welcome to Lagos* the voice-over showed the humanity of Lagosians through the very fact that they managed to stay clean, in spite of everything. Flipping the coin but not transforming the discourse, the BBC thus retained the category of dirt to visibly mark the boundary where human empathy is transformed into detachment in the form of voyeuristic surprise, articulated as "Look how clean they are!" Continuously separating observer from observed through the expression of surprise at the cleanness of this underclass, the program produced the very category of otherness it wished to transcend.

Weaving the three installments together was one common theme: rubbish, or "dirty." "Most of the dirty from the seaside, the water has pushed it down to this area, so we have to do a lot of cleaning," explained Esther as she used a makeshift shovel to dig a trench around her flooded "scrap house" on the shoreline.[6] From Makoko "slum" on the Lagoon, where, the narrator remarked emphatically, "people actually *pay* to have rubbish dumped on their doorstep [for . . .] land reclamation, Makoko-style," through to the so-called scavengers picking recyclables from the infamous dumpsite at Olusosun, the documentary placed trash at the center of attention, with a brief diversion into offal in the first episode with scenes filmed at the open-air slaughterhouse, guaranteed to disgust the BBC's home audience.[7] Almost as prominent as people's relationships with other people were their interactions with rubbish. Indeed, a theme from the outset of the program was the manner in which trash bonded humans together as a mediating substance: Joseph met Elizabeth, his future wife, on a dumpsite, for example, and Eric's workmates on the dump contributed to a fund to free him from an impossibly expensive lawsuit.

Welcome to Lagos simultaneously used and attempted to challenge representational techniques in place for a century to describe tropical cities. In

1924, invoking what had already become a familiar vision of the city, Percival Christopher Wren, author of the best-selling adventure novel, *Beau Geste*, referred dismissively to "the rubbish-heap called Lagos, on the Bight of Benin of the wicked West African Coast."[8] So pervasive was this shorthand for Lagos that by the 1950s, during a screening of an antimalaria educational film in Ilaro village, Ogun State, in 1952, a boy in the audience "called out 'Lagos,' seeing the rubbish being tipped into the swamp."[9] For its many Nigerian critics, *Welcome to Lagos* continued to feed the Western public's obsession with "tropical slums" far more than it represented the full complexity of life in Lagos. As Nobel laureate Wole Soyinka described it, the program was "jaundiced and extremely patronising. It was saying, 'Oh, look at these people who can make a living from the pit of degradation.'"[10]

Municipal officials and local commentators in Lagos expressed an equally negative but rather different response to global intellectuals such as Soyinka. In focusing exclusively on rubbish and impoverished communities, the BBC had, in the view of officials and many Lagosians, exploited the trust of the Lagos State Government, which granted the film crew access to Olusosun landfill and other key sites in the city. "You cannot use a part of Lagos to describe the whole of Lagos," one media worker complained of the documentary.[11] On the BBC TV *Blog* website, a Yoruba viewer, Adeyemi Adisa, wrote, "I wonder why western media always like to show this kind of documentary about Africa to their viewers. I am still waiting for the day when BBC and the likes will showcase the beautiful part of Africa to their viewers."[12] A Nigerian commentator in the British *Guardian* vividly stated, "Our dirty linen were yanked from our very loins and aired on the international veranda."[13]

This combination of anger and shame characterized responses in the Nigerian media. Generally, when Lagos is described in sensationalist terms as "the dirtiest city in Africa," or ranked among the "least livable" cities in the world, the country's national media react with exasperation, embarrassment, defensiveness, and an emphasis on change.[14] Some commentators express contempt for successive postcolonial governments' failures to fulfil their promises to "clean up" the city. Others, such as those cited above, are critical of the negative terminology employed by global agencies, fearing the impressions this type of representation will produce among analysts, investors, and visitors.

The memory of *Welcome to Lagos* was still strong among officials four years after the broadcast, when Olutoyosi Tokun approached the Lagos Waste Management Authority (LAWMA) and Jane Nebe approached the Ministry of Education for permits to conduct their research for the "Dirtpol" project. Suspicious managers interrogated the researchers repeatedly and were reluctant to grant access to municipal dumpsites or government schools. As Olutoyosi Tokun recalled,

> This suspicion originated to the BBC's *Welcome to Lagos* documentary.... When I went to LAWMA to get approval, it was such a difficult assignment for me. It took several months for them to approve that I access their refuse dumps, because it is exactly the same research environment that *Welcome to Lagos* was based on, because some of it was based on the refuse dump in Lagos and I was also going back to that refuse dump with an international organization.... Nobody wants a bad name. As much as things are a bit different in Nigeria, we want to promote the good aspects of the country. We don't want to be misrepresented.... We want at least a holistic, a fair, representation of what's happening in Lagos.[15]

"Because of this BBC documentary," Jane Nebe commented, "it was not surprising that people within the Ministry [of Education] were very skeptical of such research. What they felt the BBC documentary did was to hype the negatives and ignore the positives, or talk about the positives in a way that was not really hyped as positives. The skepticism was really there."[16] Arriving in Lagos with a research project focusing on dirt, we were caught up in the very media discourses we wished to analyze. Government officials were "reading" us through their negative interpretations of the BBC documentary, and they were understandably wary about the manner in which we would represent our encounters.

"Ààtàn kìí kọ ilẹ̀kílẹ̀": Public and Anti-Public Spaces of Waste

Documentaries such as *Welcome to Lagos* have the potential to reinforce historical stereotypes about the ontological status of people associated with dumpsites, but this type of voyeurism is not confined to international media coverage of Nigeria.[17] One should not assume from the above critique that Lagosians somehow have unmediated access to the city, nor that *Welcome to Lagos* articulated an exclusively Eurocentric perspective on the city. Many middle-class Lagosians have no firsthand knowledge of poor neighborhoods in the metropolis. Several of our educated, Anglophone interviewees described watching footage and documentaries about Lagos on YouTube, or reading about "slums" in the newspapers, from which they gleaned the information they reported back to us.[18] The combination of curiosity and disapproval in their commentaries on Lagos shared many features of the "us versus them" voice-over of *Welcome to Lagos*.

In his analysis of Nigerian media coverage of people abandoned at dumpsites, Patrick Oloko shows how one such educated, middle-class group, Anglophone journalists, is fascinated by the notion of "wasted humans" in liminal urban spaces, including the desertion of unwanted people at municipal dumps. Media reports regularly show the corpses of newborn babies dropped at dumps. Dumpsites are also places for leaving the corpses of murder victims, such as the young woman left at a dump beside the Lagos-Abeokuta Expressway in 2015.[19] Another sensational story described a disabled man abandoned alive by his uncle in 2014 at a dumpsite in the low-income neighborhood of Ijora, where he died.[20] In their coverage of these brutal stories, mainstream and social media often revel in descriptions of dumpsites as macabre dystopias in which people are transformed into dirt, including gory details and photographs of corpses that have been mutilated prior to disposal.[21]

Part of the media's horrified fascination with dumpsite bodies relates to older traditions whereby certain people were expelled from the social cycle to the realm of absolute uselessness, or absolute waste. In contrast to the discourse of household recycling and recuperation discussed in the preceding chapter, for newspaper reporters in Lagos, as much as for the publics for whom they write, the city dumpsite is the final stopping point for waste that has fallen off the cycle of social usefulness. Whereas trash can be recuperated, absolute waste finds its stopping point on the dump. Like the gutters into which people commonly throw effluent and unrecyclable plastics, the dumpsite is seen by many Lagosians as an untouchable urban space where irretrievable matter finds its destination (although gutters are different from dumpsites in that people participate with varying degrees of compliance in compulsory "environmental" or "sanitation" days for cleaning drains and clearing rubbish from their neighborhoods on every last Saturday of the month). The dump takes whatever is put into it, in whatever form: *Bá a gbálé, tá a gbátà, àátàn là á darí è sí* (Yoruba: after sweeping both inside and outside the house, all the trash will end up in the dumpsite).[22] Dumps are generally regarded as places where matter that is so far beyond use it has become dangerous to humans—intense dirt—belongs. "The refuse that we will find on a dump site *a à lè pè é ní pàǹtí*"(Yoruba: cannot be called litter)."[23] From this perspective, for our interviewees, true dirt was not so much "matter out of place" as hazardous matter with no further life span or use in the human life cycle. For items on the dump, "*the life don comot*" (Nigerian Pidgin: life has left it). This did not render dumpsite dirt dead or inanimate. It was considered a public health hazard with

CHAPTER SEVEN

the potential to permeate people's bodies and cause harm. As one health worker told Olutoyosi Tokun, "You just can't keep holding on to dirt like that."[24] True dirt was considered so dangerous to people that, like a tumor, it had to be excised: "It is not material now. It is not a material that you will use for production. Any danger that ought to be thrown away is waste."[25]

For most Lagosians, the dumpsite is a fixed, antisocial space, incapable of recuperation into human economies of meaning and value. Except for waste pickers, nobody would choose to spend time there.[26] The dumpsite absorbs the people who enter it into a posthuman black hole where, except for the recyclable materials retrieved by waste pickers, there is no onward passage for the matter deposited there. Historically, too, dumpsites are the antithesis of the social: traditionally located on the outskirts of villages and towns, they are regarded as "the backyard of everybody."[27] People will go there to defecate or burn rubbish, but nobody lingers on the ààtàn. Traditionally, nothing returns from the dump: "The dump does not reject any form of refuse," said Ayò Yusuff. "Bring a dead person there, he [the dump] will just accept it. Bring a dead pig, he will just take it. It doesn't reject anything," no matter how abominable.[28] The dump has the capacity to transform people into waste: "At the end of the day our garbage collectors look so, look like garbage. They are not looking different from the garbage."[29] It is this nonhuman or posthuman quality of the ààtàn that renders dumpsite communities, such as those represented in *Welcome to Lagos*, always potentially equivalent to the surrounding trash in popular opinion.

These views about the absolute dirt on dumpsites are not historically fixed or characteristic of a Yoruba worldview, but they do reflect the spatial dynamics of Yoruba cities and the social history of rubbish dumps. In towns and villages, Karin Barber argues, "the rubbish dump marks the perimeter of the town."[30] Traditionally, people would go to the dumpsite, or "dunghill," to defecate. Located on the outskirts of town, close to, permeated by, and synonymous with the "bush," or forest, this was a place associated with outcasts such as madmen, criminals, and àbíkú (children who are "born to die" many times into the same family).[31] By contrast, Barber argues, the sign of a successful city is its expansion to the point where the rubbish heap becomes the market, or center of exchange, as this praise epithet for an Ọba indicates: "*Sọgbó-dilé sògbẹ́-dìgboro / Ọba asàatàn dọjà*" (Yoruba: Turns forest into house, turns bush into town / The Ọba who turns rubbish heap into market).[32] The successful Ọba has pushed the dump away and conquered the old dump by expanding the town. When megacities such as Lagos undergo these processes of urban metamorphosis, however, the wasted humans from the old perimeter spaces may linger at the dumpsites in the heart of the city.[33] Barber writes, "When there is no forest within reach, the inhabitants have no perimeter to orient themselves to. The rubbish heaps grow inside the city, to enormous size," and outcasts, who "can't be expelled" are jettisoned in "the man-made *lgbe* of the rubbish heap, in the middle of the city."[34] What was previously pushed into the forest thus remains disturbingly present, haunting the community's imagination.

From this perspective, no matter how centrally it is located, the metropolitan dumpsite is not a public space in Lagosians' topographical imaginations, nor can anything fresh, healthy, or useful be produced there. Many people we interviewed expressed repugnance for organic matter produced on city dumpsites, describing it as inherently toxic. Chickens may flourish and lush vegetables may grow in these spaces, they said, but such material should not be introduced into the human food chain "because at times they dump dead bodies" there.[35] No matter how plump a chicken or succulent a vegetable, even after washing, people should not knowingly ingest food that had been raised on the dumpsite, a place where anything of use had already been removed.[36] "My grandmother never ate fowls," the Yoruba linguist Ayọ̀ Yusuff explained to Olutoyosi Tokun, because chickens ate maggots from corpses and "peck[ed] on any dirty thing" on the dumpsite, foraging like pigs on the *àǎtàn*.[37]

Media reports draw on this archive of untouchable matter at the heart of the city. Oloko shows how, through photographs and vivid physical descriptions of victims, the newspapers describe "wasted" humans as actually having joined the other waste matter ejected from human use. Citing Kenneth Harrow's work on trash in African cinema, Oloko suggests that "Africa seems to have produced a modernity in which 'dirt' has come to 'define not only the scraps but the eaters of scraps as well.'"[38] Alive or dead, it seems a human may be rendered an object (or become abject) on contact with the dump. While they often stress the humanity of the jettisoned subjects and express shock at perpetrators' behavior, newspaper reports combine moral outrage at the inhumanity of perpetrators with sensationalist and voyeuristic affirmations of the pariah status of the abandoned people. In doing so, in a similar manner to *Welcome to Lagos*, they ambivalently move readers' empathy in the direction of disgust. Silenced in a noisy city, dumpsite bodies form anti-publics that are anathema to the public sphere.

As indicated above, contemporary local beliefs about waste draw considerable historical authority from proverbs and maxims, which feed directly into people's perceptions of rubbish dumps, recycling, and the individuals who make their living from working with waste. In his intricately historicized account of the ways that waste, in its various Yoruba-language configurations, has come to tell stories about social class and consumption in Lagos, Ayọ̀dèjì Olukoju discusses some of the Yoruba proverbs that have the dumpsite as their focal point (see the appendix). These proverbs have a complex historicity, containing seeds of past commentary and memories to pass on. Their uses, meanings, and interpretations are not historically fixed: an expert in the use of proverbs will cite a familiar phrase or reference, embellish it artistically, and shape it to fit a particular circumstance, often without commenting directly on the situation under scrutiny. The listener completes the work by applying the proverb to the specific situation and drawing out its lessons.[39] This means, as the remainder of this chapter will suggest, that time-honored maxims about dumpsites and waste workers are available for political management and reuse, and established linguistic tools can be deployed to transform entrenched public opinions about waste and waste workers, resulting in new levels of environmental awareness among urban residents.

The Ambivalence of Buhari's Broom

As in Kitoyi Ajasa's day, sanitation and public health remain barometers of social progress for many media commentators in postcolonial Nigeria. Every rainy season, dramatic images of the flooding caused by blocked gutters dominate the national media alongside reports of collapsed buildings and fatalities from water- and sewage-borne diseases. Often focusing on low-income settlements and residents' lack of sanitary resources, these reports connect poverty and migration with disease and dirt, and, except for a handful of journalists for whom inward migration to the city and the proliferation of informal settlements is an inevitable outcome of the opportunities offered by Lagos as a regional nexus of wealth and trade, a negative language for the city's impoverished masses continues to pervade media accounts of low-income neighborhoods.

While journalists often address what should be done by urban planners, combining policy suggestions with social critique, Nigerian political discourses relating to the removal of urban dirt have become increasingly metaphorical during the long century of urban planning and public health covered by this book. In the decades since the discourse of dirt shaped colonial town-planning policies, urban dirt has accrued rich layers of double meanings in the public sphere, enabling references to objects such as the broom, or practices such as defecation and handwashing, to take on metonymic

FIGURE 7.1. "Clean and Competent Hands." Election advertisement
for the Kowa Party, 2015.

and scatological as well as literal public health value, and to become available for political deployment as symbols with moral resonance among the
electorate.[40]

   In preparation for the Nigerian presidential elections that took place in
March 2015, political strategists for the All Progressives Congress (APC)—a
coalition formed in 2013 of the People's Democratic Party, the Congress for
Progressive Change, and the Action Congress of Nigeria—chose a symbol with such deep-rooted significance in Nigerian cultural mythologies
about dirt that their candidate almost skidded over in the flow of derision
his party symbol inspired among rival candidates and voters. While other
contenders such as Professor Remi Sonaiya of the Kowa Party referenced
the handwashing associated with preventing the spread of Ebola in Nigeria, fresh in people's minds when the election campaign was under way,
and mapped it onto political metaphors for corruption relating to "people
who have soiled their hands in the past" (fig. 7.1), the APC chose the locally
made broom as its emblem, graphically depicting its intention to sweep out
corruption and other forms of immorality from the national house using
local means (fig. 7.2).[41] The party symbol seemed unequivocal, invoking
the popular euphemism "to bring out the broom" for fighting malpractice
and corruption, while also arousing affection in the electorate for the traditional palm-frond brush familiar to most Nigerian households and still
widely used. "The significant of the broom is cleaning of bad thing out to
bring in good thing," one APC supporter stated in an interview immediately
before the 2015 election. "You know, if you want to sweep the house you use

CHAPTER SEVEN

FIGURE 7.2. The APC party symbol.

broom. If you want to sweep anywhere you use broom. And if use broom to clear all things, the ground would be smooth for everybody . . . you can even sleep on the ground."[42]

Many households own two brooms, one for indoor use (a "clean" broom for sweeping light dirt such as dust and litter) and the other for sweeping organic matter into drainage channels or heaps outdoors. The symbolism was clear: the APC could sweep out corruption without requiring interventions from external, international agencies. As supporters explained, "We are trying to clear bad people out of the country."[43]

The broom seemed a perfect symbol for the presidential candidate Muhammadu Buhari, a northerner who, as military ruler of Nigeria after the coup of 1983, launched a two-year "War Against Indiscipline" (WAI) involving numerous arrests for financial and political malpractices and the enforcement of "public morality" on the streets through vigorous and often violent "clean-up" campaigns targeting street hawkers, sex workers, and other urban bodies deemed to spread immorality.[44] As most Nigerians knew, however, the humble broom symbolized a great deal more than the removal of ordinary household waste. As the popular maxim states, "The broom is not the problem. It is the person who holds the broom that is the problem."[45] And for generations of urban residents, the broom was inextricable from one of the most stigmatized bodies in Nigeria's histories of dirt, and it was linked to a substance with considerably more viscosity and odor than light domestic dirt.

The *agbépóò* (night-soil man) is a legendary urban figure in Nigeria, and the broom is a metonym for his presence.[46] Largely gone from sight in the contemporary city, this form of labor was necessitated by the British introduction of the removable bucket latrine in the early twentieth century. Promoted by colonial sanitary officials as the hygienic alternative to open-air defecation and the pit latrine, the bucket system created the *agbépóò* as one of the most stigmatized forms of "native" labor.[47] With the face completely concealed to protect the worker against contact with fecal waste—but also, according to popular belief, to prevent recognition by anybody, including members of his own family—the *agbépóò* encapsulates Frantz Fanon's description of the ontological violence and degradation experienced by the "othered" body in the colonial encounter.[48]

For many Nigerians, the *agbépóò* symbolizes and embodies a shameful aspect of the colonial encounter. Fela Kuti interpreted and memorialized night-soil men in "I.T.T., International Thief Thief," where the metaphor of shit-carrying by the corrupt postcolonial state is connected with literal shit-carrying under colonialism: "During the time them come colonize us / Them come teach us to carry shit / Long, long, long, long time ago / African man we no dey carry shit / Na European man teach us to carry shit."[49] The song ends, "We don tire to carry any more of them shit."[50] Several of our interviewees remembered this famous track. One Yoruba oral historian commented that "Fela Kuti made us to understand that it is the white people who taught us how to carry shit, otherwise we don't carry shit, what we were used to is the *ṣáláǹgá* (pit latrine). We all heard that song. It means that all their systems, their ideas which they had planted in us 'Black people' during the colonial period, they should come and pack their things, and there are lots of things."[51]

The figure of the *agbépóò* recurs in popular historical accounts of twentieth-century Lagos, but it is possible that Fela's hit of 1979 helped to consolidate local perceptions of *agbépóò* as pariahs. One interviewee in his mid-seventies suggested to John Uwa that historically there was no stigma attached to night-soil work: "In my compound in those days, around 1961, there use to be a man who does *agbépóò* business. In the afternoon he mingles with us and sometimes talks about his business. There is no shame of the job at that time."[52] A Yoruba oral historian confirmed this position, stating that late nineteenth-century *agbépóò* included members of influential families, such as "Kosoko's son" and "Dosunmu's son."[53] Their work carried no stigma, he insisted, because "when you get home, you use Dettol to bathe: *ẹní jalè ló ba ọmọ jẹ́.*[54] You see, it is the head that knows where the leg is going.[55] I have seen people who carried shit in those days who have become important people in this society today. Lagosians don't see shit carrying as dirty job. Any job a person does in Lagos which can bring home money to take care of the family is legitimate: *ẹní jalè ló ba ọmọ jẹ́.*[56]

If the *agbépòò* is a literal figure at the start of this explanation, by the end of the old man's account "shit-carrying" has taken on figurative status, signifying all the demeaning forms of labor through which a living can be made in the city while honoring Lagosians' choice of hard-work above criminality to survive in colonial and postcolonial cities.[57] The empirical details in this oral historian's account are overlaid with proverbial depth. What is important about his retrieval of the *agbépòò* as a figure for interpreting the cultural history of early colonial contact in Lagos is not so much that he makes the anachronistic reference to Dettol, a product first used in Europe in the early twentieth century, but that he names an imported disinfectant associated with European hospitals and the globalization of Western sanitation practices above locally produced soaps or disinfectants, and that he reiterates the connection between night-soil work and the colonial encounter. The *agbépòò* thus stands for—or stands in for—the new political subjectivities of chiefs in the decades following the British bombardment of Lagos in 1851 and its annexation by the British in 1861. Colonial contact is not, however, filled with the postcolonial shame of late twentieth-century representations.

By the early twentieth century—the era of colonial sanitation—*agbépòò* in Lagos were largely drawn from the Egbe people of Kwara State, approximately two hundred miles from the city, because indigenes were increasingly reluctant to undertake such work. An old man explained, "the Egbes come from a far country and no one knows them in Lagos and as such, they are not ashamed."[58] They were joined by Eguns from Benin Republic; again, we were told, "the reason the *agbépòò* job is quite common with this ethnic group is because they are not indigenes of Lagos. They are *àjòjì* (strangers) who come from elsewhere, and anyone who does not come from their town is free to know the kind of job that they are doing."[59]

This issue of indigenes' unwillingness to undertake certain types of labor was not confined to Yoruba areas of British West Africa. Throughout the region in the colonial era, the difficulty of finding local people for sanitary work led to government appeals for migrant workers to be transported across territories: in 1902, for example, the doctor responsible for malaria and sanitation work in Freetown, Matthew Logan Taylor, was asked by the governor of the Gold Coast to bring fifty men from Sierra Leone to Cape Coast for "cleansing" work due to the insufficient supply of local labor.[60]

For officials, "a properly organized permanent scavenger department" was vital to the public health of colonial West African cities, but locals refused to undertake this type of work. As a consequence, parts of the sanitary services relied on migrant laborers, and, in the process, joined a global network of other colonial countries where night-soil workers were regarded by local residents as untouchable and dirty.[61]

Well into the 1970s, night-soil workers could be seen throughout Lagos late at night or in the early hours of the morning, avoiding contact with the populations whose fecal matter they removed.[62] They are embodied in people's memories by the shadowy figure of the masked man carrying a pail on his head and a broom in his hand, on a "mission [that was] special and, at the same time, grotesque," filling large drums on carts with sewage to be wheeled off to designated dumpsites around the city.[63] "He is faceless and unknown. His mask and bandana ensured his anonymity and protected his true identity."[64] As mentioned in chapter 1, the Marina was one such site for the deposit of fecal and general waste, earning the name *Ẹhingbeh* (or *Ẹhin Ìgbẹ́*, Yoruba: Behind the shit/bush), "owing to its being the chief place in which all refuse and dirt is generally deposited in the early days of Lagos."[65] Lagos Lagoon was another site. One man remembered that "in the 1960s right here in *Èkó* (Lagos Island), around Carter Bridge and the railway station at Idumota, there used to be a road at an angle which now serves as main road. The *agbẹ́pòò* position themselves to dispose the sewage into the lagoon. This is how they manage sewage then."[66]

Night-soil workers have declined in numbers with the increase in private sewage contractors with vacuum trucks for the removal of latrine waste.[67] Operating unmasked in broad daylight with vehicles and hoses, contemporary sewage workers attract less opprobrium than their predecessors because they "don't have direct hand contact with shit," and thus exemplify municipal modernity, but some traditional *agbẹ́pòò* still operate with pails and wooden pushcarts in neighborhoods where the roads are inaccessible to sewage removal vehicles, or the residents are too poor to afford alternative services.[68]

If this already out-of-sight profession is retreating even further from visibility on the streets, *agbẹ́pòò* remain spectacularly present in popular memory, encapsulating a sensational, scatological account of Lagosian civic history through which an "aesthetics of vulgarity" combines with people's explanations of violence in the city.[69] As stigmatized bodies spawned by colonialism and urbanization, they continue to inspire ambivalence in onlookers. "How do people regard *agbẹ́pòòs* [*sic*]?" a pastor was asked by Olutoyosi Tokun. "Haa, people don't [regard them]," he answered, taking "re-gard" to mean respect as well as evaluation: "They see them as, you know, people that are dirty because they are doing a dirty job. As much as pos-sible they want to avoid them."[70] Another participant responded, "They are not regarded. They regard them with low status."[71] Night-soil work is still judged to be *iṣẹ́ ẹ̀gbin*, a degrading job. Lagos residents remember the songs they used to sing as children to taunt *agbépòò* with the threat of exposure: "You, young man, I can see you! Do not cover your face with the cap! I will tell your mother, I will tell your father. You are doing the job of *agbépòò!*"[72]

The tool of the *agbépòò*'s trade, the broom, continues to feature promi-nently in middle-class Nigerians' recollections of growing up in Lagos. "Names were called: the night soil man retaliated by dipping the short palm rib brooms in their product and spraying the closest to his tormentors with it."[73] "His little broom, short and quick, splashed generously on those who crossed his path, including children who playfully called him by his names. And his names are legion—*onishe, agbepo, ibeji, eruewo, omo adelabu,* show boy."[74] "There are some of them who are deliberately wicked—using broom stick to splash on anyone who is attempting to identify them."[75] These scat-ological anecdotes contain no comments about the cruelty of this "playful" behavior; while commentators often note that night-soil workers operated in teams rather than alone, they fail to connect this with the laborers' vul-nerability to bullying and their general social status as nonpersons. Rather, the popular formula for recollecting the presence of the night-soil man in-volves the location of all agency in the terrifying flick of his broom as he reacts to abuse, confirming the repulsive nature of the pariah in the very act of narrating his revenge while also confirming the vantage point of the *agbépòò*'s tormenter.

With the broom as their symbol, the APC was mocked by the ruling party, the People's Democratic Party (PDP), as "the gathering of *agbépòòs* [*sic*]."[76] If the simple pictorial symbolism of the broom in Buhari's election campaign facilitated surface messaging on the part of the APC about the removal of corruption, it also opened up satirical reinterpretations by rival parties. Moreover, beneath the fecal and filth symbolism lay additional, more sinister threats. According to Yoruba popular belief, "A man can lose his sexual potency if he is flogged with a broom (by a woman)."[77] As one oral historian warned John Uwa, "Nothing good has ever come out of the broom: in fact, if you use the broom to flog a male child, he can become impotent. If a broom is used to hit your leg, you may never have a good wife until your dying day. Broom is an abominable object. If a thief trespasses and a broom is used to sweep his footprint, then he is gone. The broom is not good, and those holding it are not good.[78] These layers of additional meaning positioned Buhari and the APC within the realm of *juju* as well as excrement, with the implication that they were even more corrupt than those they wished to sweep out of power.

Rotimi Amaechi of the PDP pronounced, unambiguously, "Those who carry brooms are night soil men and juju priests."[79] Amaechi had to swallow his words and carefully extricate himself from the aftermath of his statements, however, when he defected from the PDP to the APC during the 2014–15 election campaign. "Little did he know he was going to downgrade himself one day to that status and turn full circle to return to where he actually belongs," mocked Chika Onuora in the online news magazine pointblanknews.com. The APC countered with a reclamation of the *agbépóò* as a noble symbolic figure and not a literal night-soil man: "Like the true African that he is, Amaechi was speaking in parables but suffice it to say that he did not in any way contradict himself by later dumping the torn umbrella of the doomed People's Democratic Party (PDP) for the clean-sweeping broom of the APC."[80] In these and other responses to the smears, the APC demonstrated unprecedented levels of trust in the electorate's ability to appreciate and apply the nuances of symbolic representation in an election that Buhari eventually won in spite of alleged international meddling.[81] Currently, the broom has returned to surface metaphors of sweeping and cleaning in the Nigerian media. "Come, stay under the 'umbrella,' 'broom' no longer sweeping well, Makarfi tells Nigerians" ran a headline in the *Vanguard* in October 2017.[82]

As the above analysis has attempted to show, a vital transformation of the negative symbolism surrounding *agbépóò*, at least since Fela's "I.T.T.," occurred during the election campaign. It is possible that the "gathering of *agbépóòs*" openly acknowledged and endorsed what Achille Mbembe describes as the scatological aesthetics of postcolonial power, whereby "the flow of shit" from the "men in power" is attractive to ordinary people, who see signs of opulence, feasting, carnival, laughter, and sumptuous excess in the excremental symbolism—albeit satirical—surrounding political leaders.[83] But alongside this political appropriation of scatological excess, the APC's representations brought the night-soil carrier into full visibility, not as a stinking pariah or as an abject colonial body deserving to be mocked or hurt, but as a political symbol that contested historically entrenched ways of seeing the *agbépóò*. Pro-APC journalists relished and embellished the proverbial figure: "The mess by the PDP [leaves] all patriots with no other option than to join the league of proverbial night soil men. . . . [E]very Nigerian patriot needs to carry brooms to flush out this evil party and clean up the country. . . . The country desperately needs good night soil men to clean up PDP's faeces."[84] APC supporters reclaimed the epitome of dirt: they seized the opportunity to honor the stigmatized figure of the night-soil worker, and simultaneously created a metaphor out of the *agbépòò* for ordinary Nigerians' attempts to remove corruption from their daily life. In a spectacular reversal of the joke, the fecal matter became the sitting president, and his nemesis the *agbépòò* party. As the final part of this chapter will suggest, this symbolic reclamation of an old-time pariah could not have been possible without widespread transformations of public perceptions of urban waste workers.

Popular Opinion on Waste Management Workers

For Lagosians, the city furnishes a wealth of stories about dirt. Yet urban residents' descriptions of their environments are mundane by comparison with the national and international media representations discussed in previous pages. While mainstream media workers in Lagos feel the pressure, as one radio journalist put it, to "run on negativity . . . 'bad news is good news,'" the majority of interviewees for this project did not position themselves as representatives of particular positions or causes.[85] On the topics of waste and waste workers, they answered as residents and urban consumers, and, on occasion, as entrepreneurs with an appreciation for ways to make money from trash. They did not offer "bad news" to the project team, and their empathy was active in the way they told stories—often switching from the third person to the first—about waste collectors in Lagos. One man put this empathetic identification explicitly when talking to Olutoyosi Tokun about the role of *katakata* ("caterpillars") or waste pickers "on the dunghill" (municipal dump): "The reason why I am interested in getting to know about *katakata* was because most times you just want to have a feel of what they feel, like that. I want to be in their shoes. . . . I see them as me doing the thing. So, like, I can't find myself doing this thing, but how do you guys do this thing? What do you go through and all that? So that is why I am able to answer your question well."[86]

This is not to suggest that local public opinion was immune to media influences such as those described by Oloko, but among the urban residents we interviewed there was no easily available "outside" positionality from which to speak. The mediated languages of dirt discussed above—the rhetorical, symbolic, moral, political, and sensationalist discourses—were absorbed into people's reflections on the practicalities of everyday life.

Outside the informal settlements, almost every person we spoke to had access to municipal waste disposal services, either through regular visits of the LAWMA truck, or through the extensive Private Sector Participation (PSP) scheme designed to alleviate pressure on state provision. PSP contracts allow independent providers to help ensure regular waste collection in Lagos in an attempt to prevent the buildup of refuse in the streets, drains, and waterways. Costs and services varied considerably from neighborhood to neighborhood, and among our participants complaints about the irregularity of PSP provision were rife, but everybody we spoke to agreed that the expense of these services should be met by householders, not by the government. The fact that people expressed such high expectations of their service providers demonstrated the success of the local authority's efforts to generate popular support for domestic waste management.

During the period of our research, some middle-income residents had reverted to the traditional "cart-pushers" to supplement irregular PSP provision. Cart-pushers have a reputation for being "shabbily dressed, dirty, and stinking because of the kind of work they do," and in public perception they resemble the *agbépóò* of old more closely than other waste workers, even though they do not necessarily handle fecal matter.[87] In spite of attempts by the municipal authorities to outlaw them because of their reputation for dumping waste indiscriminately rather than taking it to municipal dumpsites, these private waste collectors—often Hausa men—continue to operate in Lagos, particularly in low-income areas where residents who are too poor to pay a regular monthly charge can negotiate a price on an ad hoc basis before handing over their rubbish.

Our interviewees were candid about who they believed would be willing to undertake this type of work. For many Lagosians, the shame that still attaches to handling other people's waste is exemplified by the popular belief that such workers must be migrants and strangers, not locals, in order to preserve dignity through anonymity, and to avoid disgrace. Hausa migrants from the North are often the employees of private refuse and sewage collection companies in Lagos.[88] One oral historian in his seventies told John Uwa, "Some of them do not bother to cover their faces because no one knows them around; but it is possible for someone from their town to spot them, and for this reason some of them still mask up doing the job."[89] "People will be running away from you. They don't want to stain themselves," one private sewage contractor said to Olutoyosi Tokun, describing how he was demoted to the status of "a nobody" when he started his firm, and how his staff are still popularly regarded as "stained."[90] An article in the Nigerian *Daily Times* described the phenomenal rise from *agbépòò* to successful sewage entrepreneur of Alhaji Yaya Saliu, who kept his profession a secret from his family for decades. He told the *Daily Times*, "My family lived in Ibadan while I did my 'shit' business here in Lagos. I made sure that what I did for a living was a top secret to my family and in-laws for fear of being ostracised and being looked down upon. . . . I dare not tell them the real nature of my business. . . . I was too scared to tell my wife. When some members of my family discovered, they were mad at me."[91]

In spite of these residual prejudices, many of the Lagosians the team spoke to made a keen effort to identify with the hitherto unimaginable bodies of waste workers, attempting to bridge the gap between citizen and pariah through empathy and understanding, trying to rethink "shit-carrying" and "scavenging" through the lens of waste management and profitability. Providing that human waste could be repurposed and made valuable in monetary terms, as discussed in chapter 6, those who worked with it were not regarded as abject or taboo in an ontological sense.[92] Prejudice had clearly shifted: sewage workers remained on the margins of acceptability, but if their work generated cash, and if they washed off the dirt and changed outfits at the end of the day before recirculating in society, then their incomes were seen to be as respectable as those of other legitimate workers.

This reshaping of Lagosians' perceptions of waste and waste workers can be attributed in large part to the public relations work of Ola Oresanya, managing director of LAWMA between 2005 and 2015. It took the intervention of this self-proclaimed waste management evangelist to transform popular perceptions of waste workers from untouchables into "resource managers" or "resource recovery personnel."[93] With the backing of Babatunde Raji Fashola, the popular governor of Lagos State between 2007 and 2015, renowned for his "Keep Lagos Clean" movement and for his beautification of the city, Oresanya ran a wide-ranging media campaign in which he and his staff gave radio and television interviews, supported by billboards, advertisements in newspapers, "advocacy buses," and radio jingles aimed at educating people about the correct ways to dispose of litter, household waste, and sewage.[94] Through these media campaigns, LAWMA successfully challenged Lagosians' customary perceptions of waste disposal workers as pariahs and, in the process, illustrated how local media audiences could be provoked to rethink historical prejudices through the techniques of advertising.[95] To Oresanya, waste management in Lagos meant not only the challenge of collecting and processing the city's vast quantities

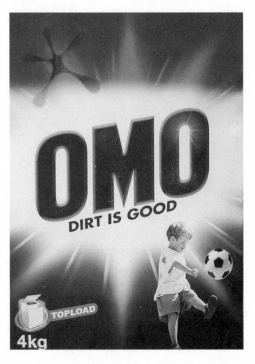

FIGURE 7.3. Advertisement for Omo washing powder.

of domestic and industrial waste, and transforming the urban environment for the better, but also media management and, through it, the management of popular perceptions about waste workers themselves.[96]

LAWMA's public relations initiative drew from a rich seam of Yoruba proverbs about dirt and waste as well as from international health campaigns such as "World Toilet Day," advertising slogans such as "Dirt Is Good" and "Shit Business Is Serious Business," and a long history of local interactions with dumpsites and waste workers (fig. 7.3).[97] The campaign helped to repopularize proverbs such as "*owó ìgbẹ́ kìí rùn*" (Yoruba: money made from shit or dirty things does not smell) and "*inú ìgbẹ́ lowó wà*" (Yoruba: it is inside feces/the bush that money can be found).[98] These proverbs, de-metaphorized and applied literally to shit, were taken up by sewage removal contractors and painted on the side of sanitation trucks around Lagos. Used as a company slogan, "*owó ìgbẹ́ kìí rùn*" is more than literal, however. It anticipates public animosity and defensively warns off harassers by reminding them that, as the Yoruba oral historian Ayọ̀ Yusuff

FIGURE 7.4. BollyLomo as an abattoir worker. Reproduced with kind permission of BollyLomo.

interprets it, "if you like [to] make jest of us, when we carry the money now, we go and feed our family, send our children to school, we buy fine dresses, we eat good food at home."[99] As a consequence of Oresanya's campaign, a maxim came into circulation that was repeated by nearly everybody we interviewed, and affected the way in which waste workers were seen: "There is no job that is dirty inasmuch as you can earn your living;"[100] "there is no dirty job so far as it is bringing in money."[101]

Nigerian online media channels also contributed to the destigmatization of waste work by showing how "it's the people you work with that determine how you enjoy your job," not the nature of the work itself.[102] In 2016, the dynamic BattaBox presenter, BollyLomo, made a number of short documentaries in which he undertook different "dirty" occupations in Lagos, including *alabaru* (head-porterage in markets), public toilet attendant, block-maker (bricks), abattoir worker, butcher, hawker (of rat poison and *Gala* sausage rolls), restaurant cleaner, and waste picker on a dumpsite (fig. 7.4).[103] "I hated it for the first thirty minutes," he told Olutoyosi Tokun of his work

FIGURE 7.5. LAWMA advertisement. Reproduced with kind permission
of the Lagos Waste Management Authority (LAWMA).

at the public toilet. "You know, just having to smell people's *pupu* all day,
and I was like 'you can't be doing this,' but after finishing the set I started
liking it because the guy was so much banter, like he would just be dancing,
and then *'Ọgá, stop there-o! No dey spoil my office'* (Dude, stop there! Don't
mess up my office). It was fun."[104]

Oresanya's chief strategy was to confront people's prejudices literally
head-on. In a culture where waste workers have been widely regarded as
shameful and unmarriageable *aṣalẹ* ("scavengers") and *agbépóò* ("night-soil
men"), who hid their faces from public view while they labored in their
degrading jobs, Oresanya employed teams of "beautiful ladies" and insisted that, if the conditions were not hazardous, they work with uncovered
faces.[105] An attractive, smiling woman was prominently featured in posters
(figs. 7.5 and 7.6). In the visual economy created by Oresanya's campaign,
there was no possibility of regarding these workers as human forms of
waste. Hugely successful as a publicity tool, this clever, high-impact campaign confronted observers with the impossibility of their own disgust, replacing the viscerality of repulsion with that of physical attraction.

In this way, the visual economy of waste work was transformed. Oresanya's teams of "neat" female laborers were no longer marked by the hyper-
visibility of the male pariah, masked and in rags, but, instead, attracted attention with their fluorescent orange LAWMA boiler suits and brooms. The

FIGURE 7.6. LAWMA advertisement. Reproduced with kind permission of the Lagos Waste Management Authority (LAWMA).

teams could not be missed as they worked along the central reservations and verges of arterial roads in Lagos, sweeping and removing waste with dense traffic on all sides.[106] Some of our male interviewees spoke about them with undisguised enchantment:

> I saw one lady one day. I said, whao, what a pretty lady! You know, she was cleaning gutter, well-dressed, fine girl. I said, whao, what is this country turning into? This lady and she is doing it in public, she doesn't give a damn, she seems to prefer that than going round to see whether there is a rich man there that can look at me, maybe I will go out with him and collect some money. No, she will say, OK, let me do this. If you want to marry me as I am, go ahead. At least I know that I have a job and I'm proud of it. Take me as I am. I will not come to your house and be a housewife, and be collecting money for soup, and then I will just be there, one day you will send me out and say what is your value-added? There is no value beyond the fact that you are a

FIGURE 7.7. LAWMA recruits "Miss Earth Nigeria" for a public
relations campaign, 2015. Reproduced with kind permission of the
Lagos Waste Management Authority (LAWMA).

wife and you are a baby-factory, there is nothing else [*laughs*]. So I saw
her, well-dressed. I looked at the [rear-view] mirror, I said, haha, this
country is changing![107]

Exploiting what John Berger famously termed the "male gaze," Oresanya successfully altered public opinion about the people who work with
trash and environmental dirt in Lagos.[108] LAWMA even recruited "Miss
Earth Nigeria" for its publicity campaign (fig. 7.7).

As the above ventriloquistic performance of a LAWMA employee's subjectivity by a male onlooker shows, the gender conspicuousness of Oresanya's "beautiful ladies" is problematic from a feminist perspective. The
campaign destigmatized waste work by harnessing women to a patriarchal
gaze, inviting pleasurable visual-sexual consumption in place of repulsion:
"I would rather have that one as a wife than someone who says 'I'm pretty,
O, so put me in your house.'"[109]

Uniformed workers gained credibility and acceptance as a result of

LAWMA's campaign: "Before now, waste management used to be the work of never-do-wells," one public health worker remarked, recalling many people's suspicions that the *akólẹ* (or *kólẹkólẹ*) might make off with one's generator as well as one's trash, but "now they are working for the government or for the organization that is employing them in a controlled working environment."[110] A side effect of Oresanya's gendered strategy, however, was that to some extent the public's progressive thinking continued to falter around male waste workers' bodies, where culturally entrenched perceptions endured, especially for "cart-pushers," "scavengers," and other men who worked with domestic waste but did not wear LAWMA or PSP overalls. "Sometimes it's difficult identifying them as normal human beings," one IT worker explained of waste pickers in Lagos. "It is only mad men who will . . . sort out those things in dirty environment. Such a person should not be accommodated in a clean environment."[111] Another said, categorically, that this work was taboo: "Nobody will allow anybody to do that kind of job."[112] The connection to the ragged madman was made by several other interviewees: "The way they are dressed, the way they appear when you see them, they don't seem any different from people that have lost their mind, people that are insane," a middle-income resident explained, referring to cart-pushers' tattered clothing.[113] "People mostly look at them like say they are mad. *Wèrè làwọn eléyìí!* (These ones are mad!) because the way they are dressed, they look tattered."[114] One interviewee repeatedly confused one of the local slang terms for cart-pushers, *Bholar* (or *Bola*) *Boys*, with Ebola, calling them "Ebola boys" throughout the interview and, in the process, powerfully but inadvertently connecting waste workers with contagion and untouchability.[115] All these responses stemmed from an idea of dirty subjectivity that was profoundly different from the domestic dirt discussed in the previous chapter, where household and nonorganic waste—removable objects—were the focus of attention.

Nevertheless, Oresanya's campaign was successful in numerous ways, affecting people's perceptions of waste as a resource with the potential for profit, and stimulating empathetic identification and environmental awareness. The vehemence of urban residents in reiterating their respect for these types of work, and the empathetic tone frequently adopted during interviews, where many stories were told about the lives of waste workers, demonstrate the success of LAWMA's effort to harness Nigerian mass media to progressive public relations work. Residents repeatedly commented on the necessity to see people differently from before. As one person said,

"You don't know that person's story, you don't know what they are coming from and you don't know what they believe in, so it's relative really."[116]

The urban geographer Matthew Gandy concluded his overview of infrastructure policy in Lagos from the early colonial period to the turn of the twenty-first century with the depressing comment that, over the 150 years covered by his article, "the periodic aspirations of successive colonial and post-colonial administrations in Lagos to improve the morphology and structure of urban space have had minimal impact."[117] Gandy's research concluded just as LAWMA commenced its campaign to transform perceptions of waste and waste workers in the city. The Lagosians we interviewed had been exposed to a decade of waste management interventions to connect the metropolis to a grid of waste disposal workers ranging from LAWMA's trucks to the PSPs. The dustbin truck had become essential to life in many homes, "flushing away" all the "dirty in the house."[118]

Nigerian media reports on infrastructural failures in the city—the annual flooding caused by blocked drains, environmental pollution around markets, the public health risks to people living in informal settlements and low-income neighborhoods, and the infamous and ubiquitous gridlock on roads—often involve appeals to metropolitan blueprints for the future of the city such as the Millennium Development Goals and the 2010 Lagos Mega-City Project with its investment in infrastructure and luxury residential accommodation.[119] Meanwhile, precarious low-income settlements such as Ikota on Lagos Island and Makoko on the Lagoon are frequently described in stark terms. As one journalist put it in terms reminiscent of those used by the producer of *Welcome to Lagos* on the BBC TV *Blog*, Ikota is "one of the most uninhabitable places in the world. Yet, human beings are living there."[120]

Nigerian scholars of urbanization and public health also frequently describe Lagos in dystopian terms as "the epitome of urban decay replete with environmental problems ranging from slums and squatter settlements, to crime and delinquency."[121] Oka Obono captures the bipolar vision of many local scholars: "On the one hand, [Lagos . . .] represents a virtual necropolis, replete with corruption, poverty, crime, and sprawling corpses. Paradoxically, however, this modern metropolis, the largest in Nigeria, is also celebrated for its life, ethos of hard work, ingenuity, and capacity for local technological innovation and adaptation."[122] But the Lagosians we interviewed offered neither utopian nor apocalyptic accounts of a city that is predicted to have 85 to 100 million inhabitants by 2100.[123] Speaking from the ground up, our interviewees offered a contrasting vision, describing micro-strategies of survival and adding a wealth of opinions and interpretations to institutional—including scholarly and mass media—theories and discourses about the megalopolis.

Contemporary African cities are characterized by urban dwellers' innovations in environments burdened with extreme poverty, scarcity, and multicultural inward migration from other regions. As AbdouMaliq Simone points out, urban subjects struggle to survive under increasingly severe constraints while continuing to produce creative responses to the flows of local and international people, commodities, and resources in their cities.[124] This provisional quality of African cities and their instability are, in many urban scholars' views, the very features that allow for the emergence of innovative responses on the streets.[125] One such response is conjured up by an eight-year-old schoolgirl from an impoverished neighborhood interviewed by Jane Nebe. The girl described how the dustbin men would bring balls, dolls, and toys retrieved from other people's rubbish to her compound to give to the youngest children, having first washed these objects so they were clean for presentation. In an important reversal of the gaze that has dominated this chapter, the girl's baby sister would continuously look out for the waste collectors, wishing them into visibility on a daily basis with her persistent, "'Motor come? Motor come?' Sometimes she will be crying when the motor does not come."[126] Retrieving objects neither for their usefulness nor for their potential commercial value, but for the pleasure they will bring to insignificant "small-smalls" such as this toddler, the dustbin men at the heart of this anecdote are so far removed from the desire for invisibility or the need for others' empathy that they give away their putative objecthood along with the gifts and demonstrate the existence of parallel, or alternative, economies of dirt besides the utilitarian logic of the dominant understanding of waste work in the city.

8

City Sexualities:
Negotiating Homophobia

A new pariah entered African legislatures in the early twenty-first century, epitomizing, for conservative moral commentators, everything that was sexually and physically dirty about the globally connected continent and its colonial heritage. By the 2010s, after decades of increasing discrimination, LGBTQ+ people had come to be regarded as an incarnation of all that was "un-African" and "ungodly" on the continent.[1] As Zimbabwean ex-president Robert Mugabe put it in 2010, in one of his milder statements on the topic, "Homosexuality . . . is contrary to our norms, values, traditions and beliefs. . . . Those that engage in such acts are insane. We cannot tolerate this; otherwise the dead will rise against us."[2] With the turn of the new millennium, the continent's wide array of nonbinary sexualities with diverse local names and, in many cases, long historical trajectories of recognition and acceptance, congealed into the singular figure of "the homosexual."[3] By 2015 homosexuality was illegal in thirty-five African states and punishable by death in Mauritania, Sudan, northern Nigeria, and southern Somalia.[4] Only two of the nineteen countries in which it remained legal, Lesotho and South Africa, were former British colonies, the latter being exceptional for recognizing same-sex relationships in its Constitution of 1996.[5]

As with homophobia in other parts of the world, the criminalization of homosexuality in many African countries was facilitated by a "dirtying" of targets that closely resembled the antihumanism of colonial officials discussed in early chapters of this book. In February 2014, for example, President Yahya Jammeh of the Gambia (1996–2017) used colonial-era categories for contagious local bodies when he described homosexuals as "vermin" who should be tackled like malarial mosquitoes.[6] In Nigeria in January 2014, President Goodluck Jonathan (2010–15) passed the "Same Sex Marriage (Prohibition) Law," which reinforced colonial-era legislation against sodomy; Jonathan promised to "cleanse" and "sanitise" society of what a previous Nigerian president, Olusegun Obasanjo (1999–2007), had labeled sexual behavior that was "unnatural" and "un-African."[7] The Nigerian law punished same-sex marriages with prison sentences of up to fourteen years, and criminalized "shows of same-sex public affection" with imprisonment for up to ten years.[8] In spite of international pressure, Jonathan's successor, Muhammadu Buhari, did nothing to repeal the law upon his election to office in 2015. In East Africa at the same time, Uganda's long-standing president, Yoweri Museveni (1986–), explained his toughened antihomosexuality legislation using associations gleaned directly from the colonial discourse of dirt and bodily contamination. He described homosexuals as "disgusting" and "abnormal," and strengthened the colonial-era law outlawing sex acts deemed to be "against the order of nature."[9] Kenya's President Uhuru Kenyatta (2013–) followed suit, criminalizing homosexuality with up to fourteen years in prison and introducing controversial anal testing to prove or disprove homosexual activities.[10] His law provoked an immediate rise in homophobic violence as well as widespread public protests against the legislation.[11]

In connecting heterosexuality with Africanity through the outright rejection of homosexuality, these presidents employed political tropes with a long history in African nationalist discourse. As numerous feminist commentators have observed, in anticolonial and anti-neocolonial rhetoric between the 1940s and 1980s, Africa was regularly metaphorized as a virgin girl or a rural mother who had been sexually violated by an invading male force.[12] In symbolism characteristic of anticolonial nationalisms elsewhere, European colonialism and its aftermath were portrayed in terms of the rape of a woman. In this manner, (male) nationalists were mustered to rescue the (feminized) continent from the (male) abuser. From Léopold Sédar Senghor in the 1940s to Ngũgĩ wa Thiong'o in the 1980s, creative writers refracted the colonial encounter through this heterosexual prism. Real women lost political agency in these representational processes, being rendered symbolic victims rather than gaining recognition for their contributions to anticolonial struggles.[13] But local hetero-masculinities were reinforced in the face of emasculating and infantilizing colonial attitudes. Any queer sexualities in these national stories took the form of feminized African masculinities yearning for postcolonial remasculinization.[14]

While they shared the category of dirt with colonial precursors, the twenty-first-century presidents listed above inverted the racialized colonial discourse and labeled Europeans dirty instead. For leaders like Mugabe, "a binary of African purity against colonial dirt" enabled "vilifying statements about the contemporary Western world."[15] They reasserted a heterosexual nationalist imaginary in their new legislation, but, in a departure from the old symbolism, the African victims of the new cultural intrusion were no longer represented as virtuous women, but as animals associated with filth. The interloper and the interloper's victim were both identified using a vocabulary of disgust and contamination. "Let the Americans keep their sodomy, bestiality, stupid and foolish ways to themselves, out of Zimbabwe," Mugabe is reported to have declared in 1995, describing gay and lesbian people as "worse than dogs and pigs."[16] Homosexuals are "very, very revolting," his chief spokesman added.[17] Arousing revulsion and thus objectified in this resexualized nationalism, "the homosexual" was given the place reserved for the pariah in all forms of hate speech.[18]

Besides the presidents and lawmakers, other commentators on homosexuality also treated it as an unwanted side effect of globalization, suggesting that it had been imported to Africa from Europe and America to challenge local principles of marriage and to break traditional taboos against same-sex relationships. Christian church leaders were especially emphatic on this point, combining biblical evidence with ideas about Africanity to reinforce the prohibition. Many of our interviewees adopted this hybrid formulation to explain their opposition: "That kind of sexual orientation is from the West. It is against our culture, our tradition. When God created man, he later created a woman, and blessed them and asked them to continue to multiply. So you can see that it's not only that it's irresponsible and dirty. It is ungodly."[19] "When God created humans, he created Adam and Eve. Why did he not create two men? I think it is a result of 'civilization,' and, you know, we Nigerians we love to copy the Western world. This is rubbish!"[20]

With systematic endorsement from denominations ranging from local Anglican to Pentecostal and evangelical churches, the legislation has strengthened grassroots homophobia among Christian communities, legitimizing spiritual interventions such as the exorcism of homosexuals and sanctioning violence against LGBTQ+ people.[21] Homosexuality, according to all these institutional reactions, is alien to Africa. Whether arising from the forces of Satan or of Westernization, or both, its presence on the continent highlights people's perceptions that their countries have been invaded by malign external forces to the detriment of Africanity.[22]

Not only has this anti-Western positioning ironically involved a resurrection of British antihomosexuality ordinances from the colonial period, but African leaders' pronouncements have also condensed centuries of nonbinary sexual behavior on the continent into the reductive dichotomy of homosexuality versus heterosexuality.[23] If anything is a Western import, it is this binary opposition, which emerged in Britain during the Oscar Wilde trials of 1895 and marked a turning point in popular European understandings of sexuality.[24] For many liberal opponents of the new legislation, the upsurge of homophobic hate speech in mainstream African media since the turn of the millennium operates in a manner similar to the racism of colonial public health officials, who employed the category of dirt to effect the transformation of people into contaminants, or waste, for removal from circulation. On a visit to Kenya in July 2015, President Barack Obama (2009–17) told President Kenyatta that the country's new laws resembled the politics of racial segregation in America's "Jim Crow" era, leaving no doubt about the connection, in his mind, between historical racism and contemporary homophobia as kindred forms of hatred.[25]

Numerous ethnographic studies and social histories of Africa demonstrate that nonbinary sexualities have existed in diverse forms—sanctioned, tolerated, hidden, or illicit—for centuries throughout the continent.[26] While useful as a tool for visibility and political activism, the word "homosexuality" barely describes the array of local nonbinary sexualities on the continent. As one Nigerian interviewee told Olutoyosi Tokun, "Our history has always had people who are attracted to same-sex people, but the embrace of religion which is a Western culture or Western belief has now influenced our people to interpret our culture in a different way. [Homophobia] has come with Western education and with Western religion."[27] From this point of view, homophobia, rather than homosexuality, is the imported, nonindigenous discourse that emerged through the impact of missionary Christianity as it morphed into indigenous churches and moral campaigns against sexual immorality.[28]

On social media platforms and in the mainstream media, as well as in the focus group discussions and in-depth interviews conducted for this book, the new laws generated considerable disagreement about acceptable and unacceptable, natural and unnatural, respectable and sinful sexual practices and behaviors. The antihomosexuality laws were fiercely opposed by LGBTQ+ and human rights activists throughout Africa, as well as by international governments and human rights groups abroad, many of whom interpreted the legislation as a politically expedient diversionary tactic to cover up other domestic issues.[29] When Mugabe shut down the Gays and Lesbians of Zimbabwe (GALZ) exhibit at the Zimbabwean International Book Fair in 1995, for example, his action was widely interpreted as a strategic deflection of attention from the "deeply raced issue of land redistribution" in Zimbabwe to the corruption of Africa by foreign cultural imperialists, giving Mugabe what Carina Ray described as his own "discursive land grab."[30] For LGBTQ+ Africans forced to live abroad out of fear for their safety, their continent has entered a period of amnesia and denial. As one exasperated Nigerian activist living in London stated, "We [should] make away with the religious fanaticism and look inwardly: where is our problem, who are the people that have siphoned our money and not built schools and good education, and why are we not having electricity? Let us look inward and challenge the people that are putting us in this suffering and stop focusing on religious value."[31]

While political and religious leaders continued their campaigns to harness public opinion against homosexuality in Lagos during the period of research for this book, a clear divide emerged between their unconditional condemnations, as reported in the media, and the deep ambivalence of many of our interviewees.[32] The people interviewed by the Dirtpol team were far more equivocal about homosexuality than about topics such as ethnicity or stigmatized forms of labor, which in their multicultural urban consciousness they combined with the positive impact of public relations campaigns, giving rise to tolerance for, if not outright approval of, hitherto vilified subjects.

Ostensibly, our 112 adult interviewees reflected the 2013 finding of the Pew Research Global Attitudes Project, with a sample of 1,031 people, that 98 percent of Nigerians are against homosexuality.[33] Only one interviewee openly identified as LGBTQ+, and in a Skype call from London revealed their reasons for living outside the country, commenting on "the total denial of homosexuality in our culture," and blaming "religious fanaticism" for the upsurge of homophobia in recent years.[34] In their view, the danger of homophobic violence was as real in Lagos as it was in other global cities where homosexuality had also been criminalized.[35]

At the other end of the spectrum, four interviewees—three focus group participants and one man in his sixties—expressed overt animosity toward people with nonbinary sexualities. "I won't do business with that kind of person except I don't know anything about the person," one businesswoman told John Uwa.[36] Another focus group participant, an investment banker in his late twenties, stated, "No, no, no, no . . . I find out you are gay, I terminate the contract, because I don't know when you will start getting attracted to me. I have this phobia for gay people. I find out you are gay, I move away."[37] Even though the other members of this man's focus group all disapproved of public displays of homosexual affection, they refused to believe that his unequivocal morality dictated his professional life: "What about if you have a contract involving millions, what will you do?" one participant asked him playfully. "Well . . . I have people around me, working for me—so that I don't strangle the gay man, I would have to bring somebody to interact with him. Just give me feedbacks on what you have decided but don't let this man . . . don't let him shake me [by the hand], don't . . . I don't want."[38] A man in his sixties also expressed extreme feelings against homosexuality, arguing that "it contradicts God's law," that homosexuals "should be thrown into prison," and that he would "report a sibling to the police, because it may appear that he has become mentally deranged."[39]

Other Christians interviewed by John Uwa cited the edicts of pastors and evidence from the Bible as reasons to reject homosexuality outright. This topic alone stimulated people to recite the institutional discourses of their various churches, to quote from the Bible, and to declare their religious affiliations. "I feel it is Satan the devil that is turning everything around. Well, I cannot talk outside my religion because that is my, that is my foundation as well. It is also my belief, so everything about homosexuality is rather wrong and repulsive."[40]

While many Christians did not wish to examine this controversial topic without the safety net of biblical quotation, for several people, biblical condemnation served as the starting point for elaborate scenarios in which homosexuality—generally figured as male by participants—was examined and understood in practical terms. "Now God created man and woman for obvious reasons to pro-create and replenish the earth," began one man in a focus group discussion: "Homosexuality is at the instance of Satan the devil who wants to challenge [us]."[41] Having established the doctrinal terms of his disapproval, this man went on to offer an elaborate scenario in which homosexuality was explained and understood in intimate and practical terms:

I know that in some prisons in some parts of the world, two years, three years, four years . . . without sex. The mind begins to go a little gaga and crazy, so now that the women are not here, which is what we all know, so what will we do? Maybe you are having a shower and there is a fat boy in the cell who is fat and he looks plumpy. Maybe he is dancing, the back-side is dancing and, you know . . . I know that in many parts of the world inside prisons . . . some of the fights that take place in prison is because I'm in cell, I'm a man, you are like my wife, if anybody goes near you, I will attack that person. It happens across the world so it's, it's a . . . it's sad that it is in Nigeria. I didn't expect that before.[42]

An unmistakably homoerotic gaze characterized the observer in this scene of empathy and desire, not least through his switch from the third person to the second to the first in describing the prisoner's possessiveness toward his "plumpy" surrogate wife.

In a similar vein, other Christian interviewees expressed curiosity about same-sex relationships and created story lines for homosexuality, or narrated their own experiences and encounters. Often bracketed by citations of biblical disapproval or statements like "it's a demonic spirit working in that person," their scenarios ranged from schoolgirl romances to stories of men who had sex with other men in order to secure gifts or employment.[43] One interviewee in his sixties told Olutoyosi Tokun how, as a young man, he experienced an unwanted sexual advance from his cousin. Reflecting on the encounter, he said, "Up till now he has not children to say 'this is my own.' So one needs to sympathise with some of them. It could be the society, it could be peer-group influence, it could be this and that, you know, so one needs not to say 'you are bad, you are good.'"[44] Another male interviewee contextualized a story about his friend's child cross-dressing by describing the ways in which "a guy in the North" will use gifts to seduce a male lover.[45]

Through stories such as these, people seemed to wish to bridge the gulf created by political leaders between nonhuman and human when they thought about homosexuality. While remaining homophobic in their intolerance of nonbinary sexualities, these participants' views were more nuanced than the prevailing institutional hate speech and media condemnations. Their disapproval was demanding as well as corrective. It necessitated cross-identification with the other, hypothesis, curiosity, and explanation as they speculated about what might motivate a person to become homosexual in the face of social disapproval and public animosity. On no other topic was the division more pronounced than it was between those who reiterated condemnations from politicians and the pulpit and those who brought their own individual consciences and imaginations to bear on the issue, the one side excoriating homosexuality as a colonial import and an outrage to God, the other musing on what made some people prefer so socially challenging a sexuality.[46]

This space of empathetic identification should not be overstated. If participants did not regard homosexuality through the ontologically fixed category of dirt in the manner of their pastors and presidents, this was often because they considered homosexuality to be a choice—arising from madness or misdirection—a bad habit that was changeable and could be cured. Christian interviewees often referred to Muslims in northern Nigeria as pro-homosexuality, over and against "anyone who is a real Christian [who] is under oath from the Bible to refute such practice."[47] And for people who did not overtly identify as Christian, the logic of sickness generally replaced that of sinfulness. "I don't think they are dirty. I think they are sick in the mind," one health worker told Olutoyosi Tokun. "That's what I just think, not necessarily dirty. They are just not in the right frame of mind. They just sick. That is my own description of them, not dirty."[48] "It's like some kind of, you know, psychological problem," stated another man.[49] A participant in one of John Uwa's focus groups stated, "They are mad people. It is even better to sleep with a mad woman than to sleep with a fellow man."[50]

For many people, one's personal morality should be governed by a combination of respect for the law and public accountability, the latter defined in terms of visibility to others. "Anything you are not able to do publicly, you know that is dirty. So for me homosexuality is dirty," one man commented, giving a normative definition of morality that rendered "anything outside the tenets of the general belief and ethics of everyday culture . . . dirty."[51] This was reiterated by many other interviewees: "Being dirty comes from being against the norm. When someone is outside the norm and is willingly doing something out of the norm, the idea of them being dirty comes out of that."[52] "If you are doing something that is good, you will always be encouraged to see people looking at you doing it. . . . Your mind can differentiate between lawful things and unlawful things."[53] Any behavior that is "socially unacceptable" should not be permitted, another participant asserted, echoing a common view among the people interviewed by the Dirtpol team.[54] "If it is a good thing, why should they be hiding behind closed doors?"[55] Closeted identities, counterpublic spaces, and sexual subcultures were invalid according to this yardstick of public visibility and accountability in which *"ẹni tó ń ṣe iwa èérí, o ń ṣe ìwà tó lòdì"* (whoever does something filthy is doing something against the norm), or "you know that what you are doing is bad and [you know] when you are doing the right thing, [because] you want people to meet you there doing it."[56]

The word "orientation" recurred among interviewees, both to delineate an array of antisocial behaviors, which were seen to result from certain people being poorly oriented, and to describe the necessary social correctives, for which "reorientation" was required. This language recalled President Buhari's first "War Against Indiscipline" (WAI) in 1984 so closely as to suggest a resurgence of public approval for his efforts to reform public morality and civic behavior in the second WAI, launched in August 2016. Both "wars" included initiatives for "behavior modification."[57] For almost all of our interviewees, people without "proper orientation" were regarded as legitimate targets for state intervention.[58] The compulsory reorientation of people with nonbinary sexualities was suggested by many interviewees as an alternative to imprisonment. "The Government could set up institutions since as a people we believe that homosexuality is something that is wrong," one person explained to Olutoyosi Tokun. "They can be trained and then help them understand what they are doing is wrong. You must come out declaring that you are straight. If you are not you will go back into the institution again."[59] In endorsing reorientation and reeducation, interviewees drew vocabulary and ideas from evangelical and Pentecostal churches, as well as from the established political discourse about "indiscipline," for which psychological or legal interventions are used to correct or remove "afflictions."[60] "Reorientation" resonates with approval for these forms of intervention, as well as with a spatial conceptualization of homosexuality as being misaligned, requiring what Danai Mupotsa characterizes, echoing Sara Ahmed, as "a straightening event."[61]

Nevertheless, as described above, many of these interviewees also showed a willingness to project themselves into nonbinary sexual narratives and to attempt to understand the other's desires. Such curiosity and equivocation are signs that Lagosian public opinion is more fluid and potentially more progressive than the official homophobia that feeds it with "dirt." While our sample was small, it does suggest that institutions such as governments and churches, rather than individuals or public opinion per se, shoulder a great deal of the responsibility for producing and fueling social stigmas and the violence they precipitate. "Our leaders should be mindful of their comments because they are leading people; and what you say can provoke a vicious reaction," observed one focus group member.[62]

For one female participant, the connection of homosexuality with dirt was not a consequence of Westernization or individual sickness so much as a result of contemporary Nigerian society's failure to accommodate alternatives to the heterosexual status quo. *"You wan hear watin dey my mouth?"* (Pidgin English: You want to find words from my mouth?), she began, laughing, when John Uwa asked about the recent criminalization of homosexuality in Nigeria.[63] The controversial point she wished to make was that

homosexuality, I don't think it is new to Nigeria or to Africa. Is not imported. We may not have heard so much about it, yea, but it is not new. I went to a boarding school, and I knew about lesbianism and you know, I knew about girls being emotionally attached to one another. . . . [Just] because you don't understand something, doesn't mean you will victimize it. Not understanding it should be a reason to say, "Okay, wait, try to understand it." How do I put it? Because you don't understand it, because you are ignorant about it, the next step is not to criminalize it, the next step is moving to that place of understanding. . . . There are so many other things to be afraid of in Nigeria than homosexuals.[64]

This participant was a married woman in her thirties, educated to master's level, with children. As she described how homosexual couples are free to work and make money, with no child-rearing duties at home or domestic obligations to their husbands, it seemed that, for her, homosexuality represented a powerful alternative to the lifestyle expectations imposed on women by the status quo, providing her with a positive vision of a successful career without the pressures of husband and children. Reflecting on the socialization of girls, she said, "I really wish I could raise my girl differently. . . . I really hope I can do it differently."[65]

"I have always wondered how gay marriages work," said another woman, before posing an extensive and speculative, and at times sexually explicit, set of questions about the physiology of gay sex.[66] As her questions layered up about how men who love men and women who love women achieve nonreproductive sexual pleasure, she too started to pose a challenge to the socialization of women in Nigeria. Like the woman discussed in the previous two paragraphs, she used the topic of homosexuality to condemn sexual double standards and the conditioning of women in Nigerian mainstream society. "It is just the hypocrisy, you know, the hypocrisy in that there are different standards given for the guys and for the girls."[67] While society regards homosexuals, promiscuous women, and prostitutes as "abominations," she concluded, "society does not really have anything against [heterosexual] men."[68]

In focus group discussions, we heard many reiterations of political leaders' condemnations of homosexuality through the dirt-related categories of disgust and animality. Away from the semipublic space of the focus group discussion, however, as the above one-on-one interviews demonstrate, a more liberal "live and let live" attitude emerged among participants, especially among women in their thirties and forties with higher education. In an interview with Olutoyosi Tokun, one female doctor stated, "You can condemn them in the church, condemn them in any religious gathering, but as far as the society is concerned, I don't think they've done anything wrong, because it's not as if they are rapists. You know, if they've got a partner it's always a mutual consent, do you understand? They are mutually involved, so why should you throw them in jail? As long as they are not constituting nuisance with this thing."[69]

Unsurprisingly, the men who were most conservative about the domestic roles of women were also the most homophobic. "My wife is not a lazy person at all," one man in his sixties told John Uwa in a Yoruba-language interview. "She takes all my dirty clothes and has them washed before I return from work. Even very early in the morning, she will have cleaned the whole house, bathed the children, washed clothes and done with everything. Before seven thirty in the morning, she has prepared breakfast, the children would have eaten and even gone to school."[70] This same man angrily described homosexuality as filthy, and became increasingly irate, voluble, and detailed in his descriptions of anal penetration. In particular, he blamed homosexuals for the spread of Ebola and other urban "filth diseases" such as tuberculosis and cholera.[71]

On the other side of this man's homophobia, implicated in his rage, were the women described above, whose vision of homosexuality saw it, at least imaginatively, as providing alternatives for heterosexual women to the gender status quo. Their curiosity about the possibilities offered by non-binary sexual lifestyles revealed the ways in which homophobia within the establishment may also be a reaction to changes in traditional heterosexual marriage roles and the emergence of greater equality between men and women in Lagos. At the very least, these women's views about homosexuality contrasted with and critiqued the gender conservatism and assertions of masculinity among male religious and political leaders.

This implicit connection between homosexuality and women's empowerment helps to explain the reactions of one of our interviewees, a long-standing officeholder in a local church. This man's faith provided the scaffolding for his interpretation of African traditions as he moved through numerous comparisons between past and present with an exclusive focus on women's morality. In a long interview, he emphasized the traditional African abhorrence for a woman having children outside wedlock, the necessity for women to be virgins at the time of marriage, and how both tradition and the Bible dictate that a woman should take care of the husband, home, and children. "The woman was created as help-mate, to assist the man, not to be on equal task with him," he explained to John Uwa, with reference to a number of biblical quotations as evidence that sexual "equality has no place in the Christian faith" and that, according to his highly biblical interpretation of "African tradition," women should not be educated to the same degree as men.[72] When asked to give an example of "dirty behavior," he became very animated on the subject of homosexuality: "It is an abomination, it's a taboo. African societies didn't have such practices. Now people who do things against the norms of society, they are ostracized and nobody wants to be ostracized. They have evil forests, they have places they keep people who have been sentenced, or forfeited to the gods and all that. Nobody could buy from you, you can't buy from anybody."[73]

A striking feature of this man's interpretation of homosexuality as taboo was the way in which it emerged out of his ultraconservative heterosexual marriage values, in which "the man is not able to have control of his home" if the woman has been to school and "feels she's equal to the man."[74] To the same extent that political condemnations of homosexuality are underwritten by the assertion of a nationalist heterosexual masculinity, one might also suggest that, paradoxically, misogyny lies at the core of many men's homophobia.

Whether Christian or secular in their approach, the sticking point for many Lagosians was the belief that homosexuality was biologically and socially un(re)productive, and thus required correction. Homosexuality rendered a person "useless" as a human being. "Producing children, it's nature of mankind," one man told Olutoyosi Tokun.[75] Much like the effect of domestic waste's use value on their opinions, the category of uselessness bound participants' various responses together and connected them with the political discourse of dirt used by political leaders. As with the types of domestic waste classified as "dirty," the category of usefulness marked out particular sexualities as productive or dirty. Somebody became a "dirty subject" through their failure, in the eyes of observers, to contribute to social reproduction.[76] Such a reductively biological understanding of usefulness rendered homosexuality ontologically closer to dirt than other urban lifestyles. Whereas the stigma of waste disposal work was dispelled through people's recognition of the use value of this type of labor, not least the capacity for waste entrepreneurs to profit from recycling schemes that allowed trash to reenter the productive economy with future potential, LGBTQ+ people were regarded by many people as useless, and thus dirty, arousing curiosity among some and disgust among others, but remaining permanently marked by the prevalent political understanding of sexuality according to an unambiguous homo- versus hetero- binary.

This chapter has attempted to show that homophobia among Lagosians is more nuanced and plural than the institutional hate speech that supports it. People's speculative narratives about the experience of homosexuality prevent the unambiguous absorption of LGBTQ+ people into the annihilating objecthood of dirt. Postcolonial African leaders have tried to mobilize homophobic hate speech for populist assertions of cultural authenticity over and against perceived political interference from the Global North. With local sexual minorities identified as the enemy within, leaders acquire a target sanctioned by thousands of Christian churches. The figure of the homosexual has become an embodiment of the dividing line between global culture and Africanity, and institutional homophobia showcases the limits and dangers of Westernization for local publics under continuous pressure from globalization. But the range of local responses reported in this chapter demonstrates that homophobia is not singular in Lagos. People who identified homosexuality as a "dirty" behavior—and many did not—expressed disparate reactions ranging from acceptance and curiosity to disapproval and disgust.

The multicultural consciousness of urban residents discussed in chapter 6 remained present in the comments of all those people who, while expressing disapproval, also sought to understand nonbinary sexual desires from the point of view of LGBTQ+ people. Akin to the views expressed by the colonial-era travelers and traders discussed in earlier chapters of the book, however, contemporary Lagosians' speculations about the other were generally marked by a sense of interpretative failure as their empathy turned back to confusion and disavowal. "I just imagine—why are they gay? I can't question their freedom but . . . I can't imagine . . . you know . . . it is something I can't even imagine."[77] As a consequence, empathy, in many interviews, ultimately conveyed a desire for the transformation of the other out of their current state and back toward supposed normalcy.

In Lagos, many people with nonbinary sexualities have been driven underground or into exile by popular homophobia, and they face extreme forms of violence for being visible in public spaces. As the Nigerian celebrity businessman Kenny Badmus (Kehinde Bademosi) wrote from the United States, where he has lived since coming out in January 2015, "Even though it can be awfully lonesome here, I'm happy I can walk down the street as a gay man without being afraid of lynching, preaching and outright hating."[78] Unlike the press in other African countries, mainstream Nigerian newspapers have not been particularly sympathetic to LGBTQ+ rights, and at best have remained neutral on the social implications of the antihomosexuality legislation.[79] In the absence of material in the mainstream media to moderate people's perceptions of this stigmatized sexuality, homophobia has a hold over public opinion in Lagos.[80]

None of the critiques of African homophobia discussed in this chapter—including the displacement theory used to explain its appearance at politically expedient moments for particular presidents—offers an understanding of the sincerity with which ordinary people express their opposition to homosexuality. The majority of Lagosians we spoke to reacted with anger, confusion, distress, and disgust as they articulated feelings that were neither partisan nor—except indirectly—strategic or economically advantageous to themselves.[81] They rearticulated political and religious interpretations of homosexuality, not in ideological ways but as feelings: their disgust was all the more real because of their embodied experience of its strength. Nevertheless, many people were conscious of the historicity and specificity of this feeling, and attempted to contextualize the new animosity to allow for diverse global sexualities: "What is considered right in a particular social setting may not necessarily be right in another social setting, and the society, they say, determines what is right and wrong. . . . Homosexuality may be considered nothing odd or abnormal in the Western world. Amongst us here, however, it is dirty."[82]

The global discourse of human rights that tracks and attacks homophobia is part of a progressive turn in public discussions of sexuality. But important questions remain unanswered. Have African publics, historically renowned for their accommodation of plural sexualities and for their intense localization of global media messages, allowed their politicians, religious leaders, and mainstream media to usurp the public sphere for homophobic statements that remain largely unchallenged by opposition parties? Have Nigerian media consumers become easier to influence—rather than more sophisticated in their tastes and interpretations—than in the early days of global media consumption discussed in previous chapters?

Previous chapters on African audiences have problematized the notion that a political or textual message can be communicated in a direct, unmediated form to intended audiences. People's minds are not blank slates on which propaganda writes its messages. Yet homosexuality has emerged as the stigma of stigmas in early twenty-first-century Africa, taking shape as one of the continent's few hegemonic discourses. But to regard homophobic people as brainwashed by political and religious propaganda is to resurrect a problematic model of media consumption in which mass audiences are seen to be naïve and manipulable, lacking agency, not subject to any other cultural countercurrents or understandings. From this perspective, the label "homophobia," like the "homosexuality" it describes, reduces the continent's diversity at precisely the global moment when "+" has been added to the proliferation of letters produced from the compound starting point of "LGBTQ."

Homophobic intolerance has been fueled by political and religious leaders in Nigeria, leaving urban residents with speculative minds to rely on their own imaginative and intellectual resources, including social media, in attempting to understand the complex sociality of people with nonbinary sexualities. The current upsurge of antihomosexual sentiment marks a shift in the queer histories of Africa and gives urgency to a set of questions. What global transformations and categorical or linguistic shifts have occurred to make homophobia thinkable now? Can we position people's anger, confusion, distress, and disgust within a history of the emotions in different African contexts? In what ways is sincerity in the public sphere historically produced and media-inflected? Perhaps the most productive question on which to end this chapter concerns the different pressures—economic, ideological, linguistic, and emotional—that Lagosian "homophobes" are processing in expressing their opposition with such feeling in a public sphere in which "anything that is foreign . . . to stability can be called dirt."[83] Just as "homosexuality" cannot be allowed to reign as the singular descriptive sign for people with nonbinary sexualities, so too "homophobia" cannot be regarded as the stopping point for people who are antihomosexual. Homophobia does not serve as a satisfactory explanatory category for advocates of LGBTQ+ rights any more than it explains the behavior of the ordinary people who express it.

The apparent singularity of homophobia arises not from "its" duplication transregionally from context to context but from its "explanatory power [as one] of our dyadic extremes—race and racism, East and West, complicity and opposition."[84] It illustrates the historical reappearance of the discourse of dirt for a new category of nonperson in twenty-first-century Africa. Its emergence in this century raises broader questions about the power and influence of all the English-language categories that circulate in global Anglophone media, and about the themes such categories generate for conceptualizing local cultural histories, questions to which the conclusion will turn.[85]

Mediated Publics, Uncontrollable Audiences

During the international media coverage of the spread of Ebola in West Africa, the British newspaper the *Telegraph* depicted the Liberian epicenter of the epidemic, New Kru Town, in apocalyptic language reminiscent of that used by Thomas Knox and his peers in the 1920s. "Sewage runs openly through its maze of corrugated shacks, and in Liberia's wet season—at its height right now—tropical torrents turn it into one vast, warm, moist, breeding pool for germs."[1] Ebola is a virus that can only be transmitted by direct contact with the body fluids of an infected person, but for the author of the piece in the *Telegraph* as for countless other Western media commentators at that time, West African cities themselves seemed to spawn the disease. As the richly adjectival language indicates, New Kru Town itself was seen as a source of contagion.

Thick with more than a century of colonialist language for urban filth, these reports presented West African cities as if they were synonymous with Ebola, and Ebola as if it were synonymous with dirt. Such places were rendered all the more terrifying by their proximity to the Global North through international air travel. "Please tell me all incoming flights are banned," wrote a British reader on the *Daily Mail*'s website after reading an item on the potential global spread of Ebola through air travel.[2] "I shudder to think the consequences of people from these areas being allowed in and out of Britain," another reader commented.[3] For one reader, the blame lay with liberal cosmopolitans in the West rather than with Africans on the continent: "The liberal will soon spread this disease to all corners of the earth," he or she stated in reaction to the British government's reluctance to impose travel prohibitions on all people entering Britain from West Africa.[4] This sentiment was not confined to conservative tabloid newspapers such as the *Daily Mail*. Commenting on the exclusion of a half-Sierra Leonean boy from a primary school in Stockport, Cheshire, in October 2014, after a Facebook campaign against him by parents terrified that he would infect his classmates with Ebola, a reader of the British liberal broadsheet the *Independent*, commented, "I hate to say it but they are similar to lepers. Touch them at the wrong time and you have it and die with the rest. So bring them here and risk possibly thousands of Deaths."[5] Another reader advised, "We should be closing our boarders [*sic*] to anyone travelling from West Africa."[6]

Deliberately or unconsciously, these British media consumers borrowed the "contagious native" verbatim from early twentieth-century colonial discourse. In a similar manner to racist town planners in colonial cities, their culturally ingrained response was to call for racial segregation and the immobilization of entire populations. Dirt had lost none of its potency as a category for interpretation that expressed the onlooker's disapproval in the form of supposed gut reactions to the proximity of a body perceived to be contaminated, making the response of the beholder appear to be natural. Whereas in the early twentieth century, the human incarnations of dirt were commonly imagined by those in power as low-income people living in poorly constructed dwellings, a new class dimension surfaced in British fears of Ebola contact and contamination in the early twenty-first century. The transmitters of the virus in West Africa and beyond were not the poor working classes or residents of informal settlements imagined by early twentieth-century town planners, but cosmopolitan business elites, diplomats, graduates, and academics, people who could afford to travel by plane to diverse global cities and stay in good hotels along the way, like the Liberian diplomat Patrick Sawyer who brought the virus to Lagos, popularly tagged in Nigeria as "the Liberian weapon of mass destruction."

Through dirt, this book has attempted to historically contextualize the phenomenon of antihumanism and understand the ways in which contemporary urban relationships resonate with past ideologies in the form of politically charged reiterations of prejudiced discourses. The category of dirt—or "dirt-as-history" as Constance Smith puts it in her ethnographic history of Kaloleni estate in Nairobi[7]—is compound and dynamic when used to evaluate other people's behavior. Dirt has a robust history as a category for the displacement of dominant groups' fears and prejudices onto others, whether expressed in the form of revulsion or fascination at the other's proximity. From such a standpoint, dirt easily becomes a vector for the expression of hatred against minorities, subcultures, and other vulnerable populations. At critical moments in the twentieth century, colonial and postcolonial governments and other institutions have activated dirt-related categories as constitutive features of racism, homophobia, and other forms of social violence and exclusion.

Dirt as Interpretive Failure

In his analysis of the rise of European "Orientalist" modes of perception in the nineteenth century, Edward Said famously describes the manner in which the repetition of particular analogies about the Arab-Islamic world "*create* not only knowledge but the very reality they appear to describe. In time, such knowledge and reality produce a tradition."[8] For Said, the recurrent use of particular categories in a dominant discourse will, over time, take hold of the existential complexity of the peoples and cultures described, and replace them with an essence that stands in for the whole. In this way, colonial power is legitimized and preserved through the production of condensed and repetitious knowledge about the other.[9]

Orientalism has attracted considerable criticism in the forty years since its publication, not least for excluding the worldviews of the actual subjects of "orientalist" discourse, and for ignoring the impact of dissident forms of knowledge on hegemonic institutional systems. But as an explanation of the formation and tenacity of dominant ideologies, *Orientalism* offers a persuasive theory of how the opinions of ruling elites become normalized through scholarship, literature, the arts, media, and public opinion. While dogmatic at times, *Orientalism* shows, via a theory of visual and textual representation, how ordinary people's realities can be produced through diverse levels of narrative and rhetoric, distributed across disparate institutions and cultural forms. In the manner of soft power, the repetition of representations slowly comes to define people's realities, contributing to the dominant group's influence and leading to the further production of knowledge through texts and other types of media.

As a category for the production of knowledge, dirt seems to exemplify the discursive hegemonies identified by Said. Numerous cross-cultural encounters in the twentieth century are mediated by it. In his classic study of colonial racism, *Black Skin, White Masks* (*Peau noire, masques blancs*), for example, Frantz Fanon reports on the traumatic moment of walking anonymously through a train carriage in France when his complex humanity is suddenly reduced to a state of epidermal filth. A white person reacts to the sight of him and, with the words "*Sale nègre!*," fixes his identity in place, skin-deep.[10] The racial descriptor *nègre* is inextricable from the adjective *sale*. There are at least twenty-two different translations of the French word *sale* (also *la saleté*), all with unfavorable connotations that resonate, cumulatively, through its most basic translation as "black," including dirty, smutty, trashy, grubby, foul, messy, oozing, depraved, obscene, greasy, nasty, unclean, disgusting, and defiled.

The fear of defilement experienced by Fanon's white observer in the 1950s is reiterated many times over in colonial racism, as shown in the early chapters of this book. Fanon describes how racist representations stick to their targets in the manner described by Said for orientalist discourse, contributing to and partly creating the realities and ideas by which people live in metropolitan and multicultural cities.[11] Sapping the subject's sense of self with powerful dismissive representations, the observer fixes the other, influencing and shaping the identity of the target *on the inside*. Fanon experiences physical nausea, or self-revulsion, at the way his skin is recast as a consequence of others' uptake of mediated representations of his race. These intimate encounters live within the psyche in the form of what Stuart Hall termed an "enigma," a "tense and tortured dialogue," and cannot simply be expunged from a culture or an encounter.[12] In Fanon's account of the colonial encounter, the dominant culture's attribution of dirt to the subject becomes a part of the other's lived experience.

Obvious, if extreme, twentieth-century examples of this conflation of dirt and cultural or racial otherness include the labeling of Jewish people as vermin by Nazis and other European anti-Semites in the 1930s and 1940s, and the Rwandan genocide of 1994 that was initiated by a media campaign on Radio Télévision Libres des Milles Collines (RTLMC) to "exterminate/crush the cockroaches."[13] In Rwanda, the media made use of the word *inyenzi* (cockroach) to relabel the Tutsi people and their sympathizers as vermin. As with Nazi ideology in Europe, the analogy with dirt became, by being propagandized, an incitement to mass murder, realigning humans with posthuman processes of waste disposal and sanitary control. The Zulu king Goodwill Zwelithini used the same incendiary language in 2015 when he encouraged xenophobic rioters in South Africa by labeling African migrants from other parts of the continent as "lice" and "ants."[14] Likewise, in January 2017, Jack Renshaw, mouthpiece for the British neo-Nazi group National Action, was arrested for speeches describing Jews and immigrants to the U.K. as vermin.[15]

Even though many decades and differences separate colonial racism from postcolonial homophobia and metropolitan racism, in all these forms of discrimination, expressions of disgust and hatred are presented by those who articulate them as natural, rather than ideological, precisely because they involve a set of visceral reactions to the appearance and behavior of others. The dirtying of particular populations remains common in numerous global locations, and these representations can become devastating under extreme political and economic conditions. When the category of dirt is taken up by policy makers in the colonial state, or by postcolonial parliamentarians and church leaders, and when it is used to rationalize the implementation of government policy, then individual conclusions or public opinion about the "dirty behavior" of others can become magnified into systemic and, in some cases, life-threatening forms of antihumanism that recall Said's analysis of knowledge production in contexts of power.

As a category for the interpretation of otherness, dirt does not originate in Europe or in European colonialism. A multitude of words can be found in African languages to describe the dirt and dirtiness of others, dating back a long time before colonialism. In southern Africa in the nineteenth century, Ndebele people used "the Shona word *tsvina* (dirt) to describe their antagonists as *chiTsvina*, 'dirty people.'"[16] Among Sotho and Tswana speakers, and in many other African cultures, evidence for the survival of precolonial concepts about dirt can be found in local ideas about ritual impurity.[17] Many African languages use dirt-related terms to describe shameful or unspeakable behaviors. And, as suggested in chapter 7, urban residents' conceptualizations of waste and waste workers can open up social histories of contamination and rubbish far older than colonial rule.

This negative aspect of dirt tells less than half the story, however. Outside the Anglophone framework that has dominated the written sources and conceptual structure of this book, one can find countless further valuations of people's bodily encounters with matter labeled dirty by Eurocentric criteria, as well as local incomprehension and rejection of Eurocentric categories. Regarded as mud, earth, dust, or reusable matter, dirt is removed from the moral, evaluative realm of disgust and presents long histories of local use in masquerade, sculpture, beautification, home decoration, skin care, recycling, farming, and medicine, as well as in expressions of reverence for chiefs and traditional leaders.[18] Whether dirt ceases to be dirty under such conditions of transformation is open to debate.[19]

In numerous African-language jokes and maxims, excrement and the presence (or absence) of vermin are recognized as signifiers of wealth rather than filth or contamination. "Aahh, you are complaining that you don't have rats in your house!," runs a Yoruba jibe, indicating that "something is fishy because the rat will come in wherever there is food. It shows that that person is living in abject poverty. You don't have food, so that is why they say, 'oh, don't mind that man, *ó tálákà bí èkúté ṣóòṣì*' (Yoruba: he is poor as a church rat)."[20] From the opposite end of the spectrum, but demonstrating a similar set of connections between dirt and prosperity (or poverty), across the continent in East Africa, British colonial officials mocked Kenyan women in the 1940s for keeping the feces of livestock in the vicinity of their homes. Whereas for sanitary inspectors this was disgusting, inviting disease, for each woman the "fine heap of dung by the doorway proclaim[ed] her husband's wealth."[21] To this day in Nairobi, scatological jokes in Sheng comment on people's enviably rich diets through references to the presence of flies on a person's mouth or around a person's anus when they fart.[22] In all of these communications, matter and behavior that should, according to a Eurocentric vision of civic modernity, be removed as noxious excesses, are conferred full presence as signifiers of affluence and social aspiration.

Questions remain, however, about what social and ideological work the English term "dirt" is capable of undertaking as a scholarly category in international contexts. Does it help to produce the very histories in which it is deployed as an explanatory and critical tool? In attempting to render dirt productive in this book, significant methodological and intellectual challenges have arisen, especially relating to the problem of what Andreas Huyssen describes as "how to reconcile the universal and the particular in the practice of cultural criticism without lapsing either into empirical particularism or abstract universalism."[23] Such challenges characterize the study of global urban cultures generally, but are of particular significance in cultural histories of postcolonial cities, in which the temptation to source the (postcolonial) present in the (colonial) past through direct, connective comparisons risks reducing the former to the latter and minimizing what Ash Amin, AbdouMaliq Simone, Arjun Appadurai, and numerous other scholars of global cities have highlighted: if there is anything essential about the global city, it is the unpredictable, productive potential of diverse urban imaginaries situated in disjunctive, globally networked contexts.[24]

When studied outside the power structures of the colonial state, the church, or postcolonial governments, the discourse of dirt contains some potential for cross-cultural understanding, at least when the onlooker recognizes the gulf separating him- or herself from the object of interpretation. The Lagosians interviewed in chapters 6 to 8 spoke fluently about dirty objects such as plastics and other types of rubbish. They readily described "dirty" behavior such as the recent rise to social unacceptability of dropping litter from car windows, but they were reluctant to publicly evaluate people in the city using categories relating to dirt. When they spoke about behavior popularly deemed to be dirty, their curiosity and empathy contrasted starkly with public discursive spaces such as newspapers, sermons, mainstream and social media, and political proclamations, where hate speech could be vehement and categorical.[25]

Except for rare individuals, the colonial commentators represented in the written archives expressed their feelings of disgust as if the dirt of others were an objective truth. By contrast, among our Lagosian interviewees for this project, dirt often stimulated an effort to cross over into the world of the other, opening a space in which frequently, but not always, the sense perceptions of revulsion and disgust were suspended out of curiosity about the other's lifestyle and a wish to understand it. Many contemporary interviewees expressed intense self-consciousness about their subjectivity and bias when addressing sensitive topics such as the domestic hygiene of others. These Lagosians expressed fascination and empathy with, or laughter and befuddlement about, local bodies that fell out of the range of social acceptability and thus attracted the label "dirty." The dehumanizing gesture that characterized colonial objectifications of the other, and that characterizes hate speech generally, was rarely allowed into their responses to the bodies of urban residents. On the contrary, dirt operated as a mediating category, rather than the stopping point, for many Lagosians' cross-cultural encounters.

In tension with the binary logic described above, many of the terms for dirt and dirtiness analyzed in this book contain within themselves a host of imaginative cultural crossings or admissions of failure, as in the colonial town planners' confessions that buildings constructed from traditional materials were, after all, more hygienic than their modern European replacements. Contemporary Lagosians' speculative cross-identifications with people labeled dirty in mainstream institutional discourses shows how the presence of dirt as an evaluative category opens up possibilities for reimaginings of the status quo. Attention to dirt can therefore help us to understand how antihumanist ideologies operate in diverse global settings and allow us to pick apart categorical labels. Whether expressed as curiosity or as hatred, or, viscerally, as physical revulsion, the category of dirt often performs a powerfully embodied failure of cross-cultural understanding on the part of commentators whose observations about other people, when expressed in the public sphere of media and popular opinion, have the power to dramatically affect a person's future.

Mediated Publics, Uncontrollable Audiences

As in many neighboring West African countries, decades of independent African and global media in Lagos have produced sophisticated urban audiences capable of filtering information and interrogating the materials before them. No matter how assertively colonial authorities strove to create a hegemonic political order using censorship and propaganda, African media producers and consumers often remained independent and critical within and against the hegemonies of representation that surrounded them. Some target populations simply continued their daily lives as before.

The particular multiculturalism of Lagos must be inserted into universalizing assumptions about media consumption in global cities. Lagos was shaped in the first half of the twentieth century by European planning efforts and locals' adjustments to policy according to their own practices; this was accompanied at all times by a vociferous and politically diverse African press containing commentaries on and critiques of government policy. In the second half of the century, Lagos developed the complex cosmopolitanism of a postcolonial society marked by extremes of wealth and poverty, accompanied by periodic curtailments of media freedoms and the burgeoning of popular film, literature, and social media.

In spite of half a century of colonial interventions in people's daily lives, by the mid-1940s the failure of officials to understand "the influences and process of mind which lead to what appear to us inexplicable reactions both on mass [sic] and by the individual" remained the primary obstacle to colonial sanitary reform in Lagos.[26] If Nigerian audiences differ from media consumers elsewhere, it may be in this propensity to render the ruling power's media messages "inexplicable" through their skeptical disregard for some messages and their appropriation of others into the plural narratives that constitute public opinion. Nigerians were by no means the compliant readers and audiences required by colonial regimes under the labels of "enlightenment and education"; nor did they resemble the emotionally volatile, vulnerable masses imagined by the Colonial Office as easy targets of political manipulation by Communists and anticolonial educated elites.[27] Neither censorship nor public relations campaigns by the Colonial Office accounted for the basic, ongoing failure of British colonial comprehension of African urban dwellers.

One ongoing implication of this critical media consumption in Nigeria is that public health initiatives will not necessarily have an impact on their intended publics in the manner anticipated by producers. As James Webb persuasively argues in his analysis of the need for African populations to be taken into account in epidemiological modeling of infectious disease transmission, "The biomedical understandings of disease processes in Africa are frequently naïve, because they lack political, social, cultural and economic historical contexts."[28] Mass media play a vital role in forming public opinion, putting arguments into circulation, but Nigerian media consumers should not be regarded either as passive or as easily vulnerable to the hegemonic forms of culture and capital that form the focus of current world literature theory.[29]

Beyond informed guesswork about local people's responses to public health messages in the colonial era, as evidenced in the written archives, critical questions remain unresolved in this book. What historical spaces are available to supplement the lack of Africans' perspectives in the colonial archives? Can printed popular narratives and other printed matter such as funeral posters and textiles help to bridge the gulf exposed by this book between African silences in the colonial archives and people's fluency as present-day media consumers? Can oral histories and resources such as proverbs and biographies serve in part to fill the gaps? If we turn away from texts and toward other types of archives, what resources are available? Might architectural configurations of space such as the location of toilets and bathrooms help us to identify historical trajectories—albeit in the form of nonlinear patterns—of African urban practice across different social groups? Beyond the last pages of this book, a question remains: how can one write an inclusive history of media audiences that takes into account the heterogeneity of urban dwellers?

If the failure of the Colonial Film Unit to achieve its health and hygiene goals through documentary narratives teaches one thing, it is that any assessment of the impact of official information campaigns must analyze not only the content of messages—stark and nonnegotiable as they often are—but also people's responses to the material in circulation. And people's imaginations are shaped by infinitely more than the messages disseminated by politicians or mainstream media. This is not to idealize or de-historicize nonelite media consumers as somehow more liberal than ruling elites. One cannot leap across centuries and cultures to connect and compare audience responses to government messaging, or to position local audiences outside the communicative and ideological power of global mass media. But a shared, broad characteristic has emerged over the century of Nigerian media consumption analyzed in this book in the shape of audiences' capacity to critically and creatively interrogate messages intended for their consumption in the public sphere, to inject them with new narratives, and to produce unexpected responses, such as laughter, that may fundamentally alter media producers' declared agendas and tip official discourses sideways into other articulations.

Words, Phrases, and Sayings Relating to Dirt in Lagos

Compiled from interviews conducted by Olutoyosi Tokun, John Uwa, and Jane Nebe, and from other sources as given. Yoruba diacritical marks and corrections by Omegalpha Consult LLC. Translations, interpretations, and further corrections with guidance from Karin Barber and sources as given.

Proverbs

Àÿtàn kìí kọ ilẹ̀ kílẹ̀

TRANSLATION: The dumpsite does not reject any form of trash.

MEANING/INTERPRETATION: This proverb describes an exceptionally tolerant person who does not want to hurt the feelings of others and who listens and accepts whatever comes his/her way. It may also describe a leader who listens too much to others, thus allowing sycophants to gain power, and who does not act decisively (Yusuff, interviewed by Olutoyosi Tokun, March 24, 2016).

Adìẹ kìí fi ibi tí kòkòrò wà láàtàn han ọmọ ẹ̀

TRANSLATION: The mother hen does not show the location of insects on the dumpsite to her chicks.

MEANING/INTERPRETATION: The one with knowledge/experience selfishly benefits from it to the detriment of those who are not mature enough to know. Some people will fill themselves up first before they remember their children, even though there might not be enough to go around (Yusuff, interviewed by Olutoyosi Tokun, March 24, 2016; Olukoju [2018]).

Àmàlà àti ẹ̀gúsí alẹ́ àná, t'ójúmọ́ bá mọ́, wọ́n á padà sáàtàn ni

TRANSLATION: The *àmàlà* and melon-seed soup from last night's dinner will return to the dumpsite at daybreak.

MEANING/INTERPRETATION: *Àmàlà* and *ẹ̀gúsí* are palatable and delicious while being eaten, but they will become feces on the refuse dump by morning; or, last night's dinner will return to the dumpsite by morning (in the villages people will defecate on the dump site). Waste comes out of useful things: I have taken the useful part into my system as nourishment, but the remainder is expelled as useless matter or dirt (Yusuff, interviewed by Olutoyosi Tokun, March 24 2016; Olukoju [2018]).

À ń gba òròmọ adìẹ lọ́wọ́ ikú, ó ní wọn kò jẹ́ kí òun lọ jayé orí òun l'áàtàn
(Commonly: *À ń gba òròmọ adìẹ lọ́wọ́ ikú, ó ní wọn ò jẹ́ kòun jẹ́ l'áàtàn*)

TRANSLATION: We rescue the chick from death; it says we're stopping it from enjoying itself [or eating] on the rubbish heap (Karin Barber, personal communication, July 2018).

MEANING/INTERPRETATION: You are being protected from endangering yourself.

Àtàrí àjànàkú, kìí ṣeru ọmọdé

TRANSLATION: (lit., the elephant's cranium is not a load for children.) The elephant's cranium is too heavy for a child to carry.

MEANING/INTERPRETATION: Some matters are too weighty for inexperienced people to handle appropriately.

Bá a gbálé, tá a gbáta, ààtàn là á darí ẹ̀ sí

TRANSLATION: After the house has been swept both inside and outside, all the trash will end up at the dumpsite.

MEANING/INTERPRETATION: The dumpsite is the inevitable end point for everything that is cleared from the house and everywhere around it, including the gutter, the street, and the garden. The dumpsite receives all forms of refuse.

Ẹni t'ó báni jẹun, ó ran'ni lẹ́rù lọ s'ààtàn ni

TRANSLATION: Whoever eats your meal with you also helps you to carry some of the load that you would take to the dumpsite.

MEANING/INTERPRETATION: You should share the good and the bad: once you share the good, you must share the bad as well (Yusuff, interviewed by Olutoyosi Tokun, March 24, 2016; Olukoju [2018]).

Ìgbẹ́ lowó wà (or Inú ìgbẹ́ ni owó wà / Inú ìgbẹ́ lowó wà)

TRANSLATION: Money can be found in the bush/in feces.

MEANING/INTERPRETATION: Things that appear unproductive may yield wealth, so one should remain alert to opportunities where others have turned away.

Inú ìkòkò dúdú lẹ̀ kọ funfun ti jáde

TRANSLATION: White corn pap comes out of a black pot.

MEANING/INTERPRETATION: A dirty person can give birth to or produce somebody or something that is neat.

Ìsàlẹ̀ ọrọ̀ lẹ́gbin

TRANSLATION: At the root of riches is dirt.

MEANING/INTERPRETATION: Unlike the proverbs about good/clean money coming out of dirty places and dirty forms of labor, this popular proverb describes the reverse process, suggesting "one should distrust great wealth because it was probably ill-gotten. This was a popular moral in Yoruba popular theatre plays of the 1980s" (Karin Barber, personal communication, July 2018).

Kàkà kí eku má jẹ sèsé, á fi ṣe àwàdànù

TRANSLATION: If the rat cannot eat the beans, it will render them useless (by urinating on them) rather than leaving the sack for somebody else to eat (Faleti 2013, 237). An alternative translation: If a rat cannot eat the beans, it will dig a hole and hide them (Abraham [1958], cited by Karin Barber, personal communication, July 2018).

MEANING/INTERPRETATION: This refers to selfish behavior: if a person cannot have something for themselves, they will spoil it for others.

Ọ̀bùn rí ikú ọkọ tìràn mọ́

TRANSLATION: A filthy woman (person) will take advantage of the customary mourning period following the death of her husband.

MEANING/INTERPRETATION: A woman (person) will turn a bad personal experience to her own advantage. That is, a slovenly woman who never likes to keep herself clean will exploit the custom of disregarding personal hygiene during a period of personal difficulty as an excuse to stop bathing and washing clothes.

Owó ìgbẹ́ kìí rùn

TRANSLATION: The money made from feces does not smell.

MEANING/INTERPRETATION: Attributed to *agbépóò*, but used generally to mean that cash has come to be more important than its source. This proverb does not apply exclusively to jobs considered demeaning. A person might use it when collecting their salary to signify that they have suffered in earning it.

Ta ló máa fi ọ̀bùn ṣaya? Kí lọ̀bùn máa bí? Or Ta ló fẹ́ fẹ́ onídọ̀tí?

TRANSLATION: Who would marry a filthy woman (person)? What would a filthy woman give birth to?

MEANING/INTERPRETATION: This is a version of "cleanliness is next to godliness."

Ṭẹni n tẹni, tàkísà n tààtàn
TRANSLATION: Everyone belongs somewhere, and rags belong to the dumpsite.
MEANING/INTERPRETATION: Appropriate things move together. What's mine is mine, and what is for the dump is its own business now (Olukoju [2018]; Yusuff, interviewed by Olutoyosi Tokun, March 24, 2016).

Tí òkété bá dàgbà tán, ọmú ọmọ rẹ̀ ló ń mú
TRANSLATION: When the giant rat grows old, it feeds on the milk of its babies (Fasoro [2012, 258]).

People

agbálẹ̀—street cleaner

agbépóò/àwọn agbépóò—(lit., "carrier of potty") night-soil men, fecal-waste workers; also used to refer to a person (esp. child) who comes in last in a competition, as in "he/she took *agbépóò*"

akógbẹ̀ẹ́—*agbépóò*, night-soil carrier

akólẹ̀ (or ***kólẹ̀kólẹ̀***)—(lit., "collector of *ilẹ̀*") refuse collector

apàlúmọ́—street cleaner

Ará Èkó—non-Lagos-born people living in Lagos

Ará Òkè—uplanders, sometimes used to connote "uncivilized" people

arómimáwẹ̀—(lit., "the person will see water but will not want to bathe") a dirty person

aṣalẹ̀—(lit., "selector/chooser from among *ilẹ̀*") waste picker, "scavenger"

Bholar Boys or ***bolas***—The term, borrowed from the Hausa language, is used for refuse collectors. An alternative term used for them is *bárò* (from "wheelbarrow pusher").

eléèérí—dirty person

jàatànyó—(lit., "someone who eats their fill off the rubbish heap") an *àbíkú* name, that is, the name given to a spirit-child who is destined to die before reaching puberty.

katakata—(Nigerian Pidgin: "caterpillar") waste worker

ọbùn—a dirty person, a person with poor personal hygiene

òjùjú—an imaginary being used to scare a child

olóòórùn—a person with poor personal hygiene

ọmọ Èkó—(lit., "a child/children of Lagos Island") Lagos-born indigene

onídọ̀tí—dirty person

oníṣẹ́—night-soil man

ṣagolo—tin pickers (on the dump)

small-small—(Nigerian Pidgin) small child, infant

tálíkà/tálákà—(loanword from Hausa) poor person

túlẹ̀túlẹ̀—(lit., "taker-apart, dismantler, scatterer of *ilẹ̀*") people who search through waste on the dump, popularly called "scavengers"

woléwolé—home inspectors, sanitary inspectors

Objects, Actions, and Places

ààtàn/àkìtàn—refuse dump, also called "the dunghill," a place for open air defecation

àlàpà—abandoned building

dirty—(Nigerian Pidgin, n.) dirt

èérí or ẹrẹ̀—dirt, filthy substance, waste matter

ẹ̀gbin—dirt, filthy substance, waste matter

Ẹ̀hìngbẹ́/Ẹ̀hìnìgbẹ̀tí—This is said to refer to an area on Lagos Island that is popular as a trading hotspot and a port. Proverb: *Bójú ò bá ti Ẹ̀hìngbẹ̀tì, ojú ò le t'Èkó* (If *Ẹ̀hìnìgbẹ̀tí* is not put to shame, *Èkó* cannot be put to shame).

eruku—dust (fine powder)

erùpẹ̀—soil

gbá òde (ìta)—remove refuse from the street

ìbòjú—mask/masquerade

ìdọ̀tí—(Yoruba, loanword from English) dirt, filthy substance, waste matter

ìgbẹ́—feces, animal waste, forest/bush

ìgbọ̀nsẹ̀—dirt, filthy substance, fecal matter

ilẹ̀—(Yoruba) earth, ground, soil, land, country. A euphemism for waste matter/filthy substances. See under *akólẹ̀* (or *kólẹ̀kólẹ̀*), *aṣalẹ̀, túlẹ̀túlẹ̀*.

iyẹ̀pẹ̀—soil (uncommon, archaic)

jẹ̀gbin—feed on decaying matter

kẹ̀/kíkẹ̀—decay, spoil, deteriorate, decompose

mọ́tò akólẹ̀—(Yoruba, with loanword from English) waste collection truck

ohun aláìnílááří—(lit., "something that is without prestige, something that is not valued") rubbish/litter

olóòórùn—something that is fragrant or smelly (including sweet or bad depending on the context of its usage). It can also refer to behavior/attitude, for example, a liar.

pàlúmọ́—remove refuse from the street

pàntí—(Yoruba) litter/debris (outdoors), untidiness (in a room), light odorless materials such as paper, cobwebs, or dry leaves that can be swept away

póò—(Yoruba, loanword from English, loanword from French) potty, *pôt de chambre*

pọ̀tọ̀pọ́tọ́/pẹ̀tẹ̀pẹ́tẹ̀—mud, boggy ground

ṣa eegun—(lit., "to pick up bones") salvage items from waste

ṣáláńgá—(Yoruba, loanword from Hausa) pit latrine

ṣalẹ̀—salvage items from waste

wòsìwósì—petty trader's goods, miscellaneous goods

Insults

ààtànkọ̀yí—(lit., "even the dunghill rejects this one") A name given to àbíkú children (children who are "born to die" many times into the same family) "to shame [them] to desist from dying" (Olukoju [2018]).

Olórí burúkú ni ẹ́—You are an unfortunate person.

Orí ẹ bàjẹ́ ni? Orí ẹ dàrú ni?—Is your brain faulty? Are you mentally unstable?

Miscellaneous

[Agbépóò] wọn máa wú kú—The agbépóò will swell up until they die.

agídí—stubbornness

àìmọ́—dirtiness (n.)

dídòtí—being dirty

èérí—dirt, dirtiness

ẹgbin—shame, ruined reputation

Ẹní jalè ló ba ọmọ jẹ́—He/she who steals will have a bad name (i.e., it is better to do menial jobs such as night-soil removal than to be renowned as a thief).

Ẹni tó ń ṣe iwa èérí, o ń ṣe iwà tó lòdì—Whoever does something filthy is doing something against the norm.

Ìlú kìì kéré kó má ní àjtàn—Every town, no matter how small, must have a dumpsite. No town is so small that it has no rubbish heap (Barber [1996, 1]).

Ìmọ́tótó ló lè ṣẹ́gun àrùn gbogbo, ìmọ́tótó ilé . . .—[incomplete saying] Good sanitation/cleanliness can overcome all diseases. The cleanliness of the house . . .

Irú wá ògìrì wá—(Yoruba: "Locust beans came, cooked melon-seeds came, i.e., all and sundry came.") This is an established Yoruba saying to indicate variety, equivalent to "every Tom, Dick, and Harry."

Ó tálákà bí èkúté ṣóòṣì—He/she is poor as a church rat.

ọ̀bùn—slovenly (person)

pọ́nṣọnpọ̀nṣọn—disgusting

rírí—dirty (e.g., ó rírí—he/she/it is dirty; or adjective, e.g., aṣọ. rírí—dirty cloth)

Tí eku bá jẹ . . . ẹni bá jẹnu eku orí ẹ̀ máa pé—Anyone that eats food nibbled by a rat will be smart.

yámayàma—filthy

NOTES

Preface

1 UN News Centre (April 5, 2012).

2 UN News Centre (March 21, 2011).

3 See chapter 6 and the appendix for the multifarious conceptualizations of dirt in Yoruba and Nigerian Pidgin.

4 See Barber (2017).

5 One of the most popular songs was "Ebola! Don't Touch Your Friends," the theme tune from *Malaria Ebola* (2014; dir. Evans Orji), one of several Nollywood movies about the virus. An American rap song, "Ebola (La La)" by Rucka Rucka Ali, was especially popular in Nairobi, with its emphasis on the racism of travel restrictions on black people, including "Don't let the Obamas on the plane."

6 See Oloko (2018); Uwa (2018). The project researchers presented their work at the workshop "Mediating Waste: Media and the Management of Waste in Lagos," held at the University of Lagos in March 2016, and Patrick Oloko and John Uwa presented their research at the workshop "The Cultural Politics of Dirt in Africa," held at Yale University in November 2016.

7 Interviews and FGDs numbered 7 to 44 were conducted and transcribed by John Uwa; interviews and FGDs numbered 45 to 58 were conducted and transcribed by Jane Nebe; interviews and FGDs numbered 59 to 121 were conducted and transcribed by Olutoyosi Tokun. All other interviews and FGDs were conducted and transcribed collectively by the team.

8 My presence, as we learned from the pilot study, distorted the dynamic of discussions. See Newell et al. (2018).

9 We discuss the ethical and methodological challenges of a project of this scope in a collective chapter in the *Routledge International Handbook of Interdisciplinary Research Methods* (Newell et al. 2018). Here, all nine members of the Dirtpol project team discuss the challenges of having a British PI subject to ethical screening by the European Research Council, over and against the choices and decisions faced by the project team in local fieldwork contexts.

Introduction

1 UAC 2/34/4/1/1 (January 9, 1925, 72).
2 UAC 2/34/4/1/1 (January 9, 1925, 72).
3 UAC 2/34/4/1/1 (January 9, 1925, 72). Knox's accounts of his travels with his employer, and Lever's own journals, leave a great deal unsaid about the use of forced labor in Lever Brothers' Congo concessions, meticulously catalogued by Marchal (2008).
4 McClintock (1995); Burke (1996).
5 Pratt (1992).
6 Whitford ([1877] 1967, 86).
7 Whitford ([1877] 1967, 142).
8 UAC 1/11/14/3/1b, 164.
9 UAC 2/34/4/1/1 (February 18, 1925, 100).
10 UAC 2/34/4/1/1 (January 9, 1925, 75).
11 UAC 2/34/4/1/1 (January 17, 1925, 81).
12 UAC 2/34/4/1/1 (January 17, 1925, 81–2).
13 UAC 2/34/4/1/1 (September 29, 1924, 3; October 21, 1924, 23; November 23, 1924, 55; January 9, 1925, 72; January 21, 1925, 85).
14 Bataille ([1970] trans. 1985); Douglas ([1966] 2002); Kristeva (1982); V. Smith (2007).
15 Douglas ([1966] 2002, 117–40).
16 Fardon (2016, 30).
17 Burke (1996); Allman and Tashjian (2000).
18 Here is what Liebig actually wrote: "The quantity of soap consumed by a nation would be no inaccurate measure whereby to estimate its wealth and civilization. . . . This consumption does not subserve sensual gratification, nor depend upon fashion, but upon the feeling of the beauty, comfort, and welfare, attendant upon cleanliness; and a regard to this feeling is coincident with wealth and civilization. . . . A want of cleanliness is equivalent to insupportable misery and misfortune" (1843, 18).
19 LSHTM Ross 82/24 (1901, 3).
20 These sanitary inspectors, or *woléwolé*, were greatly feared for their powers to remove and destroy people's possessions. See Uwa (2018).
21 Unofficial members were appointed by the governor.
22 Okere, Njoku, and Devish make the powerful argument that "all knowledge is first of all local knowledge" (2011).
23 Morris (2000, 453).
24 The Western fascination with dirt is amply illustrated by the fact that, in the first two decades of the twenty-first century, more than twenty-five books were published with "dirt," or dirt-related terms in their titles, plus in

2011 the Wellcome Institute in London held a major exhibition titled *Dirt: The Filthy Reality of Everyday Life.*

25 Recent studies include Harris (2008), Brownell (2014), and two special issues of *Social Dynamics* on the "cultural politics of dirt in Africa" (2018).

26 For anthropology, see Douglas ([1966] 2002); Masquelier (2005); C. Smith (2019). For visual cultures, see Förster (2014); Harrow (2013); Maarouf (2018); Wagner-Lawlor (2018). For soap and cleanliness, see Allman and Tashjian (2000); Burke (1996); Lewis (2012); McClintock (1995).

27 Wagner-Lawlor (2018); Förster (2014).

28 See Newell (2013).

29 See Stoler (2002); Burton (1998).

30 Economist Intelligence Unit (2017).

31 See Wim Wenders's short film *War in Peace* (2011), part of the Chacun son cinéma project. In one section, Wenders and his team film the audience in a Congolese village as they watch *Black Hawk Down* in rapt silence (http://www.veoh.com/watch/v20002583tTDYxgXt). I am indebted to Kathryn M. Lachman for alerting me to this movie. For a recent study of audience responses and the methodological questions surrounding research into African audiences, see Saint (2018).

32 Huyssen (2008, 2).

1. European Insanitary Nuisances

1 Aderibigbe (1975); Mann (2007); Falola and Afolabi (2017); Whiteman (2014); Lovejoy (2005).

2 Hopkins (1973).

3 Olukoju (2004); Falola and Heaton (2008). For studies of the "Saro" community of Brazilian and Cuban freed slaves who came to Lagos via Sierra Leone, see Spitzer (1975).

4 Bigon (2005, 259).

5 Bigon (2005, 248).

6 LSHTM, MacDonald 02/01–02a (n.d., 4).

7 Simpson (1909, 17); Ross 82/08 (September 15, 1902, 4).

8 PRO CO 592/7 (1911, 600; emphasis added). This pressure for sanitation was not as starkly racialized as implied by these examples from the colonial archives. As chapter 3 shows, from the 1880s onward, numerous educated Africans petitioned the municipal authorities for sanitary improvements to their towns. Town planning and hygiene are dominant themes in the African-owned Anglophone press of colonial West Africa, and African doctors played a critical role in improving urban sanitation (see, e.g., Adeoti and Imuoh 2016).

9 See Mann (2007); Mabogunje (1968). The numbers of "non-official natives"

increased from 84,694 in 1920 to 102,260 in 1922 ("Nigeria Medical and Sanitary Report for the Year 1922," cited in *Nigerian Pioneer*, January 25, 1924, 6).

10 See Aderibigbe (1975, 19–21); Mann (2007).

11 Bigon (2005, 248).

12 Whitford, cited by P. D. Cole (1975, 33).

13 Aderibigbe (1975, 22).

14 Diouf and Fredericks (2014, 5); Simone (2004); Myers (2011).

15 In 1911, a yellow fever epidemic on Lagos Island led the governor, Lord Lugard, to initiate discussions with London about the relocation of the colonial capital to a location close by—such as Yaba—on grounds of the impossibility of ever adequately sanitizing Lagos Island to the standard required for the health of its European population (Bigon 2005, 263). By 1924, Yaba was being proposed as a site for the relocation of Africans from the plague epicenter at Oko-Awo and other "slums" in the municipal area of Lagos (*Nigerian Pioneer*, October 3, 1924, 8).

16 M. Vaughan (1991, x, 8); Njoh (2016).

17 Seun (2015); S. H. Brown (2004); Burke (1996); Njoh (2008; 2009; 2016); Bissell (2010).

18 LSHTM Ross 76/21 (April 21, 1902, 7).

19 PRO CO 879/112—No. 177 (n.d. [1913], 296).

20 Cole (2015); Seun (2015); S. H. Brown (1992).

21 Gordon (2003, 42). Ann Laura Stoler (2010) writes about the febrile, contradictory qualities of colonial archives.

22 Gordon (2003, 42). See also M. Vaughan (1991).

23 This snapshot omits important religious and business communities in colonial West Africa, especially Syrians and settlers from the Arab world (see Rais 1988; Arsan 2014).

24 For a detailed analysis of the political space of colonial public health, see Larkin (2008).

25 See Bashford (2004); Larkin (2008). For an account of the Public Works Department, established in 1886, and the Sanitary Department, established in 1888, see Bigon (2005, 258). The Lagos Municipal Board of Health was added to the Medical Department in 1908 (PRO CO 592/5 [1910]). A Public Health (Protectorate) Ordinance initiated by the Colonial Office in 1913 attempted to consolidate provision across the whole of British West Africa. It should not be assumed that sanitary and town-planning rules distinguished British from African forms of governance. In July 1904, the Egba United Government issued an order aimed at regulating public health that included, among a range of compulsory measures, heavy penalties for noncompliance and communal cleaning of streets.

26 India was a constant reference point and comparator for colonial health personnel, many of whom were posted there prior to West Africa. Mostly, their

comparisons between the two colonial settings demonstrated "the immense inferiority of civilisation in West Africa" where one could obtain neither a punkah wallah nor ice (Ross 83/19 [1901, 13]).

27 These colonial public health interventions in the micropolitics of African bodies provide historicity to Achille Mbembe's argument about bodily surveillance of twenty-first-century migrants to the West (2018).

28 PRO CO 583/156/1 (1928, 4).

29 PRO CO 1047/651 (1913, n.p.). While this book is confined to colonial Lagos and other West African towns, it should be noted that officials in East and South African cities were equally concerned with public health. Considerable research has been published in this area (F. Cole 2015; Parle and Noble 2014; Vaughan 1991; White 1990).

30 See F. Cole (2015, 247).

31 See LSHTM Ross 76/21 (1902, 7).

32 LSHTM Ross 78/04 (1903, 20).

33 LSHTM Ross 82/08 (1902, 6).

34 PRO CO 879/112—No. 117 (1913, 156). "I have no hesitation in saying that many of the official quarters which I have seen, including, I may observe, my own official residence at Accra, would fail to secure a licence from our sanitary officers," stated Sir Hugh Clifford, governor of the Gold Coast Colony, before listing a number of institutional environments—including the hospital—where "filth diseases" were more likely to be propagated than cured (PRO CO 879/112—No. 56 [1913, 65–66]).

35 In *The Truth about the West African Land Question*, J. E. Casely Hayford presents the people's request to continue to build mud houses in Cape Coast and Axim following "sanitary principles" and advice of town councils ([1913] 1971, 169–70). Several interviewees in Lagos between 2014 and 2016 remembered similar traditional dwellings with affection: "But those days," one educated woman recalled, "they build their house with mud. Even if the weather is hot, you feel the cold, you will be comfortable in the house. And if is very cold out there, you feel the warmth within. That is the level of what they use to build the house, the mud, the clay, it helps. But now we use blocks, anything that is outside we feel it immediately, so that is the influence of the Western culture. Even our buildings it has affected" (NGO-f-112, interviewed by Olutoyosi Tokun).

36 Simpson (1909, 18). The "Simpson latrine" was very distinctive in its construction, comprising "a raised platform with cement floor, in which spaces are sunk to receive stercus pails. These spaces, 14 in each latrine, are each connected to a central cleaning channel, which in turn discharges into a bucket at the end, placed there to catch any overflow or washing-out water" (Public Works Department [Cape of Good Hope] 1901, 43).

37 Simpson (1909, 73).

38 LSHTM Ross (1922, 447).

39 PRO CO 592/7 (1911, 601).

40 PRO CO 879/112—No. 147 (1913, 230).

41 Bigon (2005, 258).

42 PRO CO 879/112—No. 169 (n.d. [1913], 272).

43 PRO CO 879/112—No. 177 (n.d. [1913], 296). One African physician allegedly supported calls for segregation in the 1890s: Patton (1996, 21, 93–122) reports that in 1893 John Farrell Easmon recommended segregation in colonial Ghana. The class dimensions of such a position are discussed in chapter 3.

44 LSHTM Ross 82/08 (1902, 7).

45 Patton (1996, 17).

46 LSHTM Ross 82/18 (1910, 3–4).

47 LSHTM Ross 76/21 (1902, 1).

48 On the topic of colonial insensitivities toward the historical meaning of particular urban spaces, Sir Hugh Clifford, governor of the Gold Coast, stated in 1913 that he housed his African servants and their families in the "dark, damp, and ill-ventilated . . . cells and dungeons" of his official residence at Christiansborg Castle, a renowned ex–slave fortress facing the Atlantic Ocean in Osu, Accra (PRO CO 879/112—No. 117 1913, 156).

49 This skepticism toward enclosed cubicle toilets persists to this day in many parts of Nigeria. In informal settlements such as Ajegunle, Lagos, where an NGO recently built toilets, people refused to use the facilities and preferred to continue open-air defecation (MIR-m-105, interviewed by Olutoyosi Tokun). One medical worker described an experience of a medical placement in a village where "no indigene would use a water closet system. They felt it was some, you know, alien discovery by the white man to come and kill them or do them harm, so they would use pit latrines. They would rather poo in the bush, that was their preferred site and the more refined ones would use pit latrines" (PHW-n-107, interviewed by Olutoyosi Tokun). One man in his seventies described how "there are some who don't even want to see 'shit' and so they go to the bush to defecate and bury it. I do this occasionally" (Misc-m-22, interviewed by John Uwa).

50 To this day many people remain convinced that the hygiene of the pit latrine is superior to that of the water closet system.

51 LSHTM Ross 78/04 (1903, 16).

52 NNA MH (Fed) 1/1—3973 (1932, 4).

53 Senior sanitary officials were qualified medical practitioners; often at variance with government officials, including governors, they regarded themselves as answerable to Whitehall rather than to local colonial authorities.

54 LSHTM Ross 82/04 (1902, n.p.).

55 LSHTM Ross 82/08 (1902, 5).

56 S. H. Brown (1994, 687).

57 LSHTM Ross 82/04 (1902, n.p.).

58 LSHTM Ross 76/21 (1902, 5).

59 LSHTM Ross 76/21 (1902, 7).

60 Adeloye (1974, 288–89).

61 Njoh (2009).

62 LSHTM Ross 83/05 (1901, 6).

63 Bashford (2004, 59).

64 NNA MH (Fed) 1/1—5561 (February 14–15 1944, n.p.). This inappropriate, Eurocentric idea of a healthy dwelling already had a long history in Nigeria. In his *Wanderings in West Africa*, Richard Burton described the British Consul building, shipped to Lagos from England, as "a corrugated iron coffin with always a dead Consul inside" (cited by Aderibigbe [1975, 23]).

65 NNA MH (Fed) 1/1—5561 (February 14–15, 1944, n.p.). Such buildings survive today in the "Face-Me-I-Face-You," or "I box you box me" type of tenement block in Lagos, constructed for low-income families, with shared kitchens and bathrooms, and with rooms directly overlooking one another. Many interviewees in Lagos between 2014 and 2016 described, or lived in, this type of accommodation where "the area is so choked up that there may not even be road to even enter to the street to pick waste" (PHW-m-97, interviewed by Olutoyosi Tokun). For such residents, the communal toilet requires water to be fetched to flush it, resulting in a build-up of "toilet disease" and a preference among some households for the potty, which is emptied into the dirty toilet or the canal.

66 LSHTM Ross 82/08 (1902, 7).

67 For Freetown in the period up to and including the First World War, see F. Cole (2015, 257).

68 Ground plans and photographs were shared between East and West Africa; see PRO CO 879/112—No. 75 (1913, 91–98). British East Africa, with its attractive climate for European farmers and settlers, generated a more explicit racialization of dirt than West Africa, where public health—especially in regard to mosquitoes—was the ostensible rationale for segregation (see chapter 2). Under the Native Passes Regulations (1903), any African hailing from a so-called Native Reserve was required to carry a permit if he or she decided to live in Nairobi. This system operated in other white settler colonies such as Rhodesia (Zimbabwe) and, most famously, in South Africa, where it became a cornerstone of apartheid.

69 Njoh (2009). Chapter 4 shows how, increasingly in the 1920s and 1930s, individuals—particularly figures of authority in the community such as chiefs and schoolteachers—were recruited to improve the cleanliness of their own homes according to European standards.

70 LSHTM Ross 83/08 (1901, 5).

71 See NNA MH (Fed) 1/1—3973 (1932, 4).

72 PRO CO 879/112—No. 117 (1913, 156).

73 LSHTM Ross 78/04 (1903, 15). Indigenous buildings were deemed to be so unhygienic that in the late 1920s the Nigerian government approved construction bylaws prohibiting the building of any new structures in the Municipal Area of Lagos using bamboo, clay, thatch, or other traditional construction materials (Izomoh 1994; R. S. Smith 1979; see also Bissell 2010). A number of prosecutions were brought against individuals for infringements of the legislation, and in one case at least, the government itself was at fault. In October 1926, Reginald Acheson Webb, the town engineer, tabled a complaint to the Lagos Town Council because the Public Works Department had erected twelve "Bush Houses" at Ikoyi with "bamboo sides and thatched roofs," intended to be "residences of the European Rodent Catchers who are arriving shortly from England" to continue the fight against bubonic plague (*Nigerian Pioneer*, February 25, 1927, 7). These houses had been approved not only by the director of medical and sanitary services, but also by Sir Graeme Thomson, governor of the colony. Such double standards, whereby bamboo-and-thatch buildings occupied by Africans were regarded as laboratories for filth and disease, but not if they were constructed for white men's habitation, need no further analysis for their message about the human source of filth in the eyes of officials at the highest level of government.

74 LSHTM Ross 79/69 (1901, 2).

75 NNA MH (Fed) 1/1—5040/T (1956, 1).

76 NNA MH (Fed) 1/1—5040/T (1956, 1).

77 NNA MH (Fed) 1/1—5040/T (1956, 1).

78 Njoh (2009); Bashford (2004); S. H. Brown (1994).

79 PRO CO 879/112—No. 18 (1913, 45).

80 For a biography of Clifford that offers a nuanced understanding of the relationship between his imperialism and his liberal humanism, see Holden (2000).

81 PRO CO 879/112—No. 77 (1913, 102).

82 Cited in F. Cole (2015, 244).

83 PRO CO 879/112—No. 177 (n.d. [1913], 102).

2. Malaria

Epigraphs: Joseph Chamberlain quoted in Ross (1922, 434); LSHTM Ross 76/20/04.

1 Ross was awarded a Nobel Prize in 1902 for his work on malaria. Grassi was nominated as cowinner of the award, but after Ross accused Grassi of fraud and Robert Koch confirmed Ross's status, Grassi was excluded (Capanna 2006). Ross's mosquito theory was not universally accepted by doctors in West Africa. In 1901, a handful of doctors on the coast wrote a letter to Francis Swanzy, chairman of the African Section of the London Chamber

of Commerce, disputing Ross's "mosquito theory of malaria" (Ross 76/01/06 [November 11, 1901, n.p.]).

2 Webb (2014, 29); Cole (2015); Oluwasegun (2017).

3 See Curtin (1985). The German bacteriologist Robert Koch is credited with discovering acquired immunity to malaria through his research into inhabitants of a German settlement in New Guinea (Webb 2014, 25).

4 PRO CO 879/112—No. 56 (1913, 66).

5 LSHTM, MacDonald 02/01–02b (n.d., 1).

6 LSHTM, MacDonald 02/01–02b (n.d., 2).

7 See Seun (2015).

8 PRO CO 879/112—No. 132b (n.d. [March 1913]). F. G. Hopkins's papers are held at the Bodleian Library, Oxford.

9 Webb (2014).

10 PRO CO 879/112—No. 83 (1913, 114). "Carried to its logical conclusion," Sir Hugh Clifford commented of the policy of segregation, "the acceptation of this contention [that segregation is necessary on grounds of European health] would entail the abandonment of many, if not all, of our West African Colonies and possessions. It is clearly more conducive to the preservation of health to reside in Europe than to live in great discomfort on the Gold Coast" (PRO CO 879/112—No. 83 [1913, 114]).

11 Webb (2014, 14).

12 Sutphen and Andrews (2003, 4).

13 Ross (1922, 448). For a discussion of the ethics of health and medical interventions in colonial Africa, see Tilley (2016).

14 In 1901, the authors of the *Report of the Malaria Expedition to Nigeria* reported consistent "misuse" of mosquito netting by Europeans. "We very rarely met with one who used the curtains in a careful and proper manner," they reported, and the mode of hanging netting, untucked and frequently torn, over the mattress, in fact served "as a trap for those mosquitoes which have taken shelter during the day-time under the bed" (cited in Webb [2014, 22–23]).

15 LSHTM Ross 76/21 (1902, 10).

16 LSHTM Ross 83/13 (1901, 5). For a detailed description of the European "Hill Station" at Freetown in the early twentieth century, see F. Cole (2015). Spencer H. Brown (1994, 693, 695) makes the important point that European and North American cities were just as odoriferous as Lagos for the majority of their populations, if not more so with the vast quantities of horse urine and dung.

17 LSHTM Ross 82/16 (1901, 6). The British traders in Lagos are discussed by Olukoju (2004) and Lynn (1997).

18 PRO CO 879/112—No. 56 (1913, 66). In spite of his passionately antisegregationist views, Clifford's assumption that Europeans could never go mad

offers a glimpse into how "reason" and "sanity" were racialized at all levels of colonial governance. For outstanding studies of the relationship between colonial psychiatry and theories of race in Africa, see Keller (2001); M. Vaughan (1991, 100–128).

19 A 1940 propaganda movie made by the Colonial Health Unit for screening in Africa, *Mr. English at Home*, demonstrates this colonial desire to remodel African lives and minds along British domestic patterns. The film was a favorite with colonialist film programmers for its promotion of modern family life through interior shots of Mr. English's semidetached suburban home, complete with a smiling housewife, electric appliances, and clean, healthy children with their own gender-segregated bedrooms. It was part of an ongoing postwar campaign "to inform the African peoples, either directly or indirectly, of the British way of life, British ideals and the Colonial Policy common to all British Governments which aims at self-government for the Colonial People *when they are of sufficient education and responsibility to undertake it*" (PRO CO 875/72/4 [1952, 125; emphasis added]). According to a 1943 survey of information officers by the Colonial Film Unit in London, "amongst literate audiences" in the Gold Coast, *Mr. English at Home* aroused "more interest and comment than any other" (PRO CO 875/10/11 [1943, A1]). The film's value, for the reporting officer, was in the contrast between African and English ways of life. The way in which the film "present[s] them with the English counterpart of a flash of their own African life . . . is highly entertaining to the audiences and at the same time self explanatory" (PRO CO 875/10/11 [1943, 2]). See "Mr. English at Home," Colonial Film, http://www .colonialfilm.org.uk/node/1808 (accessed June 12, 2019).

20 This is how Viscount Lewis Harcourt, secretary of state for the colonies (1910–15), described West African urban environments in 1913 (PRO CO 879/112—No. 177 [295]).

21 Commiserating with his compatriots in West Africa, one British official in Nairobi described the sensory overload faced by Europeans in East African coastal towns: they "have their out-of-office hours rendered hideous by tom-toms, gramophones, street cries, goats, fowls, traffic, and native children," he complained, because their rented offices were in "immediate proximity to native property" (PRO CO 879/112—No. 75 [1913, 95]). At least West African government employees could enjoy "considerably higher salaries . . . for posts of equivalent responsibility on the East," he added with a note of envy (91).

22 PRO CO 879/62/13 (1900, 4).

23 PRO CO 592/3 (1906, 314).

24 Viscount Harcourt, secretary of state for the colonies, describing West African urban environments in his "Memorandum on the 'Segregation Principle' in West Africa" (PRO CO 879/112—No. 177 [1913, 295]).

25 See Oloko (2018).

26 LSHTM Ross 78/04 (1903, 15).

27 In an early example of public relations work, aimed not so much at destigmatizing general perceptions of the colonial night-soil man as eulogizing the "pariah," Ronald Ross wrote the following paean to sanitary workers in the British colonial world:

> Great is Sanitation—the greatest work, except discovery, I think, that a man can do. Here is a city seething with filth and disease. What is the use of preaching high moralities, philosophies, policies, and arts to people who dwell in these appalling slums—sometimes whole families of them crowded into one cell, mixed with cattle, vermin, and ordure? Your job, Sanitarian, is plain! You must wipe away those slums, that filth, these diseases. You shall work in the darkness while others sleep. None shall know of your labour, no one shall thank you, you shall die forgotten. The great ones of the earth shall despise you, shall hamper you, shall even punish you. The lofty rulers of the world shall not deign even to look at you; but shall prate of gods and virtues, liberties and laws. . . . But you, O Cleanser, shall always be a Pariah. Fret not, however; for these dying children shall live, and some day this hideous slum shall become a city of gardens and it is you who will have done it. (Ross 1922, 186)

> For all these fine words, as chapter 7 will discuss in more detail, Ross and his colonial colleagues—"lofty rulers" all—did little to address entrenched local convictions that contributed to the scarcity of sanitary labor in the early twentieth century.

28 This is not to set all traders against colonial officials, but to highlight the differences between travelers through and residents of African cities. As the example of Wilson clearly demonstrates, European traders who had settled in colonial cities were capable of violent and unchecked racial loathing.

29 LSHTM Ross 82/24 (1901, 10).

30 White (1990).

31 NNA CSO 26: File no. 30314 (1943, n.p.).

32 NNA CSO 26: File no. 30314 (1943, n.p.).

33 Webb (2014). Webb's study of malaria in sub-Saharan Africa contains a section on African antimalarial treatments (45–49). I am grateful to Michael Cappello, Professor of Pediatrics, Microbial Pathogenesis, and Public Health at the Yale School of Medicine, for providing the following clarification:

> All age groups contribute to transmission within communities. . . . Young children often experience higher burdens of infection and hence greater disease and mortality, up until they develop some degree of immunity. That's why early investigators assumed that they were the only reservoir, leading to the misguided attempts to segregate children as a means of protecting

others. However, the immunity does not protect people from infection, although it does make it far less likely that they will die from the disease. In that sense, the larger numbers of older children and adults walking around with asymptomatic infections are now recognized as a significant source of transmission to mosquitoes. So while the statement [that "children are neither more nor less likely to transmit the parasite to mosquitoes than adults"] . . . is probably true at the population level (i.e., both children and adults are responsible for transmission), it may not be true when looking at a single bite of a mosquito (i.e., heavily parasitized child vs. moderately parasitized adult). On this latter point, the fact is that we still don't really know. (personal communication, February 2019)

34 Webb (2014, 65–66) argues that infant mortality from malaria was often overlooked by European researchers in tropical Africa in favor of a view of infants as having acquired immunity in their first months of life.

35 PRO CO 879/112—No. 177 (1913, 294).

36 PRO CO 879/112—No. 177 (1913, 295). Harcourt was an "enthusiastic practising paedophile" and child pornographer until his suicide in 1922 after being exposed by the irate mother of one of his victims (Parris 1995).

37 Floyd (2014); Wynne (2015).

38 For a discussion of the connections between segregation, race, and hygiene, see Bashford (2004); Njoh ([2012] 2016).

39 PRO CO 879/112—No. 132b (1913, 197).

40 Webb (2014, 27–28); Seun (2015); Oluwasegun (2017).

41 Simpson (1909).

42 Ironically, the cosmopolitan Nigerian port city of Port Harcourt was named after Viscount Harcourt at the request of Lord Lugard.

43 PRO CO 879/112—No. 83 (1913, n.p.). See Bissell (2010) for analysis of similar approaches in colonial Zanzibar.

44 PRO CO 879/112—No. 177 (1913, 293). From this ideological starting point, Harcourt carefully prepared the ground for his proposed solution: racial segregation on grounds of health (294).

45 PRO CO 879/112—No. 177 (1913, 296).

46 PRO CO 879/112—No. 177 (1913, 296). The annual reports from the Nigerian Medical and Sanitary Department tell a different story about mortality. In the report for 1922, 7 European officials are reported to have died out of total resident population of 4,406, whereas 88 African officials died out of 2,706 (*Nigerian Pioneer*, January 25, 1924, 6).

47 Bragard (2018); Njoh (2008); Bissell (2010); Curtin (1985).

48 Gale (1980). For a study of West African newspapers' critiques of colonial racism, see Newell (2013).

49 PRO CO 879/112—No. 83 (1913, 114).

50 Clifford reiterated many of the points made by Governor William Mac-Gregor earlier in the century; see Oluwasegun (2017, 223–24).

51 PRO CO 879/112—No. 51a (1913, 55).

52 LSHTM Ross 76/21 (1902, 1).

53 Baderoon (2018).

54 M. Vaughan (1991, 43).

3. African Newspapers

1 Newell (2016).

2 For studies of West African newspapers in the colonial era, see Adebanwi (2016); Omu (1978); Newell (2013). Prosecutions for sedition were rare in British West Africa; when they occurred, they generated great publicity (see Newell 2013). In 1925, Thomas Horatio Jackson, one of the editors of the anticolonial *Lagos Weekly Record*, was sent to prison for six months with hard labor for an article accusing Mr. Justice Webber of government bias, rather than independent judgment, in the controversial "Eleko of Lagos" case. Legislation requiring editors to disclose the names of pseudonymous contributors was not passed until the early 1930s (Newell 2013).

3 PRO CO 879/112—No. 144 (1913, 143).

4 PRO CO 879/112—No. 133a (1913, 203).

5 Otero (2010). Patton (1996, 97) describes the unfulfilled British promises to the African settlers of Freetown, who were liberated slaves, including Nova Scotians who were promised land in return for their British loyalty in the American War of Independence. See Cole (2015, 250).

6 For a study of the Yoruba press, see Barber (2012). For studies of Nigerian newspapers and political engagement later in the colonial period, see Adebanwi (2016); Omu (1978).

7 See James (2015).

8 Bigon (2005, 254–55).

9 Bigon (2005).

10 See Omu (1978); Barber (2012); Newell (2013). Marcus Garvey's *Negro World* and George Padmore's *Negro Worker* were banned by colonial censors in the late 1920s (James 2015).

11 By 1924, there were fourteen newspapers in Nigeria with weekly circulations ranging from two hundred (*Advanced Opinion*) to two thousand (*Lagos Weekly Record*) (Omu 1978, 261).

12 Adebanwi (2016); Newell (2013). Several of the pro-colonial editors were "unofficial members" of the Legislative Council, and editors frequently used their newspapers as mouthpieces for their political parties.

13 Newell (2013).

14 The *Daily Times* was not the first Nigerian daily. One of the reasons it was established was to counter the *Lagos Daily News* (est. 1925), which it de-

scribed as a "purveyor of fictitious sensational news" (*Daily Times*, October 21, 1930, 4). With a strongly pro-European editorial voice, the *Daily Times* was one of the few West African newspapers to refer to "the natives" as a homogeneous block, as in "the natives love to harbor [smallpox] to their own detriment" (*Daily Times*, March 22, 1930, 3).

15 *Nigerian Pioneer*, January 25, 1924, 6.

16 *Nigerian Pioneer*, July 18, 1924, 8–9. For a discussion of one of the most significant crises of the mid-1920s in Lagos, the Eleko affair, see Barber (2016, 104–5).

17 *Nigerian Pioneer*, July 18, 1924, 8–9; see also October 23, 1925, 7. Ajasa was not alone in his views about Nigerians who had not passed through the colonial education system. In June 1924, the Nigerian *Spectator* (1923–30), founded and edited by the physician and fellow gradualist on the topic of decolonization, Dr. Richard Akinwande Savage (1874–1935), was of the opinion that "the voice of the majority is sometimes the voice of the devil itself" (cited in *Nigerian Pioneer*, June 27, 1924, 6). The conservative press carefully avoided references to W. E. B. Du Bois, except for articles on why Du Bois failed (he was seen as too dogmatic).

18 *Nigerian Pioneer*, October 23, 1925, 7.

19 *Nigerian Pioneer*, June 27, 1924, 6. See also editorials in the *Nigerian Pioneer*, November 14, 1924, 8; February 13, 1925, 8; May 22, 1925, 8. The first African to be knighted, Ajasa held a leadership position in the conservative People's Union Party (est. 1908). The *Nigerian Pioneer* reserved its "highest," most alliterative language for condemnations of John Payne Jackson's *Lagos Weekly Record*. Thus, in November 1924, the editor condemned "the pursuit, by these persons, of the meaner passions of their nature, of their petulant arrogance and diseased vanity—all under the guise of patriotism" (November 14, 1924, 8). In July 1925, he attacked the editors of the *Record* for their "obnoxious exhibition of mendacity, misrepresentations and misconceptions" (July 3, 1925, 8). Ajasa used his full arsenal of English bombast to belittle his political enemies and attack the leadership credentials of his opponents. While his vision of the masses was extreme, it also encapsulated other editors' beliefs in the leadership role played by the press.

20 Izomoh (1994, 4, 18).

21 *Nigerian Pioneer*, July 2, 1926.

22 Dr. I. Ladipo Oluwole in the *Nigerian Pioneer*, November 5, 1926, 4, 6.

23 *Eko Akete*, May 9, 1925, 9.

24 *Eko Akete*, May 9, 1925, 7.

25 "Atari Ajanaku," *Eko Akete*, May 9, 1925, 8. "Atari Ajanaku" are the opening words of a popular Yoruba proverb, *Àtàrí àjànàkú kìí ṣẹrù ọmọdé*, which refers to the elephant's cranium being too heavy for a child to carry or play with, meaning some matters are too weighty for inexperienced people to handle

appropriately. Karin Barber notes the quarrel in the Yoruba newspapers about whether this was one of Herbert Macaulay's pseudonyms (2016, 111). *Eko Akete* had a circulation of 1,500 in 1925, rising to 1,600 in May 1925 (May 9, 1925, 9).

26 *Eko Akete*, March 7, 1925, 8. Karin Barber notes that this was "one of repeated efforts by the Yoruba newspapers to get the Lagos Town Council and government to attend to the poorer areas of Lagos. The pot-holed and untarred roads suffered from flooding and became impassable during the rainy season." Deniga's complaint was, in her view, not so much an endorsement of imperialist health and hygiene ideology as the expression of "disgruntlement on behalf of the poor" (personal communication, July 2018).

27 *Nigerian Pioneer*, February 15, 1924, 6.

28 *Nigerian Pioneer*, October 3, 1924, 8.

29 LSHTM Ross 83/02 (1901).

30 *Nigerian Pioneer*, January 25, 1924, 6.

31 *Nigerian Pioneer*, November 5, 1926, 8.

32 In October 1925, *Eko Akete* published an open letter to Dr. Thomas Blane Adam, the acting director of sanitary and medical services in Lagos, condemning his and others' arguments for racial segregation on grounds of health (October 17, 1925, 7). Ajasa never attacked European officials in this way.

33 In his study of colonial sanitation and hygiene in Freetown in the early twentieth century, Festus Cole discusses how "by 1916 'filth' was a regular feature of life in Freetown. The condition of Smythe Street, in the west end, was [according to official reports] 'loathsome and disease creating,' punctuated by 'a mosquito factory,' a 'frog depot,' 'stagnant pools' and 'the evils attendant to health and human life'" (2015, 244).

34 Olukoju (2004). For a history of the Nigerian railway, see Ayoola (2016); Jaekel (1997). For discussion of earlier outbreaks of bubonic plague, see Echenberg (2007).

35 *Eko Akete*, May 9, 1925, 10.

36 The 1931 census figures are analyzed by Perham (1933). The Nigerian *Daily Times* published regular tables of new cases of plague deaths in Lagos, with revisions to previous estimates: by October 1930, as the epidemic tailed off, the official figures were given as 46 deaths in 1930, 86 deaths in 1929, 342 deaths in 1928, 102 deaths in 1927, and 323 deaths in 1926 (*Daily Times*, October 21, 1930, 4). This can be compared with fatalities from the influenza epidemic that swept the United States in the winter of 1928–29, with 50,000 deaths recorded (Collins 1930, 120).

37 Bigon (2016).

38 See Gray (1910, 387); Schneider (2009).

39 Luggage in first class was treated differently from luggage in third class,

and all Africans had their goods disinfected whether in first class or not (CSO 26: File no. 13001a; CSO 26: File no. 13001b).

40 For those with sufficient cash, within a month of the outbreak forgeries of these "red tickets" could be purchased for two shillings in the streets (*Nigerian Pioneer*, September 5, 1924, 4).

41 *Nigerian Pioneer*, July 25, 1924, 6.

42 *Nigerian Pioneer*, July 25, 1924, 6.

43 *Nigerian Pioneer*, August 8, 1924, 6, 9.

44 Speaking for African business and trade interests, conservative newspaper editors were far more vocal than government officials about the economic, rather than the health, rationale for investment in sanitary infrastructure. While the effects of plague were largely confined to poor urban districts, the effects of quarantine on trade were a terrible blow to many local business people.

45 *New York Herald Tribune*, April 12, 1925, 19.

46 *Nigerian Pioneer*, April 17, 1925, 6. In fact, a second Reuters telegram was issued one day after the first, reinstating the visit to Nigeria "in view of the intense disappointment caused in Nigeria by the news of the abandonment of the Prince's tour" (*Guardian*, April 13, 1925, 12).

47 *Nigerian Pioneer*, March 27, 1925, 6.

48 *Nigerian Pioneer*, March 27, 1925, 6.

49 Economic and infrastructural advances in the Gold Coast were followed with a keenly competitive and critical eye by the business and political community in Nigeria.

50 *Nigerian Pioneer*, October 2, 1925, 7.

51 *Nigerian Pioneer*, August 28, 1924, 6; September 5, 8.

52 *Nigerian Pioneer*, October 3, 1924, 8. In spite of frequent discussion, during the plague outbreak, of the purchase of land at Yaba for an ambitious African housing scheme, it was not until the mid-1940s, with the rise of welfarism in the U.K., that the government financed housing schemes such as that at Yaba. Proposals always expressed concerns about local chiefs' ownership of the land and the complexity of negotiations for land purchase.

53 *Nigerian Pioneer*, October 3, 1924, 8.

54 *Nigerian Pioneer*, November 21, 1924, 8. The "garden city" concept, introduced to Britain in the 1890s, with its emphasis on open public spaces, influenced Nigerian urban planners over the course of the twentieth century and into the twenty-first, from Ikoyi in Lagos for European residency in the 1920s to Victoria Garden City in Lekki today.

55 *Nigerian Pioneer*, August 28, 1924, 6.

56 *Nigerian Pioneer*, August 28, 1924, 6.

57 *Nigerian Pioneer*, October 31, 1924, 3.

58 *Nigerian Pioneer*, October 31, 1924, 3. See Burke (1996); McClintock (1995).

59 See, e.g., Dr. J. Everett Dutton's description of racial types in the Gambia: "The Jollofs and Mandingoes . . . are much superior to those met with in Nigeria. They are very clean" (LSHTM Ross 75/05 [1906, n.p.]).

60 See chapters 6 and 7.

61 No evidence could be found of overt religious bias in the English-language press.

62 *Nigerian Pioneer*, February 13, 1925, 8.

63 *Nigerian Pioneer*, March 18, 1927, 6 (emphasis in original).

64 For Ajasa, dirt and contamination were located in the spaces occupied by "itinerant hawkers of foodstuffs" in Lagos, who rendered the anti-rat campaigns futile by throwing unsold vegetables into the drains at the end of each day and needed to be removed into enclosed markets (*Nigerian Pioneer*, April 29, 1927, 3). Similar associations of hawkers with insanitary behavior a century later motivated Akinwunmi Ambode, the governor of Lagos State, to enforce a total ban on street hawking in 2016.

65 *Nigerian Pioneer*, September 5, 1924, 3.

66 *Nigerian Pioneer*, May 22, 1925, 12.

67 MIR-m-121, interviewed by Olutoyosi Tokun.

68 MIR-m-121, interviewed by Olutoyosi Tokun.

69 MIR-m-121, interviewed by Olutoyosi Tokun. Other proverbs relating to rats include, *tí òkété bá dàgbà tán, ọmú ọmọ rẹ̀ ló ń mú* ("When the giant rat grows old, it feeds on the milk of its young ones"), and *kàkà kí eku má je sèsé, á fi se àwàdànù* ("If the rat cannot eat the beans, it will render them useless [by urinating on them] rather than leaving the sack for somebody else to eat"). See Fasoro (2012, 258); Faleti (2013, 237).

70 "Interim Report by the Director of Medical and Sanitary Service, Nov 20 1925," cited by Olutoyosi Tokun (Project Researcher's Report, August 5, 2016, n.p.).

71 *Daily Times* (Nigeria), March 22, 1930, 4.

72 "Discussions of government response to epidemics in the Yoruba papers included resistance to *kọrọnti* (quarantine) and complaints about the intervention of public health officials in funerals—they would apparently take the body away to the cemetery in Ikeja before the pre-burial rites had been completed. Being taken to Ikeja [therefore] meant both being taken to the hospital and also being buried in the Ikeja cemetery" (Karin Barber, personal communication, July 2018).

4. Screening Dirt

Epigraph: William Sellers quoted in Strickland (1940, 211).

1 Mamdani (2012); Said (1978).

2 PRO CO 875/10/11 (1943, B17).

3 PRO CO 875/10/11 (1943, B17).

4 NNA CSO 26: File no. 30314 (1937, 2).

5 Ambler (2001).

6 *Colonial Cinema* (1947); PRO CO 875/52/3 (1952–53).

7 Larkin (2008); Reynolds (2015).

8 NNA CSO 26: File no. 30314 (1937, 3); PRO CO 1045/227a (1940, 4).

9 Meyer (2015, 41–42); Garritano (2013, 27–28); Ambler (2001).

10 PRO CO 875/10/4a (1943, 1). For studies of cinema in French West Africa in this period, see Diawara (1992); Frindéthié (2009); Ouoro (2011); Stoller (1992).

11 PRO CO 875/10/4a (1943, 1).

12 PRO CO 875/10/4b (1943).

13 PRO CO 875/10/4a (1943, 1); PRO CO 875/10/4b (1943, 3); Ambler (2001). A detailed account of double-censorship can be found in Newell (2016); for discussions of Hollywood movies in southern Africa, see Reynolds (2015, 89–115).

14 Most sources list 1929 for the release of *Plague*, but Sellers claimed to have toured Nigeria with the film in 1926 (Sellers 1953, 830).

15 PRO CO 1045/227a (1940, 1). Release dates are not available for most of Sellers's amateur movies in the late 1920s and early 1930s.

16 See Commission on Educational and Cultural Films (1932, 115); Smyth (2013); Larkin (2008, 77).

17 NNA CSO 26: File no. 30314 (1937, 1938). See Larkin (2008).

18 Huxley ([1931] 1936, 59–60).

19 Smyth (2008).

20 PRO CO 1045/227a (1940, 8).

21 PRO CO 1045/227a (1940, 3).

22 Morton-Williams (ca. 1953, 134).

23 Morton-Williams (ca. 1953, 73). See Larkin (2008).

24 Unfortunately, these log books could not be located in the national archives of Nigeria or the U.K., nor was it possible to locate the materials referred to by information officers in British African colonies when they claimed to have read "over a thousand" essays on the topic. See "Which film did you like best and why?" in PRO CO 875/10/11, B16.

25 PRO CO 1045/227a (1940, 1).

26 PRO CO 1045/227a (1940, 2). See Larkin (2008); Smyth (2013). By 1950, the CFU boasted twelve production units in eight British African territories, with a total of 339 reels circulating for free in the colonies; see PRO CO 875/52/3 (1952–53, 35). For a detailed history of the changing faces of the CFU between 1939 and the early 1950s, see Smyth (2011, 155–75).

27 *Colonial Cinema* (1947, 27).

28 Reynolds (2015, 171–95). For a discussion of missionary- and Christian-sponsored films intended for African audiences, see Reynolds (2015, 79–83).

For research into Hollywood films in West African cities in the 1930s, see Newell (2002).

29 This short film was reworked by the original filmmaker, Sellers, in 1937 as *Anti-Plague Operations in Lagos*, including new footage of scenes from the Infant Welfare Exhibition in Lagos (the film can be viewed at http://www.colonialfilm.org.uk/node/1526; M. Vaughan [1991]).

30 Burns (2000).

31 See Burns (2000); Smyth (2011; 2013).

32 McClintock (1995); Burke (1996).

33 Alongside the figure of the blundering chief, this pantomime baddie appears as a stock type in several CFU films, most famously *Mr Wise and Mr Foolish Go to Town* (1944) and *Amenu's Child* (1950). He appears as the evil "Rainmaker" in the instructional film *Fear to Faith* (1946, Southern Rhodesia), sponsored by the Religious Film Society for British audiences. Often holding a fly whisk as the symbol of his primitiveness, this figure is influenced less by empirical observation than by the portrayal of African authority figures in pro-colonial movies and novels such as the Korda Brothers' adaptation of Edgar Wallace's *Sanders of the River* (1935), where the bad chief, King Mofolaba, is characterized by his fly whisk. Interestingly, similar stock figures pervade Nigerian popular literature and Nollywood films such as *Ebola in Kingdom* (2015)—a topic ripe for further research.

34 NNA CSO 26: File no. 30314 (1938, n.p.).

35 NNA CSO 26: File no. 30314 (1938, n.p.).

36 NNA CSO 26: File no. 30314 (1938, n.p.).

37 NNA CSO 26: File no. 30314 (1938, n.p.). Sellers had been invited to the podium during C. F. Strickland's lecture titled "Instructional Films in India" at the Royal Society of Arts. He showed clips from *Machi Gaba*, performed sections of the voice-over, and described Nigerian audience reactions.

38 NNA CSO 26: File no.30314 (1938, n.p.).

39 NNA CSO 26: File no.30314 (1938, n.p.).

40 PRO CO 1045/227b (n.d. [1951], 9).

41 PRO CO 1045/227a (1940, 6).

42 PRO CO 1045/227a (1940, 6). In practice, Sellers's pre-scripted commentaries were subject to great variation. In Yoruba areas of Nigeria, for example, alterations were required to the commentator's original English script when the film *Smallpox* was shown, not least a modification of the recommendation for infant vaccination at the age of three months, for no Yoruba adult would allow a baby to be injected before it was at least one year—and more probably five years—old.

43 PRO CO 1045/227a (1940, 6).

44 Larkin (2008, 100).

45 PRO CO 1045/227a (1940, 6).

46 PRO CO 875/10/11 (1943, A1, 6).

47 PRO CO 875/10/11 (1943, A1, 6).

48 PRO CO 875/10/11 (1943, A1, 6).

49 A focus group in Lagos in April 2015 contained a fascinating critique, by a Yoruba man, of Igbo Nollywood film producers' representations of eastern Nigerian traditions and what he saw as the responsibilities of movie-makers to educate viewers in positive aspects of Igbo culture:

The thing is that the Igbo have failed to show us their culture in a positive way. The only way the Yorùbá and other Nigerians can access their real tradition is in movies; but unfortunately the only platform they have is what they use to show the negative parts of their tradition—which is doing juju, getting angry with your brother that is progressing, poisoning this person with your eyes, shaving hair [of widows] and drinking water [out of a dead body]. . . . You know, the only platform we have to see your tradition, see your culture, you show us evil in it. (FGD-23-28, interviewed by John Uwa)

The response from an Igbo man in the focus group was to say, "trust me, things are getting better, people are getting more aware and civilized, and some of these cultures are being taken out of the system" (FGD-23-28, interviewed by John Uwa). Nobody challenged whether these Igbo filmmakers' exaggerated representations were of "real tradition"; rather, participants agreed that such traditions have "faded with time and civilization" (FGD-23-28, interviewed by John Uwa).

50 Morton-Williams (ca. 1953, 72).

51 PRO CO 875/52/3 (1952–53).

52 PRO CO 875/52/3 (1952–53, 38).

53 Pearson (1948, 26).

54 Pearson (1948, 26; emphasis in original).

55 PRO CO 875/10/11 (1943, D21).

56 For a discussion of the sexual health movie *Mr Wise and Mr Foolish Go to Town*, see Burns (2000); Reynolds (2015).

57 PRO CO 1045/227a (1940, 8).

58 L. H. Ross, cited in Burns (2000, 200).

59 Beale (1948, 19).

60 Morton-Williams (ca. 1953, 42).

61 Morton-Williams (ca. 1953, 44–45).

62 PRO CO 875/52/3 (1951, 39), PRO CO 875/10/13 (1943, 32), NNA CSO 26: File no. 30314 (1937, n.p.).

63 PRO CO 875/10/11 (1943, D21).

64 PRO CO 875/10/11 (1943, D21).

65 PRO CO 875/10/11 (1943, D21).

66 Morton-Williams (ca. 1953, 65–66)

67 Morton-Williams (ca. 1953, 66).

68 Morton-Williams (ca. 1953, 66).

69 Morton-Williams (ca. 1953, 64, 70, 72, 76).

70 Morton-Williams (ca. 1953, 74).

71 Morton Williams (ca. 1953, 42).

72 See Stein (2013, 315–45).

73 Morton-Williams (ca. 1953, 72).

74 Morton-Williams (ca. 1953, 79).

75 Morton-Williams (ca. 1953, 31).

76 Morton-Williams (ca. 1953, 78).

77 Morton Williams (ca. 1953, 78).

78 Morton-Williams (ca. 1953, 79).

79 In 1940, a similar failure of "authenticity" was given as the reason for audiences' laughter in northern Nigeria. L. H. Ross noted that people laughed not because of their "primitive psychology" but because the village portrayed in *Machi Gaba* was implausible; it was "so utterly miserable, so utterly destitute" that it failed to "arouse the sympathy and understanding of the audience" (cited in Burns [2000, 200]). Charles Ambler describes how when *Cry, the Beloved Country* was screened in the Zambian Copperbelt, "uproarious laughter greeted the scene in which the wealthy white landowner Mr Jarvis is informed of the murder of his son and audience members were 'visibly delighted when Mrs Jarvis was grief-stricken at the news of the death of her son,'" leading to the demand "we want cowboys" in place of *Cry, the Beloved Country* (Ambler 2001, 98). Ambler (2001, 98) says this laughter was not an expression of antiwhite political sentiment; audience members were less interested in character or plot than "extreme facial expressions," which caused laughter.

80 Stein (2013).

81 Morton-Williams (ca. 1953, 53). Among Berom audiences, one man commented wittily at this scene, "Why didn't he remember God before?" (Morton-Williams ca. 1953, 55).

82 Morton-Williams (ca. 1953, 29).

83 Morton-Williams (ca. 1953, 136).

84 Morton-Williams (ca. 1953, 136).

85 Morton-Williams (ca. 1953, 27).

86 Morton-Williams (ca. 1953, 60).

87 Morton-Williams (ca. 1953, 59).

88 The word "foolish" is repeated countless times in the British voice-overs of Christian missionary and colonial health films intended for African spectators. See *Towards Wholeness* (1952), made by the Overseas Film Unit of the Church Missionary Society.

89 Morton-Williams (ca. 1953, 30).

90 Morton-Williams (ca. 1953, 31).

91 See Newell (2002).

92 PRO CO 875/10/4b (1943, 1–2).

93 PRO CO 875/10/11 (1943, A1); Hofmeyr (2003).

94 PRO CO 875/10/11 (1943, 5).

95 Morton-Williams (ca. 1953, 5).

96 PRO CO 875/10/11 (1943, A1, 6, A2, 1).

97 PRO CO 875/10/11 (1943, D21).

98 PRO CO 875/10/11 (1943, D21, A2, 2).

99 PRO CO 875/10/11 (1943, D21, A2, 2).

100 PRO CO 875/10/11 (1943, D21, A2, 2).

101 Dickie (2011, 49).

102 Dickie (2011, 49).

103 African audiences were often highly alert to making faux pas in the face of foreign films and controlled their own reactions accordingly. One of the more sensitive observers who worked for the CFU, Norman F. Spurr, noted of one rural Tanzanian audience's responses to the South African musical film *Zonk*, "The most surprising reaction was the almost complete absence of chatter . . . there was almost silence. This suggested at first glance that the film was not being followed in the sense that even visually it made no sense, or that it was not liked. Nothing was further from the truth" (PRO CO 875/51/7a [1950, 4]).

104 See M. Vaughan (1991).

105 PRO CO 875/10/11 (1943, A2, 3). When the colonial secretary, Arthur Creech-Jones, gave the opening address at the British Film Institute conference "The Film in Colonial Development" in March 1948, he attempted to prize open the hermetically sealed colonial optic. "Sometimes," he suggested, "I have been told that, for practical purposes, a primitive African audience is quite as appreciative, say, of the antics of Charlie Chaplin as is the British audience (there is a certain common humanity there) but we do not know really the effects of films on the unsophisticated, the general reaction, nor are we quite happy about the place of commercial films and whether it is altogether wise in certain societies for the modern British or American film to be introduced at all" (Creech-Jones 1948, 6).

106 Morton-Williams (ca. 1953, 52); Smyth (2013, 96).

107 Morton-Williams (ca. 1953, 53).

108 Morton-Williams (ca. 1953, 59).

109 PRO CO 1045/227a (1940, 4). See Potter (2012).

110 PRO CO 875/51/7b (1950, 1).

111 PRO CO 875/51/7b (1950, 6).

112 Ambler (2001, 101).

5. Methods

Epigraph: Joseph Conrad ([1899] 1922, 137–38).

1 Morton-Williams (ca. 1953).
2 See also Reynolds (2015, 125–26).
3 CO 875/51/7a (1950, n.p.).
4 NNA CSO 26: File no. 30314 (1937, 2).
5 Warner (2002, 65–70).
6 Warner (2002, 67, 72, 88; emphasis in original).
7 Larkin (2008).
8 Larkin (2008, 94, 99).
9 Larkin (2008, 85).
10 Larkin (2008, 94).
11 Larkin (2008, 80).
12 Larkin (2008, 86).
13 See NNA CSO 26: File no. 303143 (1937, 3); PRO CO 1045/227a (1940, 4).
14 Warner (2002, 68). It is important to note that Warner does not offer his theory of publics and counterpublics as a universal account of public spaces applicable across cultures or histories.
15 Larkin (2008, 77–78); Burns (2000).
16 Hartley (1987, 5).
17 Larkin (2008, 89).
18 One of the few exceptions to this is Procter and Benwell (2015).
19 Morton-Williams (ca. 1953, 137).
20 hooks (1992, 128). See also Diawara (1988).
21 Reynolds (2015, 2).
22 Sherzer (1996, 2).
23 James Burns regards the voluminous archives of British speculation about African audiences as forming a body of "colonial film spectatorship theory" (Burns 2000).
24 I am indebted to Michael Veal for this observation.
25 Morton-Williams (ca. 1953, 30).
26 Morton-Williams (ca. 1953, 91).
27 Morton-Williams (ca. 1953, 165).
28 PRO CO 875/51/7c (1950, 6). These are the same colonial subjects who were condemned as mimics by colonial educators (see Newell 2002).
29 Spivak (1988, 271–313). In practice, there was no rigid divide between rural and urban areas, as individuals exercised a great deal of geographical mobility in colonial West Africa; there was no "native permit" system as in the settler colonies of East and southern Africa.
30 See Gikandi (2012, 309–28).
31 Willems (2014, 80–96).

32 See Peterson, Hunter, and Newell (2016).

33 Willems (2014, 80).

34 Morton-Williams (ca. 1953, 49–52, 65).

35 Peterson (2013, 4).

36 Morton-Williams (ca. 1953, 57).

37 Smyth (2011).

38 See, e.g., WREC (2015).

6. Popular Perceptions of "Dirty"

1 New Humanitarian (2006); Gandy (2006, 371). The Nigerian project team of researchers was based at the University of Lagos and conducted the interviews between February 2014 and December 2016.

2 Reynolds (2015); Quayson (2014).

3 Permits to carry out research in health centers and schools were obtained from the relevant government departments. Informed consent was obtained from gatekeepers and stakeholders and from each of the individuals interviewed for the project. Prior to the commencement of research, ethical clearance was obtained from the research ethics committees of the European Research Council (ERC) and the University of Lagos. For a team-authored account of these ethical considerations and challenges in the field, see Newell et al. (2018).

4 NEPA, or the National Electric Power Authority, is the old name for the Power Holding Company of Nigeria, but it is still widely used.

5 The Private Sector Participation scheme is discussed in chapter 7.

6 ES-f-47, interviewed by Jane Nebe.

7 Olutoyosi Tokun, Project Researcher Report (August 8, 2014, n.p.).

8 PHW-n-107, interviewed by Olutoyosi Tokun.

9 PHW-n-109, interviewed by Olutoyosi Tokun.

10 MIR-f-36, interviewed by John Uwa.

11 The term "scavenger" is discussed in chapter 7.

12 PHW-n-109, interviewed by Olutoyosi Tokun.

13 PHW-f-117, interviewed by Olutoyosi Tokun.

14 MIR-f-36, interviewed by John Uwa.

15 PHW-f-110, interviewed by Olutoyosi Tokun.

16 MIR-m-105, interviewed by Olutoyosi Tokun.

17 FGD-7–11, interviewed by John Uwa.

18 FGD-7–11, interviewed by John Uwa.

19 FGD-40–42, interviewed by John Uwa.

20 MIR-m-105, interviewed by Olutoyosi Tokun.

21 PHW-f-106, interviewed by Olutoyosi Tokun.

22 PHW-n-107, interviewed by Olutoyosi Tokun.

23 PHU-m-61, interviewed by Olutoyosi Tokun.

24 FGD-23–28, interviewed by John Uwa. Many people pointed out that Yoruba contains many foul words and phrases. Some blamed touts and bus drivers in Lagos for turning it into a "gutter language"; others blamed Lagosian common parlance, such as when friends may greet each other using insults, or respond to one another with "*Orí ẹ bàjẹ́ ni? Orí ẹ dàrú ni?*" (Is your brain faulty? Are you mentally unstable?) and "*Olórí burúkú ni ẹ́, orí ẹ ti*" (You are an unfortunate person). Out of more than 120 interviews in Yoruba and English, however, only one woman and one man used the word "fuck" in English, further illustrating the effects of the environment produced by our interview processes.

25 Misc-m-114, interviewed by Olutoyosi Tokun.

26 Misc-m-114, interviewed by Olutoyosi Tokun.

27 FGD-7–11, interviewed by John Uwa.

28 FGD-23–28, interviewed by John Uwa.

29 MW-f-12, interviewed by John Uwa.

30 MW-f-12, interviewed by John Uwa.

31 LIR-2m-20–21, interviewed by John Uwa.

32 LIR-2m-20–21, interviewed by John Uwa.

33 FGD-15–19, interviewed by John Uwa.

34 Olufemi Vaughan argues that Yoruba-speaking nationalist leaders worked hard to construct a "new pan-Yoruba communal identity" in the 1950s, bringing together conflicting "myths, traditions and local histories, centered on chieftaincy institutions" (2000, 20).

35 LIR-mf-34–35, interviewed by John Uwa. Yoruba: locust beans came, cooked melon-seeds came, that is, all and sundry came. This is an established Yoruba saying to indicate variety.

36 MW-m-39, interviewed by John Uwa.

37 SG-m-54, interviewed by Jane Nebe.

38 LIR-mf-34–35, interviewed by John Uwa.

39 Newell et al. (2018, 262).

40 FGD-40–42, interviewed by John Uwa.

41 Newell et al. (2018, 265).

42 Faluyi Muyiwa, interviewed by John Uwa (June 5, 2015).

43 Faluyi Muyiwa, interviewed by John Uwa (June 5, 2015).

44 Faluyi Muyiwa, interviewed by John Uwa (June 5, 2015). For discussion of the *agbẹ́pòò*, or night-soil worker, see chapter 7.

45 Misc-m-22, interviewed by John Uwa.

46 Curtis (2007). See also Menninghaus (2003).

47 Curtis (2007; 2013).

48 Curtis (2003).

49 Curtis (2003).

50 Olutoyosi Tokun, Project Researcher Report (December 16, 2016, n.p.).

51 PHU-f-63, interviewed by Olutoyosi Tokun.

52 MIR-m-105, interviewed by Olutoyosi Tokun.

53 HS-f-55, interviewed by Jane Nebe.

54 PHW-f-110, interviewed by Olutoyosi Tokun.

55 "Shot-put" involves directing urine and feces into a "nylon" (plastic bag), ty-
ing a knot at the top, and throwing it in the vicinity of a canal or drain. In
low-income settlements in Nairobi, this is known as the "flying toilet."

56 Punch (2002); Nesbitt (2000).

57 Newell et al. (2018, 252).

58 ES-f-57, interviewed by Jane Nebe.

59 ES-f-57, interviewed by Jane Nebe.

60 ES-f-57, interviewed by Jane Nebe.

61 ES-f-57, interviewed by Jane Nebe.

62 These stories were not confined to schoolchildren. A female media worker
aged 25–35 described how the recent death of a king in Ikeja led to a curfew
among residents who were afraid that "if you are caught walking around
late, you might be unlucky to lose your head. They [Yoruba] still practice it!
It is a dirty practice . . . it is diabolical, barbaric, because it's the twenty-first
century for crying out loud!" (interview, MW-f-37). Other interviewees told
stories about Igbo cannibalism.

63 Yoruba: ulcer. Sense unclear in this usage.

64 ES-f-52, interviewed by Jane Nebe.

65 ES-f-47, interviewed by Jane Nebe.

66 ES-f-57, interviewed by Jane Nebe.

67 All the girls interviewed for this study were from low-income neighborhoods. Some of them had witnessed sexual assaults on girls by "area boys,"
and some of the older girls lived in terror of rape (interview, ES-f-47). Nearly
all of the children and young people interviewed for this project had experienced the death of a parent or sibling.

68 See Gandy (2006).

69 HS-f-55, interviewed by Jane Nebe.

70 HS-f-55, interviewed by Jane Nebe.

71 De Boeck and Plissart (2004, 155–56).

72 De Boeck and Plissart (2004, 156–57).

73 ES-f-47, interviewed by Jane Nebe. This participant was still in elementary
school in spite of her age as a result of numerous relocations and removals
from schools during her childhood.

74 TS-m-87, interviewed by Olutoyosi Tokun.

75 Hausa, Igbo, and other Nigerian-language participants chose to be interviewed in English.

76 MIR-m-101, interviewed by Olutoyosi Tokun.

77 LIR-m-78, interviewed by Olutoyosi Tokun.

78 MIR-m-82, interviewed by Olutoyosi Tokun.

79 TS-m-87, interviewed by Olutoyosi Tokun.

80 TS-m-87, interviewed by Olutoyosi Tokun.

81 WW-m-92, interviewed by Olutoyosi Tokun.

82 PHW-m-97, interviewed by Olutoyosi Tokun.

83 PrWW-f-73, interviewed by Olutoyosi Tokun. This professionalized recycling mentality has a long history in West Africa. Colonial sanitary inspectors complained regularly about the health hazards caused by the retention of tin cans, bottles, and other discarded receptacles in African households as storage vessels for water or for use as containers for products such as palm oil and groundnuts (see chapter 1). Seen through the lenses of today's recycling culture, such people were the first "zero waste" entrepreneurs in Nigeria (PrWW-f-73, interviewed by Olutoyosi Tokun).

84 PHU-f-63, interviewed by Olutoyosi Tokun.

85 PHW-m-97, interviewed by Olutoyosi Tokun.

86 PHW-n-107, interviewed by Olutoyosi Tokun.

87 LIR-m-72, interviewed by Olutoyosi Tokun.

88 PHW-m-93, interviewed by Olutoyosi Tokun.

89 FGD-40–42, interviewed by John Uwa.

90 SG-f-56, interviewed by Jane Nebe.

91 FGD-7–11, interviewed by John Uwa.

92 PHW-f-100, interviewed by Olutoyosi Tokun.

93 MW-m-43, interviewed by John Uwa.

94 Douglas (1966, 117–40).

95 FGD-40–42, interviewed by John Uwa.

96 FGD-40–42, interviewed by John Uwa.

97 In her PhD dissertation on "the politics and poetics of electricity" in Accra during the electricity crisis of 2014–16, Pauline Destrée analyzes the ways in which words connoting "brightness" indicate people's social and economic success or aspirations. Her work can be used to shed new light—literally—on the recurrent motif of the "gleam" in Ayi Kwei Armah's iconic novel of postcolonial political and urban deterioration, *The Beautyful Ones Are Not Yet Born* (1968).

98 FGD-23–28, interviewed by John Uwa.

99 FGD-23–28, interviewed by John Uwa. Three interviewees mentioned the violence at Ketu/Mile 12 Market in March 2016 when at least fifteen people were killed. This is a prominent market in Lagos where people from different ethnic groups buy and sell goods. Problems arose when the long-standing Hausa market heads were challenged by a group of Yoruba traders. See Eribake (2016b).

100 See Korieh (2013) and Onuoha (2016) for examinations of the role played by ethnic labeling as well as ethno-nationalism in the Biafran conflict.

101 Misc-m-88, interviewed by Olutoyosi Tokun.

102 Aliyi and Amadu (2017, 149–58); Oke et al. (2017); Olorunfemi (2007).

103 The exact population of Lagos is disputed. According to the online World Population Review 2018, "the Lagos State Government estimates the population of Lagos at 17.5 million, although this number has been disputed by the Nigerian Government and found to be unreliable by the National Population Commission of Nigeria, which put the population at over 21 million in 2016." "Lagos Population," World Population Review, http://worldpopulationreview.com/world-cities/lagos-population/ (accessed April 29, 2018).

104 HIR-f-83, MIR-m-86, MIR-m-82, HW-m-92, interviewed by Olutoyosi Tokun.

105 MIR-m-105, interviewed by Olutoyosi Tokun.

7. Remembering Waste

Epigraph: Jackson and Robins (2018, 73).

1 Anderson (2010).

2 MW-f-44, interviewed by John Uwa.

3 BBC, *Welcome to Lagos* (2010, episode 2; emphasis in script).

4 BBC, *Welcome to Lagos* (2010, episode 1).

5 Anderson (2010).

6 BBC, *Welcome to Lagos* (2010, episode 3).

7 The use of trash for land reclamation is nothing new in African cities. In his *Lagos Report* of 1909, Professor W. J. Simpson complained that "in a number of instances . . . the compounds of the houses were being raised by the deposit of garbage and refuse from the streets instead of clean sand. Some of the refuse that was supposed to be taken into the middle of the Lagoon and dumped into the water was finding its way instead into the compounds and was being used in the manner described. Practices of this kind can only lead to a very unhealthy state of things. They should be stopped by the enforcement of strict regulations and by regular inspection" (Simpson 1909, 71–72). One of our interviewees, a literacy facilitator for children in an informal settlement named "Dustbin Estate," said of her working environment, "I work on the refuse dump so it's like the raw material in which I build things. . . . My kids see waste as bare floor; they can play with it, jog on it, sleep on it, go to the toilet on it. In this community right now, it's a necessity for them to have waste because this people cannot afford to buy sand . . . right now it's not waste in this community: it is useful" (NGO-f-120, interviewed by Olutoyosi Tokun). Her comments explain the common saying in Lagos that there is "too much dirt under soil" (Misc-m-22, interviewed by John Uwa).

8 Wren (1924, 6).

9 Morton-Williams (ca. 1953, 162).

10 Cited in Dowell (2010).

11 MW-f-44, interviewed by John Uwa.

12 Anderson (2010).

13 Nwaubani (2010).

14 Economist Intelligence Unit (2017).

15 Newell et al. (2018).

16 Newell et al. (2018).

17 The Yoruba proverb in the subhead above literally means "the dump does not reject any form of refuse." This proverb describes an exceptionally tolerant person who does not want to hurt the feelings of others and who listens and accepts whatever comes his/her way. It may also describe a leader who listens too much to others, thus allowing sycophants to gain power, and who does not act decisively (Ayọ̀ Yusuff, interviewed by Olutoyosi Tokun [March 24, 2016]).

18 PHU-m-61, interviewed by Olutoyosi Tokun.

19 Oloko (2018, 61).

20 Oloko (2018, 61).

21 Oloko (2018, 61–62).

22 Ayọ̀ Yusuff, interviewed by Olutoyosi Tokun (March 24, 2016).

23 Ayọ̀ Yusuff, interviewed by Olutoyosi Tokun (March 24, 2016).

24 PHW-n-107, interviewed by Olutoyosi Tokun.

25 PHU-m-64, interviewed by Olutoyosi Tokun. Karin Barber suggested the metaphor of the tumor (personal communication, July 2013).

26 The dump is not entirely cut off. Olukoju notes that traditionally people would retrieve items for ritual use from the dump, or they would collect ceramic pieces for use in household decoration (Olukoju 2018).

27 PHW-m-97, interviewed by Olutoyosi Tokun.

28 Interviewed by Olutoyosi Tokun (March 24, 2016).

29 MIR-2m-68–69, interviewed by Olutoyosi Tokun.

30 Barber (1996, 2).

31 Barber (1996, 2). Several *àbíkú* names refer to dirt and the dumpsite. *Jàátànyó* is described by Oluseye Adesola as an *àbíkú* name appealing to its holder not to die again, literally translated by Ayọ̀dèjì Olukoju as "someone who lived off the dumpsite." *Ààtànkọ̀yí* is an *àbíkú* name that can be translated as "even the dunghill (dumpsite) rejects this one," a name given "to shame the children to desist from dying" (Olukoju 2018; Adesola, personal communication, May 2018).

32 Barber (1996, 1).

33 Barber's argument about the forest, the dumpsite, and the town is upheld by A. B. Aderibigbe in his history of Lagos in the early nineteenth century. He describes how the Isale Eko quarter of Lagos was originally named "Ehin Ogba" ("outside the fence") and was associated with the "jungle." Used for

dumping "the corpses of paupers" and *àbíkú* children, it was described by one 1920s Yoruba historian as "a jungle then and seldom traversed" (Deniga, cited by Aderibigbe [1975, 19]). For empirical studies of the impact of urban dumpsites on proximate populations, see Adetaye-Ekundayo (2010); Olorunfemi (2007).

34 Barber (1996, 4).

35 HIR-f-83, interviewed by Olutoyosi Tokun.

36 Olukoju (2018).

37 Interviewed by Olutoyosi Tokun (March 24, 2016).

38 Kenneth Harrow, cited by Oloko (2018, 56).

39 Yankah (1989); Newell (2002).

40 Urban filth and feces have also become literary tropes for the critique of postcolonial regimes. See, e.g., Abani (2004); Armah (1968).

41 The Kowa Party's slogan, "Clean and Competent Hands," may also be a concealed reference to the popular euphemism for witchcraft. If a person is suspected of witchcraft, others will say, "This person, his/her hand is not clean."

42 PrWW-f-115, interviewed by Olutoyosi Tokun.

43 PrWW-f-115, interviewed by Olutoyosi Tokun.

44 In the newspapers, Buhari's current "War Against Indiscipline" is regularly compared with his earlier WAI.

45 Faluyi Muyiwa, interviewed by John Uwa (June 5, 2015).

46 See Uwa (2018). *Agbépòò* are referred to as male in this chapter because all of the examples are of men, and interviewees did not refer to any female night-soil workers. Note: the plural for *agbépòò* is also *agbépòò*, but some participants Anglicized it as *agbépòòs*. This latter spelling has been retained in interview transcripts and quotations from the media.

47 There is significant scope for comparison with colonial India and the "sweeper," or *Dalit* caste. See Sultana and Subedi (2016); Teltumbde (2017).

48 Fanon ([1952, 1967] 1986, 109–62).

49 Fela Kuti ([1979] 1984). See Uwa (2018).

50 See Uwa (2018).

51 Faluyi Muyiwa, interviewed by John Uwa (June 5, 2015). To "pack" something is to remove it from the vicinity, for example, the *agbépòò* "packs" shit. Fela ventriloquized as the shit-flicking *agbépòò* in the final verse of another song, "You Gimme Shit I Give You Shit," where the chorus threatens, "Him go get his shit / Plenty plenty shit / We go give am shit / Ten pockets full of shit" (Kuti 1984).

52 Misc-m-14, interviewed by John Uwa.

53 Faluyi Muyiwa, interviewed by John Uwa (June 5, 2015). Kosoko (d. 1872), Oba of Lagos from 1845 to 1851, was an important figure in the early colonial history of Lagos, having been forced to flee during the British bombard-

ment of Lagos. His son was called Atin (P. D. Cole 1975, 58). Dosunmu (1823–85) was appointed Oba of Lagos by the British from 1853 until 1885, and he is listed as having approximately forty children (P. D. Cole 1975, 58). For a detailed political history of Kosoko and Dosunmu, see Aderibigbe (1975); P. D. Cole (1975); Mann (2007).

54 *Ẹní jalè ló ba ọmọ jẹ́*: he/she who steals will have a bad name (i.e., it is better to do menial jobs such as night-soil removal than to be renowned as a thief). If you do a dirty job, you can go home and clean off the dirt, but thieving and other immoral activities spoil the decency and responsibility of the person and cannot simply be washed off.

55 Karin Barber explains this phrase as you have a plan, a destiny, to earn money and take care of your family (head), and this dictates your actions (leg), suggesting purposeful activity with a goal. Your leg is the mechanism for reaching your destiny (personal communication, July 2018).

56 Faluyi Muyiwa, interviewed by John Uwa (June 5, 2015).

57 In contemporary Lagos, by contrast, the word *agbépóò* is often used as a metaphor for political corruption and criminality, as dramatized in Nollywood movies such as *Agbépóò Laja* (2016; dir. Segun Owolabi).

58 Misc-m-14, interviewed by John Uwa.

59 Misc-m-22, interviewed by John Uwa. Many Lagosians perceive the Eguns to be inferior or "uncivilized," and they will say, "He/she is Egun" or "Are you Egun?" as an insult. Other sanitary workers in Lagos, such as cleaners, are also from other states. One man explained, "You can hardly find a Yorùbá person in certain jobs. Those working in the cleaning area, in cleaning, there are more Calabar people than Yorùbá, than Igbos. The domestic helps as well" (MIR-m-91, interviewed by Olutoyosi Tokun).

60 LSHTM Ross 76/13/01 (1902, n.p.).

61 LSHTM Ross 76/13/01 (1902, n.p.). See Sultana and Subedi (2016); Teltumbde (2017). Untouchability is a major topic in twentieth-century Indian fiction. See Anand ([1935] 2003); Pillai ([1947] 1994); Roy (1998).

62 Ajayi (2005).

63 Ajayi (2005).

64 Ajayi (2005).

65 *Eko Akete*, April 11, 1925, 1.

66 Misc-m-22, interviewed by John Uwa. Details of the colonial "sewage tram" can be found in Bigon (2007). This tradition of dirt-imbued place-names continues into the present, with one community in Ajegunle named "Dustbin Estate" because it was built on a refuse dump.

67 Pit latrines are discouraged in Lagos, but they still exist in large numbers.

68 Misc-m-14, interviewed by John Uwa; LIR-f-79, interviewed by Olutoyosi Tokun.

69 Mbembe (2001).

70 MIR-m-85, interviewed by Olutoyosi Tokun.

71 MIR-2m-68–69, interviewed by Olutoyosi Tokun.

72 John Uwa singing, during interview with Muyiwa Faluyi (June 5, 2015).

73 Chigbo (2010).

74 Ajayi (2005). The diacritical marks are missing from the original printed text, for example, *Oníṣẹ́, Agbépòò*, etc. Some of the names are Yoruba slang names for night-soil workers: *ìbejì* means "twins"; *ẹrú owo* means "a slave of money"; and *ọmọ adélabú* translates as "son of Adélabú."

75 Misc-m-22, interviewed by John Uwa.

76 Faluyi Muyiwa, interviewed by John Uwa (June 5, 2015).

77 John Uwa, personal communication, March 23, 2018.

78 Faluyi Muyiwa, interviewed by John Uwa (June 5, 2015). Karin Barber notes the gender dimension in the use of the broom for admonition: the broom is a woman's weapon for sweeping a man out of the house, and thus cursing him (personal communication, July 2018).

79 Ofiebor (2014).

80 Ofiebor (2014).

81 See Cadwalladr (2018).

82 Nwafor (2017).

83 Mbembe (2001, 107).

84 Ofiebor (2014).

85 MW-m-38, interviewed by John Uwa.

86 MIR-m-86, interviewed by Olutoyosi Tokun.

87 PHU-n-62, interviewed by Olutoyosi Tokun.

88 PrWW-f-115, interviewed by Olutoyosi Tokun.

89 Misc-m-22, interviewed by John Uwa.

90 PrWW-m-118, interviewed by Olutoyosi Tokun.

91 *Daily Times* (Nigeria) (2016).

92 For discussion of a series of "rubbish to riches" stories, see Olukoju (2018).

93 PWW-f-117, interviewed by Olutoyosi Tokun; Olukoju (2018).

94 PWW-f-117, interviewed by Olutoyosi Tokun; NGO-f-119, interviewed by Olutoyosi Tokun.

95 Fashola's many other initiatives were celebrated in Lagos by numerous project participants. In particular, people mentioned his 2008 introduction of "bus rapid transit" (BRT) and light rail transport and his 2010 development of Freedom Park on the site of the old prison (and subsequent rubbish dump). Fashola enforced environmental sanitation laws, including the compulsory "environmental" days on the last Saturday of every month, continuing an old tradition from the early twentieth century of compulsory community participation in urban waste removal. With changes in leadership, there have been changes to waste management policy in Lagos State, including new initiatives (see www.cleanerlagos.org).

96 Okoroayanwu and Sanyaolu (2010).

97 See Uwa (2018).

98 The correct translation of *ìgbẹ́* is "bush," but a secondary meaning is "shit." This proverb has been repurposed into a maxim about sewage work.

99 Ayọ̀ Yusuff, interviewed by Olutoyosi Tokun (March 24, 2016).

100 SG-m-54, interviewed by Jane Nebe.

101 SG-f-56, interviewed by Jane Nebe. The producer of the BBC's *Welcome to Lagos* labeled it "preferring a life of grime to a life of crime" (Anderson 2010).

102 BollyLomo, interviewed by Olutoyosi Tokun (May 17, 2018).

103 *How to Be a Waste Collector* (2016) and *How to Collect Trash in Nigeria* (2016) are available on YouTube (BattaBox).

104 BollyLomo, interviewed by Olutoyosi Tokun (May 17, 2018).

105 Oresanya, interviewed by Dirtpol team (January 8, 2016). See also Adeyemi (2015).

106 Numerous men are also employed as waste workers by LAWMA, but the public relations and advertising materials in Oresanya's campaign featured smiling young women.

107 MIR-m-91, interviewed by Olutoyosi Tokun.

108 Berger (1972); Mulvey (1975).

109 MIR-m-91, interviewed by Olutoyosi Tokun.

110 PHW-m-97, interviewed by Olutoyosi Tokun.

111 MIR-m-101, interviewed by Olutoyosi Tokun.

112 MIR-m-99, interviewed by Olutoyosi Tokun.

113 MIR-2m-68–69, interviewed by Olutoyosi Tokun.

114 MIR-m-82, interviewed by Olutoyosi Tokun.

115 LIR-f-74, interviewed by Olutoyosi Tokun.

116 PHW-f-117, interviewed by Olutoyosi Tokun.

117 Gandy (2006, 389).

118 ES-f-57, interviewed by Jane Nebe.

119 The LMCP began in 2005 with a presidential committee "for the redevelopment of Lagos mega-city region" and the establishment of the Lagos Mega-City Region Development Authority (Ilesanmi 2010, 247). Among the project's commitments were the improvement of infrastructure, the beautification of Lagos State, residential housing construction in the Lekki Peninsula (Lekki Garden City), and the development of Eco Atlantic City with provisions for a quarter-million residents with its own electricity generating plant (Ilesanmi 2010, 248).

120 Bayo Olupohunda, cited by Olukoju (2018).

121 Akinwale et al. (2013, 37). In their study of public health in three "slum" settlements in metropolitan Lagos, O. P. Akinwale and colleagues surveyed 2,434 residents of largely low-income households in Ajegunle, Ijora Oloye, and Makoko.

122 Obono (2007, 31).

123 Hoornweg and Pope (2017).

124 Simone (2004; 2005).

125 Barber (1987); de Boeck and Plissart (2004).

126 ES-f-52, interviewed by Jane Nebe.

8. City Sexualities

1 For the purposes of this chapter, the polymorphous identifier LGBTQ+ is adopted instead of the term "homosexual" to indicate the plurality of non-binary sexualities generally theorized as "queer."

2 Mugabe, cited in the *Zimbabwe Independent*, November 27, 2015, https://www.theindependent.co.zw/2015/11/27/mugabe-comes-face-to-face-with-gays/ (accessed April 30 2018).

3 For indicative historical studies of Africa's plural sexualities, see Epprecht (1998; 2009) and Amadiume (1987); for indicative studies of contemporary sexualities, see the essays in Bennett and Tamale (2017).

4 Amnesty International (2015). Homosexuality is illegal in Algeria, Angola, Botswana, Burundi, Cameroon, Comoros, Egypt, Eritrea, Ethiopia, Gambia, Ghana, Guinea, Kenya, Liberia, Libya, Malawi, Mauritania, Mauritius, Morocco, Namibia, Nigeria, São Tomé and Principe, Senegal, Seychelles, Sierra Leone, Somalia, South Sudan, Sudan, Swaziland, Tanzania, Togo, Tunisia, Uganda, Zambia, and Zimbabwe. The law was under review in Kenya in spring 2019.

5 Section Nine of the South African Constitution prohibits discrimination on the basis of "race, gender, sex, pregnancy, marital status, ethnic or social origin, colour, sexual orientation, age, disability, religion, conscience, belief, culture, language and birth" (Outright Action International n.d.).

6 Reuters (2014).

7 Nossiter (2014); BBC News Online (2014).

8 The Same Sex Marriage (Prohibition) Act, 2014. For a legal description and interpretation of the Act, see "Same Sex Marriage (Prohibition) Act, 2014," Centre for Laws for the Federation of Nigeria, http://www.lawnigeria.com/LawsoftheFederation/Same-Sex-Marriage-Prohibition-Act,-2014.html (accessed April 30, 2018).

9 Landau, Verjee, and Mortensen (2014).

10 Cooper (2015).

11 Buchanan (2015).

12 Stratton (1994); Boehmer (1991).

13 Stratton (1994); Boehmer (1991).

14 The South African author Bessie Head famously represented the impact of apartheid on mixed-race men in her novel *A Question of Power* (1973): a hallucinatory scene shows effeminate "Coloured" homosexual men—or *moffies*—falling passively to their deaths in a pit. Head set this against the

hypermasculinity of an Afrocentric, nationalist character called Dan, who towers over the broken-down protagonist, Elizabeth, in displays of sexual aggression she is powerless to halt.

15 Harris (2008, 44). See Spurlin (2001).

16 Duke (1995).

17 Duke (1995).

18 See Schweppe and Walters (2016).

19 NGO-m-90, interviewed by Olutoyosi Tokun.

20 FGD-7–11, interviewed by John Uwa.

21 The Anglican Synod continues to be divided by an unresolved disagreement between African and Euro-American clergy on the topic of homosexuality.

22 The terms used to dismiss homosexuality bear a striking resemblance to the dismissal of "feminism" as "un-African" in previous decades. From the early twentieth century onward, male cultural nationalists rejected feminism as alien to heterosexual gender relations on the continent. In the 1910s, the Ghanaian anticolonial nationalist Kobina Sekyi described suffragettes as "unsexed abortions" (Newell 2002). Decades later, Chinweizu's antifeminist tract, *Anatomy of Female Power: A Masculinist Dissection of Matriarchy*, used a similar language of loathing for feminists (Chinweizu 1990).

23 See Beriss (1996) on colonial antihomosexuality (sodomy) laws.

24 Belcher and Kleiner (2015); Belcher (2016); Spurlin (2001).

25 See Baker (2015); Dovere (2015). For work on the connections between race and sexuality in relation to hate speech and hate crimes, see Human Rights Watch (2010); Nyong'o (2012); Schweppe and Walters (2016).

26 Belcher and Kleiner (2015); Achebe (2000); Amadiume (1987).

27 Misc-m-104, interviewed by Olutoyosi Tokun.

28 Belcher (2016). See also Adenekan (2012); Ray (2015b).

29 Ray (2015b).

30 Ray (2015b, 12–13).

31 Misc-m-104, interviewed by Olutoyosi Tokun.

32 Online Nigerian media were polarized about the legislation. The case of Kenny Badmus, mentioned further on in the text, gave rise to a number of sympathetic or neutral articles on online forums such as pulse.ng and ynaija.com. See Daniel (2014); Dede (2015); Peters (2016).

33 Pew Research Global Attitudes Project (2013). None of the children and young people interviewed for this project referred to homosexuality when asked to describe behavior they considered "dirty," and we did not suggest it to them as a topic.

34 Misc-m-104, interviewed by Olutoyosi Tokun.

35 Misc-m-104, interviewed by Olutoyosi Tokun. See Amnesty International (2013); Human Rights Watch (2010).

36 FGD-40–42, interviewed by John Uwa.

37 FGD-23–28, interviewed by John Uwa.

38 FGD-23–28, interviewed by John Uwa. Unexpectedly, this man had undertaken a considerable amount of research into homosexuality, showing a fascination for its apparent acceptance in the Islamic north of the country. He gave a detailed history of northern Nigerian sexual practices, concluding, "I won't say it's a foreign thing. I believe it has been in Africa and it is present in Nigeria a long time" (FGD-23–28, interviewed by John Uwa).

39 LIR-mf-34–35, interviewed by John Uwa.

40 FGD-40–42, interviewed by John Uwa.

41 FGD-29–33, interviewed by John Uwa.

42 FGD-29–33, interviewed by John Uwa.

43 NGO-f-112, interviewed by Olutoyosi Tokun.

44 Misc-m-88, interviewed by Olutoyosi Tokun.

45 PHU-m-61, interviewed by Olutoyosi Tokun.

46 Few of our Muslim interviewees commented on homosexuality, and nobody reported imams' proclamations on this topic. For detailed discussion of homosexual and nonbinary sexualities in northern Nigeria, see Pierce (2016).

47 OH-m-13, interviewed by John Uwa; PHU-m-61, interviewed by Olutoyosi Tokun; NGO-f-119, interviewed by Olutoyosi Tokun; FGD-15–19, interviewed by John Uwa.

48 PHW-f-106, interviewed by Olutoyosi Tokun.

49 NGO-m-84, interviewed by Olutoyosi Tokun.

50 FGD-7–11, interviewed by John Uwa.

51 MIR-m-105, interviewed by Olutoyosi Tokun.

52 MS-m-43, interviewed by John Uwa.

53 HS-m-53, interviewed by Jane Nebe.

54 PHW-f-108, interviewed by Olutoyosi Tokun.

55 FGD-40–42, interviewed by John Uwa.

56 HS-f-55, interviewed by Jane Nebe.

57 Buhari established the National Orientation Agency (NOA) during his first term as president in 1983 "to fight against indiscipline, disorderly behaviour in public and private places, disobedience to traffic rules and regulations, disrespect for constituted authorities, filthy environment, bribery, corruption and other social vices" (Eribake 2016a). The "National Re-Orientation Campaign" that is part of Buhari's second "War Against Indiscipline" (WAI) varies little from the first; it also includes an emphasis on behavioral transformation through the "Change Begins with Me" campaign. The NOA issues regular bulletins in the form of the *National Mobilizer*, which include reports from the director of the "Department of Orientation and Behaviour Modification." See the NOA website at http://www.noa.gov.ng/downloads/.

58 PHU-m-61, interviewed by Olutoyosi Tokun.

59 PHU-n-62, interviewed by Olutoyosi Tokun.

60 In the early 1980s, when Nigeria was under military rule with stringent media censorship, Buhari's "War Against Indiscipline" and General Ibrahim Babangida's extension of the "war" during his long period in power from 1985 to 1993 generated unanimously supportive media coverage. Today, however, while the fight against bribery and corruption generally attracts positive media coverage, the press is more cynical about the government's targeting of street vendors, beggars, and ordinary people, rather than addressing corruption and inefficiency among those in political power.

61 Mupotsa (2014). In her discussion of the political and emotional resonances surrounding the figure of the bride at "white" weddings in South Africa, Mupotsa sees weddings as occasions for the social coercion and correction of brides through heightened performances of praise and threats of violence.

62 FGD-23–28, interviewed by John Uwa.

63 This phrase is commonly used to indicate that the speaker holds views contrary to popular opinion, particularly relating to taboos and socially unsanctioned practices; the phrase can also be used to say, "I refuse to be implicated" (John Uwa, personal communication, February 6, 2015).

64 MS-f-12, interviewed by John Uwa.

65 MS-f-12, interviewed by John Uwa.

66 MS-f-37, interviewed by John Uwa.

67 MS-f-37, interviewed by John Uwa.

68 MS-f-37, interviewed by John Uwa.

69 PHW-f-110, interviewed by Olutoyosi Tokun.

70 LIR-mf-34–35, interviewed by John Uwa.

71 LIR-mf-34–35, interviewed by John Uwa.

72 Misc-m-39, interviewed by John Uwa.

73 Misc-m-39, interviewed by John Uwa.

74 Misc-m-39, interviewed by John Uwa. This rationale for men's opposition to the education of women was common in Nigeria up until the mid-1990s, but these days it is rare, especially among younger men.

75 PHU-m-61, interviewed by Olutoyosi Tokun.

76 Many participants classified prostitution alongside homosexuality as "dirty."

77 FGD-23–28, interviewed by John Uwa.

78 Akahinews.com (April 4, 2016). Another prominent Nigerian gay rights activist and creative writer, Jude Dibia, was forced into exile by the 2014 legislation. Dibia's first novel, *Walking with Shadows* (2005), was boycotted by many Nigerian literary reviewers for its pro-homosexual content. See ICORN (2015); *Sampsonia Way* (2016); and Jude Dibia's website at http://judedibia-jd.blogspot.com/. For further discussion of queer scenes in African literature and films, see Osinubi (2016).

79 See the Reports section of the Bisi Alimi Foundation website, http://www.bisialimifoundation.org/reports/.

80 In an off-the-record conversation in 2016, the founder of a new charity aimed at tackling the stigmatization of people with HIV/AIDS in Nigeria refused to consider homosexuality as part of his organization's remit (personal communication, August 2016).

81 Among our participants, the only group who could be said to benefit materially from homophobia was the handful of ultraconservative men for whom any transformation of already anachronistic gender norms was an "abomination" because of their loss of domestic power as heads of household.

82 FGD-40–42, interviewed by John Uwa.

83 PHU-n-59, interviewed by Olutoyosi Tokun.

84 Xiang (2018, 89).

85 While Nigerian middle-class households are increasingly Anglophone, an exclusive reliance on English terms for describing multicultural contexts can produce conceptual and historical erasures. As one senior interviewee commented reflectively to Olutoyosi Tokun, "We have lost so many things to civilization. You and I, we are Yorùbá, errr . . . and [the fact] we are conversing now in English language, it itself speaks volumes on what we have lost. If I say okay, you now finish this proverb, I speak it in Yorùbá, I'm sure you won't know" (NGO-m-90, interviewed by Olutoyosi Tokun). See Yusuff (2015).

Conclusion

1 Freeman (2014).

2 Robinson (2014).

3 Robinson (2014).

4 Robinson (2014).

5 Eleftheriou-Smith (2014).

6 Eleftheriou-Smith (2014).

7 C. Smith (2018, 109).

8 Said (1978, 94; emphasis in original).

9 Said (1978, 94).

10 Fanon ([1952, 1967] 1986, 109–40).

11 Fanon ([1952, 1967] 1986, 109–40).

12 Hall (1994, 400).

13 Prunier (1998). The derogatory use of *inyenzi* (cockroach) at the outset of the Rwandan genocide is incontrovertible, but some scholars suggest that the Tutsis used *inyenzi* positively to describe themselves when they entered Rwanda and moved south in the 1960s (K. Harrow, personal communication, July 2018).

14 Magaziner and Jacobs (2015).

15 Collins (2019).

16 Timothy Burke, cited by Harris (2008, 44).

17 Brown and Beinart (2013).

18 In 1900, during a trip to Ibadan, Governor William MacGregor of Lagos Colony witnessed the traditional Yoruba practice for acknowledging the power and authority of political leaders: "Whilst I was there the two highest Chiefs in the land, one of them the *Bashorun* of Oyo, next in rank to the *Aláàfin* [supreme ruler, king] himself, presented themselves before the *Aláàfin*," dressed in beautiful satin robes (PRO CO 879/62/13 [1900, 10]). "They threw themselves in the dust in the open court, each pressed his right cheek into the earth, then the left cheek, then the chin: each then spread out his arms and hands on the earth, rolled over on to his back and clapped his hands over his face so that it was covered with dust: they then rolled on the face again, and finally pressed the forehead into the dust before they rose up in front of the *Aláàfin*" (PRO CO 879/62/13 [1900, 10]).

Coated with dirt, the two chiefs visibly and publicly embodied their subordination to the *Aláàfin* at that moment, above all other marks of social status. Arguably, however, the two chiefs who prostrated themselves before the *Aláàfin* in Ibadan did not enter the domain of "dirt" that is the focus of the chapters in this book. By coating themselves with dust in a customary salutation, they showed the highest level of deference in a deliberate and momentary spectacle of self-abnegation in their own eyes, in the eyes of onlookers, and in the eyes of the *Aláàfin*. But their mode of salutation only qualifies as "dusty" according to the dirt-related discourses analyzed in this book, because it was a voluntary act of abasement performed as a requirement of political etiquette within the clearly bounded confines of institutional authority. This kind of dirt does not stick: it falls back into its natural place, easily brushed off one's clothing in the manner of household dust.

19 Whiteley (2011).

20 MIR-m-121, interviewed by Olutoyosi Tokun.

21 FCO 141/6436 (1944).

22 Maranga-Musonye (2014).

23 Huyssen (2008, 4).

24 Amin (2012, 68); Simone (2004); Appadurai (1996).

25 There is LGBTQ+ friendly media in Nigeria, and, as interviews for this book demonstrate, there was considerable opposition to the antihomosexuality legislation within Nigeria at the time. A recent opinion piece in the Nigerian *Guardian* "urged a rethink" among the country's politicians (Igwe 2018; see also Nwaubani 2017). Likewise, social media offer spaces of contestation and activism (Adenekan 2012).

26 NNA MH (Fed) 1/1—5890 (1946, n.p.).

27 Newell (2016).

28 Webb (2013, 10).

29 WReC (2015).

REFERENCES

Note on interviews: Please consult the list of abbreviations at the beginning of the book to interpret the interview coding used.

Archival Sources

KENYA NATIONAL ARCHIVES AND DOCUMENTATION SERVICES

AP/1/400. "Letter from F. W. Isaac, Ag Provincial Commissioner, to Secretary to Administration, Nairobi via Treasurer, Mombasa, 8th July 1907." *Prostitute Nairobi (1907): Removal of Undesirable Nandi and Lumbwa Women.* July 1907.

AP/1/400. "Memo to the Provincial Commissioner, Nairobi, from His Excellency the Governor, RMC, 6th August 1907." *Prostitute Nairobi (1907): Removal of Undesirable Nandi and Lumbwa Women.* August 1907.

LONDON SCHOOL OF HYGIENE AND TROPICAL MEDICINE (LSHTM)

MacDonald 02/01–02a. "Balfour Kirk: 'The Filth Diseases.'" n.d.

MacDonald 02/01–02b. "Balfour Kirk: 'Protection from Malaria.'" n.d.

Ross 75/05. "Letters to Ross from Dr. J. Everett Dutton." 1906.

Ross 76/01/02. "Letter dated 20 Sept 1901 from Swanzy to Ross." September 1901.

Ross 76/01/06. "Gold Coast Expedition: Letter dated Nov 11th 1901 from F. Swanzy to Dr Ross." November 1901.

Ross 76/12/02. "Letter dated 25 Dec 1901 from Balfour Stewart to Ross." December 1901.

Ross 76/13/01. "Letter dated 12 March 1902 from Matthew Nathan to Antrobus." March 1902.

Ross 76/20/04. "Letter from Matthew Nathan, GC Governor to Ross." n.d.

Ross 76/21. "Dr Matthew Logan Taylor: Report on the Sanitary Conditions of Cape Coast." April 21, 1902.

Ross 78/04. "Sanitation of Lagos: Conference with His Excellency Sir William MacGregor." 1903.

Ross 79/69. "Letter from M. Logan Taylor to Ross." November 12, 1901.

Ross 82/04. Extract from the *Liverpool Courier*, April 16, 1902, n.p.

Ross 82/08. "Dr Matthew Logan Taylor: 'Second Progress Report on the Campaign against Mosquitoes in Sierra Leone.'" September 15, 1902.

Ross 82/16. *The African Trade Section of the Incorporated Chamber of Commerce of Liverpool. Health and Sanitation, West Africa. Deputation to the Rt Hon. J. Chamberlain* MP *(HM Secretary of State for the Colonies) at the Colonial Office 15 March 1901.* Liverpool: Lee and Nightingale.

Ross 82/18. "R. H. Kennan: 'Freetown 1800 to 1870 from a Sanitarian Point of View.'" January 13, 1910.

Ross 82/24. "The African Trade Section." January 1901.

Ross 83/02. "The Lagos [Literary] Institute: Proceedings in Inaugural Meeting (Paper Read to the Lagos [Literary] Institute: Proceedings in Inaugural Meeting by President Sir William MacGregor, 16 Oct 1901)." *Visit to Lagos.* 1901.

Ross 83/05. "Commission of Enquiry into Infant Mortality, by Sir William MacGregor, to C. H. Harley Moseley, Ag Colonial Secretary. Chaired by Dr Francis Gethin Hopkins, Acting Chief Medical Officer, Dr Orisadipe Obasa, Assistant Colonial Surgeon and the Rev Jacob Henry Samuel, Principal of Wesleyan Boys High School." January–February 1901.

Ross 83/08. "Dr Strachan, Chief Medical Officer, 'Diseases and How to Prevent Them: Lecture 4,'" *A Course of Simple Lectures on Elementary Hygiene.* 1901.

Ross 83/13. "Notes on a Tour." October 25, 1901.

Ross 83/19. "'The Africa Trade Section of the Incorporated Chamber of Commerce of Liverpool': Address by Ronald Ross." October 21, 1901.

NIGERIAN NATIONAL ARCHIVES, IBADAN (NNA)

CSO 26: File no. 13001a. "Memorandum: 'Plague in Lagos' from Deputy Director of Sanitary Services, Accra, to the Honorable Director of Sanitary Services, Accra." *Outbreak of Plague in Lagos, Vol. III.* September 23, 1924.

CSO 26: File no. 13001b. "Memorandum: 'Plague in Lagos' from Deputy Director of Sanitary Services, Lagos, to Director of Medical and Sanitary Services, Lagos." *Outbreak of Plague in Lagos, Vol. III.* October 29, 1924.

CSO 26: File no. 30314. "[William] Sellers: Health Propaganda Unit: Tour of Southern Provinces." *Health Propaganda.* March 11–April 28, 1937.

CSO 26: File no. 30314. "[William] Sellers: Health Propaganda Unit Tour of Northern Provinces." *Health Propaganda.* November 3, 1937–February 11, 1938.

CSO 26: File no. 30314. "General Manager's Circular No. 816: GM 1446: Ebute Metta Compound, Signed C. E. Rooke, General Manager, Railway HQ, Ebute Metta." *Health Propaganda.* January 12, 1943.

MH (Fed) 1/1—3973. "Village Health: A Pamphlet." *Equipment and Books for Training of Sanitary Inspectors.* 1932.

MH (Fed) 1/1—5040/T. "Report by M. W. Service, 'Mosquito Survey of Ikeja District.'" *Medical Department Nigeria: Mosquito and Malaria Control—Ikeja.* February 3, 1956.

MH (Fed) 1/1—5561. "Extract from the Report of the Second Conference of the West African Labour Officers: Address by Major Orde Brown." *Lagos Housing Committee Minutes, 1944–50*. February 14–15, 1944.

MH (Fed) 1/1—5890. "Letter from J. W. P. Harkness, Director of the Medical Services in Nigeria to the Chief Secretary to Government in Lagos." *Alienist: Appointment of (ii) Duties of 1944–53*. February 12, 1946.

PUBLIC RECORD OFFICE, THE NATIONAL ARCHIVES, KEW, U.K. (PRO)

CO 583/156/1. "Ordinance to Make Provision for the Re-Planning, Improvement and Development of Lagos." *Town Planning in Lagos*, 1928.

CO 592/3. *Southern Nigeria Annual Reports, Vol. 1*. 1906.

CO 592/5. "Annual Report on the Medical Dept for the Year 1908 by the Principal Medical Officer, Lagos, 3rd May 1909." *Annual Reports of the Colony of Southern Nigeria for the Year 1908*. Lagos: Printed by the Government Printer, 1910.

CO 592/7. "Report upon the First Year's Work of the Medical Research Institute by W. M. Graham, Director MRI, Yaba." *Annual Reports of the Colony of Southern Nigeria for the Year 1909*. Lagos: Printed by the Government Printer, 1911.

CO 875/10/4a. "Extract from Report of Conference of West African Information Officers." *Cinema Propaganda—West Africa*. 1943.

CO 875/10/4b. "Fletcher and Wilson: 'Report on The Development of the Cinema in Nigeria,' Enclosure in Letter to H. V. Usill, Colonial Secretary, Ministry of Information, from Ministry of Information Representative." *Cinema Propaganda—West Africa*. June 8, 1943.

CO 875/10/11. "Replies to Questionnaire." *Cinema Propaganda. Colonial Film Unit*. 1943.

CO 875/10/13. "VD Film." *Cinema Propaganda. Colonial Film Unit*. 1943.

CO 875/51/7a. "Norman F. Spurr: 'A Report on the Reactions of an African Urban and Rural Audience to the Entertainment Film *Zonk*.'" *CFU: Audience Research (Dar-Es-Salaam)*. August 26, 1950.

CO 875/51/7b. "Letter from R. O. H. Porch to Mr Hammer, 'Film in Use in the Community Development Field.'" *CFU: Audience Research*. October 31, 1950.

CO 875/51/7c. "Letter from P. Morton-Williams to D. N. Leich." *CFU: Audience Research*. July 25, 1952.

CO 875/52/3. "Annual Report of the Colonial Film Unit, 1951." *Colonial Film Unit: Policy*. 1952–53.

CO 875/72/4. "Answers to Circular Savingram of 29 May 1952." *Interdepartmental Enquiry on Effectiveness of Overseas Information Services*. 1952.

CO 879/62/13—No. 1. "Governor Sir William MacGregor to Mr Chamberlain, July 20 (received) 1900." *Lagos: Reports of Two Journeys in the Lagos Protectorate by Governor Sir William MacGregor African (West), No. 627, Colonial Office*. 1900.

CO 879/112—No. 18. "Enclosure 4: Sanitary Report on Axim, December 1912 by G. C. Walker, Acting Senior Sanitary Officer, dated 2 January 1913." *African No. 999 Confidential: Africa, Further Correspondence January to June, 1913 Relating to Medical and Sanitary Matters in Tropical Africa.* 1913.

CO 879/112—No. 51. "Egba United Government, Order in Council, Regulating Towns Police and Public Health, 27th July 1904." *African No. 999 Confidential: Africa, Further Correspondence January to June, 1913 Relating to Medical and Sanitary Matters in Tropical Africa.* March 3 (received), 1913.

CO 879/112—No. 51a. "Gold Coast: The Secretary of State to the Governor, November 1913." *African No. 999 Confidential: Africa, Further Correspondence January to June, 1913 Relating to Medical and Sanitary Matters in Tropical Africa.* November 1913.

CO 879/112—No. 56. "Gold Coast: The Governor to the Secretary of State." *African No. 999 Confidential: Africa, Further Correspondence January to June, 1913 Relating to Medical and Sanitary Matters in Tropical Africa.* February 24 (received), 1913.

CO 879/112—No. 57. "Gold Coast: The Governor to the Secretary of State: Petition from the Gold Coast Auxiliary of the Anti-Slavery and Aborigines Protection Society re: non-employment of native medical practitioners in Government Service." *African No. 999 Confidential: Africa, Further Correspondence January to June, 1913 Relating to Medical and Sanitary Matters in Tropical Africa.* March 3 (received), 1913.

CO 879/112—No. 75. "East Africa Protectorate. Mr W. M. Ross (Director of Public Works, East Africa Protectorate): 'Memorandum on Housing and Town-Planning in the East Africa Protectorate.'" *African No. 999 Confidential: Africa, Further Correspondence January to June, 1913 Relating to Medical and Sanitary Matters in Tropical Africa.* March 26 (received), 1913.

CO 879/112—No. 77. "Gold Coast: The Governor to the Secretary of State." *African No. 999 Confidential: Africa, Further Correspondence January to June, 1913 Relating to Medical and Sanitary Matters in Tropical Africa.* March 24 (received), 1913.

CO 879/112—No. 83. "Gold Coast: The Governor to the Secretary of State." *African No. 999 Confidential: Africa, Further Correspondence January to June, 1913 Relating to Medical and Sanitary Matters in Tropical Africa.* March 31 (received), 1913.

CO 879/112—No. 117. "Gold Coast: The Governor to the Secretary of State." *African No. 999 Confidential: Africa, Further Correspondence January to June, 1913 Relating to Medical and Sanitary Matters in Tropical Africa.* April 1913.

CO 879/112—No. 132a. "Gold Coast: The Governor to the Secretary of State." *African No. 999 Confidential: Africa, Further Correspondence January to June, 1913 Relating to Medical and Sanitary Matters in Tropical Africa.* April 14, 1913.

CO 879/112—No. 132b. "Enclosure 1, Enclosure 2: Memorandum by F. G. Hopkins (Principal Medical Officer)." *African No. 999 Confidential: Africa, Further Correspondence January to June, 1913 Relating to Medical and Sanitary Matters in Tropical Africa.* n.d. [March 1913].

CO 879/112—No. 133a. "Sierra Leone: The Governor to the Secretary of State." *African No. 999 Confidential Africa, Further Correspondence January to June, 1913 Relating to Medical and Sanitary Matters in Tropical Africa.* May 5 (received), 1913.

CO 879/112—No. 133b. "Enclosure 1, Enclosure 2: Re: Native Doctors Attending Native Staff: by J. Wallace Collett, Ag Principal Medical Officer, Freetown." *African No. 999 Confidential: Africa, Further Correspondence January to June, 1913 Relating to Medical and Sanitary Matters in Tropical Africa.* n.d. [1913].

CO 879/112—No. 144. "Southern Nigeria: The Governor to the Secretary of State for the Colonies received 12 August 1913, Confidential." *African No. 999 Confidential: Africa, Further Correspondence January to June, 1913 Relating to Medical and Sanitary Matters in Tropical Africa.* August 1913.

CO 879/112—No. 147. "Gambia: The Governor to the Secretary of State." *African No. 999 Confidential: Africa, Further Correspondence January to June, 1913 Relating to Medical and Sanitary Matters in Tropical Africa.* May 12 (received), 1913.

CO 879/112—No. 169. "Enclosure 2: Memorandum from Senior Sanitary Officer, Southern Nigeria." *African No. 999 Confidential: Africa, Further Correspondence January to June, 1913 Relating to Medical and Sanitary Matters in Tropical Africa.* n.d. [1913].

CO 879/112—No. 177. "Memorandum on the 'Segregation Principle' in West Africa." *African No. 999 Confidential: Africa, Further Correspondence January to June, 1913 Relating to Medical and Sanitary Matters in Tropical Africa.* n.d. [1913].

CO 1045/227a. Sellers, William. "Enclosure 1 in Circular Dispatch." January 30, 1940.

CO 1045/227b. Sellers, William. "Memorandum, 'Non-Commercial Films, Film Strips and Film Slides in the Colonial Empire.'" n.d. [1951].

CO 1047/651. "Plan of Town of Lagos Revised to August, 1911." *Sanitary Report 1913.*

FCO 141/6436. "Arthur M. Champion, 'Native Welfare in Kenya,' September 1944." Item 4.

UNILEVER ARCHIVES AND RECORD MANAGEMENT, PORT SUNLIGHT

UAC 1/11/14/3/1. "Anonymous Memoires of a Trading Post at Sapele." n.d.

UAC 2/34/4/1/1. "Niger Company Ltd: Diary of Tour through the Congo and West Africa."

UAC/2/34/4/1/3. Knox TM (1929) Niger Company Ltd: Reports of TM Knox to Chairman and Board on His Tour through West Africa. *Knox TM (1924–1927).*

UAC LBC Box 1376 TT 3810 location SRI. "Nigerian Tour 1921: Letter No. 5, 5 August 1921." *Lever, WH (1921) Letters from William Hulme Lever to Lord Leverhulme.*

Interviews with Oral Historians and Linguists

Agboola, Ola. 2015. Interviewed by John Uwa, September 4.

BollyLomo. 2018. Interviewed by Olutoyosi Tokun, May 17.

Dosunmu, Henry. 2014. Interviewed by John Uwa, October 24.

Muyiwa, Faluyi. 2015. Interviewed by John Uwa, June 5.

Okoro, Robert. 2015. Interviewed by John Uwa, October 30.

Oresanya, Ola. 2016. Interviewed by Dirtpol team, January 8.

Yusuff, Ayọ̀. 2016. Interviewed by Olutoyosi Tokun, March 24.

Published Sources

Abani, Chris. 2004. *GraceLand*. New York: Farrar, Straus and Giroux.

Abraham, Roy C. 1958. *Dictionary of Modern Yoruba*. London: University of London Press.

Achebe, Nwando. 2000. "Farmers, Traders, Warriors and Kings: Female Power and Authority in Northern Igboland." PhD diss., University of California.

Adebanwi, Wale. 2016. *Nation as Grand Narrative: The Nigerian Press and the Politics of Meaning*. Rochester, NY: University of Rochester Press.

Adeloye, Adelola. 1974. "Some Early Nigerian Doctors and Their Contribution to Modern Medicine in West Africa." *Medical History* 18 (3): 275–93.

Adenekan, Olorunshola. 2012. "African Literature in the Digital Age: Class and Sexual Politics in New Writing from Nigeria and Kenya." PhD diss., University of Birmingham.

Adeoti, Ezekiel Oladele, and Augustine Uvu Imuoh. 2016. "The Contribution of Dr. Oguntola Odunbaku Sapara Williams to Colonial Medical Service in Lagos." *Journal of Humanities and Social Science* 21 (4): 50–54.

Aderibigbe, A. J. 1975. "Early History of Lagos to about 1850." In *Lagos: The Development of an African City*, edited by A. J. Aderibigbe, 1–26. Ibadan: Longman Nigeria.

Adetaye-Ekundayo, Odutimirola A. 2010. "Waste Collection Management in Developing Countries: A Case Study of the Lagos PSP Waste Collection Programme." PhD diss., Cardiff University.

Adeyemi, Laolu. 2015. "Oresanya: 10 Years of Managing LAWMA." *Guardian* (Lagos), May 23. https://guardian.ng/saturday-magazine/c105-saturday-magazine/oresanya-10-years-of-managing-lawma/ (accessed April 30, 2018).

Ajayi, Babs. 2005. "A Strange and Fascinating Nation: My Early Years in Nigeria (III)." *Nigeriaworld*, February 22. http://nigeriaworld.com/feature/publication/babsajayi/030805.html (accessed March 28, 2018).

Ajisafe, A. K. 1924. *The Laws and Customs of the Yoruba People*. London: Trubner and Company.

Akinwale, O. P., et al. 2013. "Living Conditions and Public Health Status in Three Urban Slums of Lagos, Nigeria." *South East Asia Journal of Public Health* 3 (1): 36–41.

Aliyi, Alhaji A., and Lawal Amadu. 2017. "Urbanization, Cities, and Health: The Challenges to Nigeria—a Review." *Annals of African Medicine* 16 (4): 149–58.

Allman, Jean M., and Victoria B. Tashjian. 2000. *"I Will Not Eat Stone": A Women's History of Colonial Asante*. Oxford: James Currey.

Amadiume, Ifi. 1987. *Male Daughters, Female Husbands: Gender and Sex in an African Society*. London: Zed Books.

Ambler, Charles. 2001. "Popular Films and Colonial Audiences: The Movies in Northern Rhodesia." *American Historical Review* 106 (1): 81–105.

Amin, Ash. 2012. *Land of Strangers*. Cambridge, U.K.: Polity Press.

Amnesty International. 2013. "Making Love a Crime: Criminalization of Same-Sex Conduct in Sub-Saharan Africa." June 24. https://www.amnestyusa.org /reports/making-love-a-crime-criminalization-of-same-sex-conduct-in-sub -saharan-africa/ (accessed April 30, 2018).

Amnesty International. 2015. "Mapping Anti-Gay Laws in Africa." July 22. https://www.amnesty.org.uk/lgbti-lgbt-gay-human-rights-law-africa -uganda-kenya-nigeria-cameroon (accessed March 13, 2018).

Anand, Mulk Raj. (1935) 2003. *Untouchable*. London: Penguin.

Anderson, Will. 2010. "Welcome to Lagos—It'll Defy Your Expectations." *BBC TV Blog*, April 15. http://www.bbc.co.uk/blogs/tv/2010/04/welcome-to-lagos -itll-defy-you.shtml (accessed April 2, 2018).

Appadurai, Arjun. 1996. *Modernity at Large*. Minneapolis: University of Minnesota Press.

Armah, Ayi Kwei. 1968. *The Beautyful Ones Are Not Yet Born*. Oxford: Heinemann.

Arsan, Andrew. 2014. *Interlopers of Empire: The Lebanese Diaspora in Colonial French West Africa*. Oxford: Oxford University Press.

Ayoola, Tokunbo A. 2016. "Establishment of the Nigerian Railway Corporation." *Journal of Retracing Africa* 3 (1): 21–42.

Baderoon, Gabeba. 2018. "Surplus, Excess, Dirt: Slavery and the Production of Disposability in South Africa." *Social Dynamics* 44 (2): 257–72.

Baker, Aryn. 2015. "Obama Defends Gay Rights on Kenya Trip." *Time Magazine*, July 26. http://time.com/3972445/obama-kenyatta-gay-rights/ (accessed January 15, 2018).

Barber, Karin. 1987. "Popular Arts in Africa." *African Studies Review* 30 (3): 1–78.

Barber, Karin. 1996. "Forests as Sites of Transformation." Unpublished research paper. Contesting Forestry in West Africa Workshop, University of Birmingham.

Barber, Karin. 2012. *Print Culture and the First Yoruba Novel: I. B. Thomas's "Life Story of Me, Segilola" and Other Texts.* Leiden: Brill.

Barber, Karin. 2016. "Authorship, Copyright and Quotation in Oral and Print Spheres in Early Colonial Yorubaland." In *Copyright Africa: How Intellectual Property, Media and Markets Transform Immaterial Cultural Goods,* edited by U. Roeschenthaler and M. Diawara, 105–27. Canon Pyon, U.K.: Sean Kingston.

Barber, Karin. 2017. *A History of African Popular Culture.* Cambridge: Cambridge University Press.

Bashford, Alison. 2004. *Imperial Hygiene: A Critical History of Colonialism, Nationalism and Public Health.* Basingstoke, U.K.: Palgrave Macmillan.

Bataille, Georges. (1977) 1985. *Visions of Excess: Selected Writings, 1927–1939.* Edited and translated by Allan Stoekl. Manchester: Manchester University Press.

BBC News Online. 2014. "Nigeria Anti-Gay Laws: Fears over New Legislation." January 14. http://www.bbc.com/news/world-africa-25728845 (accessed February 8, 2016).

Beale, Colin. 1948. "The Commercial Entertainment Film and Its Effect on Colonial Peoples." In *The Film in Colonial Development: A Report of a Conference,* edited by the British Film Institute, 16–21. London: British Film Institute.

Belcher, Wendy L. 2016. "Same-Sex Intimacies in the Early African Text *Gädlä Wälättä Petros* (1672): Queer Reading an Ethiopian Woman Saint." *Research in African Literatures* 47 (2): 20–45.

Belcher, Wendy L., and Michael Kleiner. 2015. *The Life and Struggles of Our Mother Wälättä Petros: A Seventeenth-Century African Biography of an Ethiopian Woman.* Princeton, NJ: Princeton University Press.

Bennett, Jane, and Sylvia Tamale, eds. 2017. *Research on Gender and Sexualities in Africa.* Oxford: African Books Collective.

Berger, John. 1972. *Ways of Seeing.* London: Penguin.

Beriss, David. 1996. "Introduction: 'If You're Gay and Irish, Your Parents Must Be English.'" *Identities* 2 (3): 189–96.

Bigon, Liora. 2005. "Sanitation and Street Layout in Early Colonial Lagos: British and Indigenous Conceptions, 1851–1900." *Planning Perspectives* 20 (3): 247–69.

Bigon, Liora. 2007. "Tracking Ethno-Cultural Differences: The Lagos Steam Tramway, 1902–1933." *Journal of Historical Geography* 33 (3): 596–618.

Bigon, Liora. 2016. "Bubonic Plague, Colonial Ideologies, and Urban Planning Policies: Dakar, Lagos, and Kumasi." *Planning Perspectives* 31 (2): 205–26.

Bissell, William Cunningham. 2010. *Urban Design, Chaos, and Colonial Power in Zanzibar.* Bloomington: Indiana University Press.

Boehmer, Elleke. 1991. "Stories of Women and Mothers: Gender and Nationalism in the Early Fiction of Flora Nwapa." In *Motherlands: Black Women's Writing from Africa, the Caribbean and South Asia*, edited by Susheila Nasta, 3–23. London: Women's Press.

Booth, William. (1890) 1970. *In Darkest England and the Way Out*. London: Charles Knight.

Born, Megan, Helene M. Furján, and Lily Jencks, with Phillip M. Crosby. 2012. *Dirt*. Philadelphia: PennDesign; Cambridge, MA: MIT Press.

Bragard, Véronique. 2018. "Reclaiming the Future: (In)visible Dirt Borders in Sammy Baloji's Mining Photomontages." *Social Dynamics* 44 (2): 273–90.

British Broadcasting Company (BBC). 2010. *Welcome to Lagos*. Documentary in 3 episodes, broadcast April 15, 22, 29. Prod. Will Anderson, Exec. Prod. Andrew Palmer. KEO Films.

Brown, Karen, and William Beinart. 2013. *African Local Knowledge and Livestock Diseases: Diseases and Treatments in South Africa*. Oxford: James Currey; Johannesburg: Wits University Press.

Brown, Peter J. 1997. "Culture and the Global Resurgence of Malaria." In *The Anthropology of Infectious Disease: International Health Perspectives*, edited by Marcia C. Inhorn and Peter J. Brown, 119–41. Amsterdam: Gordon and Breach Science.

Brown, Spencer H. 1992. "Public Health in Lagos, 1850–1900: Perceptions, Patterns, and Perspectives." *International Journal of African Historical Studies* 25 (2): 337–60.

Brown, Spencer H. 1994. "Public Health in U.S. and West African Cities, 1870–1900." *The Historian* 56 (4): 685–98.

Brown, Spencer H. 2004. "A Tool of Empire: The British Medical Establishment in Lagos, 1861–1905." *International Journal of African Historical Studies* 37 (2): 309–43.

Brownell, Emily. 2014. "Seeing Dirt in Dar es Salaam: Sanitation, Waste, and Citizenship in the Postcolonial City." In *The Arts of Citizenship in African Cities: Infrastructures and Spaces of Belonging*, edited by Mamadou Diouf and Rosalind Fredericks, 209–29. Basingstoke, U.K.: Palgrave Macmillan.

Buchanan, Elsa. 2015. "LGBT in Kenya: 'Government Needs to Stop Violent Anti-Gay Attacks.'" *International Business Times*, September 28. http://www.ibtimes.co.uk/lgbt-kenya-government-needs-stop-violent-anti-gay-attacks-1521533 (accessed February 8, 2016).

Burke, Timothy. 1996. *Lifebuoy Men, Lux Women: Commodification, Consumption, and Cleanliness in Modern Zimbabwe*. Durham, NC: Duke University Press.

Burke, Timothy. 2002. "'Our Mosquitoes Are Not So Big': Images and Modernity in Zimbabwe." In *Images and Empires: Visuality in Colonial and Postcolonial Africa*, edited by Paul Landau and Deborah Kaspin, 41–55. Berkeley: University of California Press.

Burns, James. 2000. "Watching Africans Watch Films: Theories of Spectatorship in British Colonial Africa." *Historical Journal of Film, Radio and Television* 20 (2): 197–211.

Burns, James. 2002. *Flickering Shadows: Cinema and Identity in Colonial Zimbabwe.* Athens: Ohio University Press.

Burton, Antoinette. 1998. *At the Heart of the Empire: Indians and the Colonial Encounter in Late-Victorian Britain.* Berkeley: University of California Press.

Cadwalladr, Carole. 2018. "Cambridge Analytica's Ruthless Bid to Sway the Vote in Nigeria." *Guardian* (U.K.), March 21. https://www.theguardian.com /uk-news/2018/mar/21/cambridge-analyticas-ruthless-bid-to-sway-the-vote -in-nigeria (accessed March 21, 2018).

Capanna, Ernesto. 2006. "Grassi *versus* Ross: Who Solved the Riddle of Malaria?" *Perspectives: International Microbiology* 9 (1): 69–74.

Casely Hayford, J. E. 1903. *Gold Coast Native Institutions: With Thoughts upon a Healthy Imperial Policy for the Gold Coast and Ashanti.* London: Thoemmes Press.

Casely Hayford, J. E. 1911. *Ethiopia Unbound: Studies in Race Emancipation.* London: C. M. Phillips.

Casely Hayford, J. E. (1913) 1971. *The Truth about the West African Land Question.* London: Routledge.

Chigbo, Gilbert. 2010. "Improving Sanitary Conditions in Nigeria." *Vanguard,* July 14. https://www.vanguardngr.com/2010/07/improving-sanitary -conditions-in-nigeria/ (accessed March 28, 2018).

Chinweizu. 1990. *Anatomy of Female Power: A Masculinist Dissection of Matriarchy.* Lagos: Pero Press.

Cohen, William A., and Ryan Johnson, eds. 2005. *Dirt, Disgust, and Modern Life.* Minneapolis: University of Minnesota Press.

Cole, Festus. 2015. "Sanitation, Disease and Public Health in Sierra Leone, West Africa, 1895–1922: Case Failure of British Colonial Health Policy." *Journal of Imperial and Commonwealth History* 43 (2): 238–66.

Cole, P. D. 1975. "Lagos Society in the Nineteenth Century." In *Lagos: The Development of an African City,* edited by A. B. Aderibigbe, 27–57. Ibadan: Longman Nigeria.

Collins, Matthew. 2019. "I Helped Stop a Far-Right Terror Plot. Are UK Police Ready for the Next One?" *Guardian* (U.K.), April 3. https://www.the guardian.com/commentisfree/2019/apr/03/far-right-terror-plot-police-jack -renshaw-rosie-cooper-mp (accessed April 12, 2019).

Collins, Selwyn D. 1930. "The Influenza Epidemic of 1928–1929 with Comparative Data for 1918–1919." *American Journal of Public Health and the Nation's Health* 20 (2): 119–29.

Colonial Cinema. 1947. Editorial. 5 (2): 26–27.

Comaroff, Jean. 1982. "Medicine: Symbol and Ideology." In *The Problem of Medi-*

cal Knowledge: Examining the Social Construction of Medicine, edited by
P. Wright and Amal Treacher, 49–69. Edinburgh: Edinburgh University
Press.

Commission on Educational and Cultural Films. 1932. The Film in National Life.
London: George Allen and Unwin.

Conrad, Joseph. (1899) 1922. Youth, and Two Other Stories. New York: Doubleday,
Page and Co.

Cooper, Jonathan. 2015. "Kenya Anti-Gay Laws Are Leaving LGBT Community at the Mercy of the Mob." Guardian (U.K.), October 8. http://www
.theguardian.com/global-development/2015/oct/08/kenya-anti-gay-laws-lgbt
-community-mercy-of-mob (accessed February 8, 2016).

Creech-Jones, Arthur. 1948. "Opening Address." In The Film in Colonial Development: A Report of a Conference, edited by the British Film Institute, 4–8.
London: British Film Institute.

Curtin, Philip D. 1985. "Medical Knowledge and Urban Planning in Tropical
Africa." American Historical Review 90 (3): 594–613.

Curtis, Valerie. 2003. "Talking Dirty: How to Save a Million Lives." International Journal of Environmental Health Research 13: 73–79.

Curtis, Valerie. 2007. "Dirt, Disgust and Disease: A Natural History of Hygiene." Journal of Epidemiology and Community Health 61 (8): 660–64.

Curtis, Valerie. 2013. Don't Look, Don't Touch, Don't Eat: The Science behind Revulsion. Chicago: University of Chicago Press.

Curtis, Valerie, and A. Biran. 2001. "Dirt, Disgust, and Disease: Is Hygiene in
Our Genes?" Perspectives in Biology and Medicine 44 (1): 17–31.

Daily Times (Nigeria). 2016. "The Very Serious and Lucrative Business of Shit
Carrying." March 3. https://www.newsghana.com.gh/the-very-serious-and
-lucrative-business-of-shit-carrying/ (accessed April 30, 2018).

Daniel, Jo. 2014. "'I've Lived with HIV the Last 15 Years'—Brand Expert, Kenny
Badmus." Information Nigeria, December 1. http://www.informationng.com
/2014/12/brand-expert-kenny-badmus-shares-his-amazing-story-of-living
-with-hiv-in-the-last-15-years.html (accessed June 13, 2019).

Dankwa, Serena O. 2014. "Doing Everything Together: Female Same-Sex In-
timacy in Postcolonial Ghana." PhD diss., Institute of Social Anthropology,
University of Bern.

de Boeck, Filip, and Marie-Françoise Plissart. 2004. Kinshasa: Tales of the Invisible City. Leuven: Leuven University Press.

Dede, Steve. 2015. "HIV-Positive Brand Expert Comes Out as Gay." pulse.ng,
January 9. http://www.pulse.ng/gist/kenny-badmus-hiv-positive-brand
-expert-comes-out-as-gay-id3395543.html (accessed June 13, 2019).

Destrée, Pauline. 2018. "Recalcitrant Infrastructures: The Politics and Poetics of
Electricity in Accra, Ghana." PhD diss., University College London.

Diawara, Manthia. 1988. "Black Spectatorship." Screen 29 (4): 66–79.

Diawara, Manthia. 1992. *African Cinema: Politics and Culture*. Bloomington: Indiana University Press.

Dickie, Simon. 2011. *Cruelty and Laughter: Forgotten Comic Literature and the Unsentimental Eighteenth Century*. Chicago: University of Chicago Press.

Diouf, Mamadou, and Rosalind Fredericks. 2014. "Introduction." In *The Arts of Citizenship in African Cities*, edited by Mamadou Diouf and Rosalind Fredericks, 1–23. New York: Palgrave Macmillan.

Douglas, Mary. (1966) 2002. *Purity and Danger: An Analysis of the Concept of Pollution and Taboo*. London: Routledge.

Dovere, Edward-Isaac. 2015. "Obama, Kenyatta Clash on Gay Rights in Kenya." *Politico*, July 25. https://www.politico.com/story/2015/07/obama-kenyatta -clash-on-gay-rights-in-kenya-120621 (accessed January 30, 2018).

Dowell, Ben. 2010. "Wole Soyinka Attacks BBC Portrayal of Lagos 'Pit of Degradation.'" *Guardian* (U.K.), April 28. https://www.theguardian.com/media /2010/apr/28/soyinka-bbc-lagos-documentaries-criticism (accessed April 29, 2018).

Duke, Lynne. 1995. "Mugabe Makes Homosexuals Public Enemies." *Washington Post*, September 9. https://www.washingtonpost.com/archive/politics/1995/09 /09/mugabe-makes-homosexuals-public-enemies/94008c9a-c402–48ad-b99d -7a4176217e43/?utm_term=.0cf24c466da9 (accessed March 21, 2018).

Duschinsky, Robbie, Simone Schnall, and Daniel H. Weiss, eds. 2016. *Purity and Danger Now: New Perspectives*. London: Routledge.

Echenberg, Myron. 2007. *Plague Ports: The Global Urban Impact of Bubonic Plague, 1894–1901*. New York: NYU Press.

Economist Intelligence Unit. 2017. *The Global Liveability Report 2017*. http:// pages.eiu.com/rs/753-RIQ-438/images/Liveability_Free_Summary_2017.pdf (accessed April 30, 2018).

Eleftheriou-Smith, Loulla-Mae. 2014. "Ebola Virus: Sierra Leone Boy's UK School Placement Cancelled over 'Misguided Hysteria' by Parents over the Disease." *Independent* (U.K.), October 8. http://www.independent.co.uk/news /uk/home-news/sierra-leone-boys-uk-school-placement-cancelled-over -misguided-hysteria-by-parents-over-ebola-9781366.html (accessed October 8, 2014).

Ellis, Alfred Burdon. 1881. *West African Sketches*. London: Samuel Tinsley.

Epprecht, Marc. 1998. "The 'Unsaying' of Indigenous Homosexualities in Zimbabwe: Mapping a Blindspot in an African Masculinity." *Journal of Southern African Studies* 24 (4): 631–51.

Epprecht, Marc. 2009. "Sexuality, Africa, History." *American Historical Review* 114 (5): 1258–72.

Eribake, Akintayo. 2016a. "Breaking: Buhari Relaunches War Against Indiscipline Brigade." *Vanguard*, August 8. https://www.vanguardngr.com/2016/08 /buhari-relaunches-war-indiscipline-brigade/ (accessed May 30, 2018).

Eribake, Akintayo. 2016b. "Mayhem in Ketu: Gov Slams Curfew, Shuts Market." *Vanguard*, March 4. https://www.vanguardngr.com/2016/03/mayhem-in-ketu-gov-slams-curfew-shuts-market/ (accessed April 29, 2018).

Faleti, Ayo. 2013. *Yoruba Proverbs and Their Contexts: A Simplification*. Online source: Lulu.com.

Falola, Toyin, and Niyi Afolabi. 2017. *The Yoruba in Brazil, Brazilians in Yorubaland: Cultural Encounter, Resilience, and Hybridity in the Atlantic World*. Durham: Carolina Academic Press.

Falola, Toyin, and Matthew M. Heaton. 2008. *A History of Nigeria*. Cambridge: Cambridge University Press.

Fanon, Frantz. (1952) 1986. *Black Skin, White Masks*. London: Pluto Press.

Fardon, Richard. 2016. "Purity as Danger: '*Purity and Danger* Revisited' at Fifty." In *Purity and Danger Now: New Perspectives*, edited by Robbie Duschinsky, Simone Schnall, and Daniel H. Weiss, 23–33. London: Routledge.

Fasoro, J. O. 2012. "Myth and Proverb as a Vehicle of Moral Education among Traditional Yoruba." *International Journal of Arts and Commerce* 1 (5): 255–62.

Feierman, Steven. 1985. "Struggles for Control: The Social Roots of Health and Healing in Modern Africa." *African Historical Review* 28 (2–3): 73–147.

Field, Alan. 1913. *"Verb. sap": On Going to West Africa, Northern Nigeria, Southern, and to the Coasts*. 3rd ed. London: Bale, Sons and Danielsson.

Floyd, David. 2014. *Street Urchins, Sociopaths and Degenerates: Orphans of Late-Victorian and Edwardian Fiction*. Cardiff: University of Wales Press.

Förster, Till. 2014. "On Creativity in African Urban Life: African Cities as Sites of Creativity and Emancipation." In *Popular Culture in Africa: The Episteme of the Everyday*, edited by Stephanie Newell and Onookome Okome, 27–46. London: Routledge.

Fraser, Nancy. 1990. "Rethinking the Public Sphere: A Contribution to the Critique of Actually Existing Democracy." *Social Text* 25–26: 56–80.

Freeman, Colin. 2014. "The Liberian Slum Where Ebola Spreads Death among Killer Virus 'Deniers.'" *Telegraph* (U.K.), August 8. http://www.telegraph.co.uk/news/worldnews/africaandindianocean/liberia/11020768/The-Liberian-slum-where-Ebola-spreads-death-among-killer-virus-deniers.html (accessed October 16, 2014).

Frindéthié, K. Martial. 2009. *Francophone African Cinema: History, Culture, Politics and Theory*. Jefferson, NC: McFarland.

Gale, T. S. 1980. "Segregation in British West Africa." *Cahiers d'Études Africaines* 20: 495–507.

Gandy, Matthew. 2006. "Planning, Anti-Planning and the Infrastructure Crisis Facing Metropolitan Lagos." *Urban Studies* 43 (2): 371–96.

Garritano, Carmela. 2013. *African Video Movies and Global Desires: A Ghanaian History*. Athens: Ohio University Press.

Gikandi, Simon. 2012. "Realism, Romance, and the Problem of African Literary History." MLQ: *Modern Language Quarterly* 73 (3): 309–28.

Gold Coast Leader. 1902. Editorial. July 1: 2.

Gordon, David. 2003. "A Sword of Empire? Medicine and Colonialism at King William's Town, Xhosaland, 1856–91." In *Medicine and Colonial Identity*, edited by Mary Sutphen and Bridie Andrews, 41–60. London: Routledge.

Gray, Albert. 1910. "West Africa." *Journal of the Society of Comparative Legislation* 10 (2): 382–87.

Grierson, John. 1948. "The Film and Primitive Peoples." In *The Film in Colonial Development: A Report of a Conference*, edited by the British Film Institute, 9–15. London: British Film Institute.

Hall, Stuart. 1994. "Cultural Identity and Diaspora." In *Colonial Discourse and Postcolonial Theory: A Reader*, edited by Patrick Williams and Laura Chrisman, 392–403. Harlow, U.K.: Harvester Wheatsheaf.

Hampton, Mark. 2004. *Visions of the Press in Britain, 1850–1950.* Urbana: University of Illinois Press.

Harris, Ashleigh. 2008. "Discourses of Dirt and Disease in Operation Murambatsvina in Zimbabwe." In *The Hidden Dimensions of Operation Murambatsvina*, edited by Maurice T. Vambe and Tendai Chari, 40–50. Harare: Weaver Press.

Harrow, Kenneth. 2013. *Trash: African Cinema from Below.* Bloomington: Indiana University Press.

Hartley, John. 1987. "Invisible Fictions: Television Audiences, Paedocracy, Pleasure." *Textual Practice* 1 (2): 1–18.

Head, Bessie. 1973. *A Question of Power.* Oxford: Heinemann.

Hofmeyr, Isabel. 2003. *The Portable Bunyan: A Transnational History of* The Pilgrim's Progress. Princeton, NJ: Princeton University Press.

Holden, Philip. 2000. *Modern Subjects/Colonial Texts: Hugh Clifford and the Discipline of English Literature in the Straits Settlements and Malaya, 1895–1907.* Greensboro, NC: ELT Press.

hooks, bell. 1992. *Black Looks: Race and Representation.* London: Routledge.

Hoornweg, Daniel, and Kevin Pope. 2017. "Population Predictions for the World's Largest Cities in the 21st Century." *Environment and Urbanization* 29 (1): 195–216.

Hopkins, A. G. 1973. *An Economic History of West Africa.* London: Routledge.

Human Rights Watch. 2010. *Criminalizing Identities: Rights Abuses in Cameroon Based on Sexual Orientation and Gender Identity.* New York: Human Rights Watch.

Huxley, Julian. (1931) 1936. *Africa View.* London: Chatto and Windus.

Huyssen, Andreas. 2008. "Introduction: World Cultures, World Cities." In *Other Cities, Other Worlds*, edited by Andreas Huyssen, 1–23, Durham, NC: Duke University Press.

ICORN. 2015. "A Voice for LGBTI People in Africa." July 26. https://icorn.org/article/voice-lgbti-people-africa.

Igwe, Leo. 2018. "Nigeria: Time to Re-Think Opposition to LGBT Rights." *Guardian* (Nigeria), March 26. https://guardian.ng/opinion/nigeria-time-to-re-think-opposition-to-lgbt-rights/ (accessed March 27, 2018).

Ilesanmi, Adetokunbo Oluwole. 2010. "Urban Sustainability in the Context of Lagos Mega-City." *Journal of Geography and Regional Planning* 3 (10): 240–52.

Inhorn, Marcia C., and Peter J. Brown, eds. 1997. *The Anthropology of Infectious Disease: International Health Perspectives*. Amsterdam: Gordon and Breach Science.

Izomoh, S. O. 1994. *Nigerian Traditional Architecture*. Benin City, Nigeria: S. M. O. Aka and Brothers.

Jackson, Shannon, and Steven Robins. 2018. "Making Sense of the Politics of Sanitation in Cape Town." *Social Dynamics* 44 (1): 69–87.

Jaekel, Francis. 1997. *The History of the Nigerian Railway: Network and Infrastructures*. Ibadan: Spectrum Books.

James, Leslie. 2015. *George Padmore and Decolonization from Below: Pan-Africanism, the Cold War, and the End of Empire*. Basingstoke, U.K.: Palgrave Macmillan.

James, Leslie. 2016. "Transatlantic Passages: Black Identity Construction in West African and West Indian Newspapers, 1935–1950." In *African Print Cultures: Newspapers and Their Publics in the Twentieth Century*, edited by Derek Peterson, Emma Hunter, and Stephanie Newell, 49–74. Ann Arbor: University of Michigan Press.

Jones, Rebecca. 2014. "Writing Domestic Travel in Yoruba and English Print Culture, Southwestern Nigeria, 1914–2014." PhD diss., University of Birmingham.

Keller, Richard. 2001. "Madness and Colonization: Psychiatry in the British and French Empires, 1800–1962." *Journal of Social History* 35 (2): 295–326.

Killingray, David. 2008. "'A Good West Indian, a Good African, and, in Short, a Good Britisher': Black and British in a Colour-Conscious Empire, 1760–1950." *Journal of Imperial and Commonwealth History* 36 (3): 363–81.

Koolhaas, Rem (voice). 2002. *Lagos Wide and Close: An Interactive Journey into an Exploding City*. Dir. Bregtje van der Haak. Amsterdam: Pieter van Huystee Film.

Korieh, Chima J. 2013. "Biafra and the Discourse on the Igbo Genocide." *Journal of Asian and African Studies* 48 (6): 727–40.

Kristeva, Julia. 1982. *Powers of Horror: An Essay on Abjection*. New York: Columbia University Press.

Kuti, Fela. (1979) 1984. "I.T.T., International Thief Thief." *Fela Anikulapo Kuti & Egypt 80: Live in Amsterdam*. London: EMI Records.

Landau, Elizabeth, Zain Verjee, and Antonia Mortensen. 2014. "Uganda Presi-

dent: Homosexuals Are 'Disgusting.'" *CNN*, February 25. http://edition.cnn
.com/2014/02/24/world/africa/uganda-homosexuality-interview/ (accessed
October 15, 2014).

Larkin, Brian. 2008. *Signal and Noise: Media, Infrastructure, and Urban Culture in Nigeria*. Durham, NC: Duke University Press.

Lewis, Brian. 2012. *So Clean: Lord Leverhulme, Soap and Civilisation*. Manchester: Manchester University Press.

Liebig, Justus von. 1843. "Liebig's Letters on Chemistry." *Spectator*, October 14, 18–19.

Lovejoy, Paul E. 2005. *Slavery, Commerce, and Production in West Africa*. Trenton, NJ: Africa World Press.

Lynn, Martin. 1997. *Commerce and Economic Change in West Africa: The Palm Oil Trade in the Nineteenth Century*. Cambridge: Cambridge University Press.

Maarouf, Moulay Driss El. 2018. "Waste's Dominion: The Gymnastics of Value in Informal Markets." *Social Dynamics* 44 (1): 38–54.

Mabogunje, Akin L. 1968. *Urbanization in Nigeria*. London: University of London Press.

Macqueen, Adam. 2011. *The King of Sunlight: How William Lever Cleaned Up the World*. London: Corgi.

Magaziner, Daniel, and Sean Jacobs. 2015. "South Africa Turns on Its Immigrants." *New York Times*, April 24. https://www.nytimes.com/2015/04/25/opinion/south-africa-turns-on-its-immigrants.html (accessed April 12, 2019).

Mamdani, Mahmood. 2012. *Define and Rule: Native as Political Identity*. Cambridge, MA: Harvard University Press.

Mann, Kristin. 2007. *Slavery and the Birth of an African City: Lagos, 1760–1900*. Bloomington: Indiana University Press.

Maranga-Musonye, Miriam. 2014. "Literary Insurgence in the Kenyan Urban Space: *Mchongoano* and the Popular Art Scene in Nairobi." In *Popular Culture in Africa: The Episteme of the Everyday*, edited by Stephanie Newell and Onookome Okome, 195–218. London: Routledge.

Marchal, Jules. 2008. *Lord Leverhulme's Ghosts: Colonial Exploitation in the Congo*. London: Verso.

Masquelier, Adeline, ed. 2005. *Dirt, Undress, and Difference*. Bloomington: Indiana University Press.

Masterman, Charles F. G., ed. 1901. *The Heart of the Empire: Discussions of Problems of Modern City Life in England*. London: T. Fisher Unwin.

Mbembe, Achille. 2001. *On the Postcolony*. Berkeley: University of California Press.

Mbembe, Achille. 2018. "Borders in the Age of Networks." 2018 Tanner Lectures on Human Values, Whitney Humanities Center, Yale University, March 27–29.

McClintock, Anne. 1995. *Imperial Leather: Race, Gender and Sexuality in the Colonial Contest.* London: Routledge.

Menninghaus, Winfried. 2003. *Disgust: Theory and History of a Strong Sensation.* Albany: State University of New York Press.

Meyer, Birgit. 2015. *Sensational Movies: Video, Vision, and Christianity in Ghana.* Oakland: University of California Press.

Morris, Kate. 2000. *British Techniques of Public Relations and Propaganda for Mobilizing East and Central Africa during World War Two.* London: Edwin Mellen.

Morton-Williams, Peter. [ca. 1953]. *Cinema in Rural Nigeria: A Field Study of the Impact of Fundamental-Education Films on Rural Audiences in Nigeria.* Zaria, Nigeria: Federal Information Service and Gaskiya Corporation.

Mulvey, Laura. 1975. "Visual Pleasure and Narrative Cinema." *Screen* 16 (3): 6–18.

Mupotsa, Danai S. 2014. "White Weddings." PhD diss., University of the Witwatersrand.

Murillo, Bianca. 2012. "'The Modern Shopping Experience': Kingsway Department Store and Consumer Politics in Ghana." *Africa* 82 (3): 368–92.

Murray, David A. B. 2009. *Homophobias: Lust and Loathing across Time and Space.* Durham, NC: Duke University Press.

Myers, Garth. 2011. *African Cities: Alternative Visions of Urban Theory and Practice.* London: Zed Books.

Nesbitt, E. 2000. "Researching Eight to Thirteen Year-Olds' Perspectives on Their Experience of Religion." In *Researching Children's Perspectives*, edited by A. Lewis and G. Lindsay, 135–49. Buckingham, U.K.: Open University Press.

Newell, Stephanie. 2002. *Literary Culture in Colonial Ghana: "How to Play the Game of Life."* Manchester: Manchester University Press.

Newell, Stephanie. 2006. *The Forger's Tale: The Search for Odeziaku.* Athens: Ohio University Press.

Newell, Stephanie. 2008. "Dirty Whites: 'Ruffian-Writing' in Colonial West Africa." *Research in African Literatures* 39 (4): 1–13.

Newell, Stephanie. 2013. *The Power to Name: A History of Anonymity in Colonial West Africa.* Athens: Ohio University Press.

Newell, Stephanie. 2016. "Paradoxes of Press Freedom in Colonial West Africa." *Journal of Media History* 22 (1): 101–12.

Newell, Stephanie, et al. 2018. "Dirty Methods as Ethical Methods? In the Field with 'The Cultural Politics of Dirt in Africa, 1880–Present.'" In *Routledge International Handbook of Interdisciplinary Research Methods*, edited by Celia Lury et al., 248–65. London: Routledge.

New Humanitarian. 2006. "Lagos, the Mega-City of Slums." September 5. http://www.thenewhumanitarian.org/news/2006/09/05/lagos-mega-city-slums.

New York Herald Tribune. 1925. "Prince Alters Trip to Avoid Danger from Plague in Lagos." April 12, 19.

Nigerian Pioneer. 1924. Editorial. September 5, 3.

Njoh, Ambe J. 2008. "Colonial Philosophies, Urban Space, and Racial Segregation in British and French Colonial Africa." *Journal of Black Studies* 38 (4): 579–99.

Njoh, Ambe J. 2009. "Urban Planning as a Tool of Power and Social Control in Colonial Africa." *Planning Perspectives* 24 (3): 301–17.

Njoh, Ambe J. (2012) 2016. *Urban Planning and Public Health in Africa: Historical, Theoretical, and Practical Dimensions of a Continent's Water and Sanitation Problematic.* London: Routledge.

Nossiter, Adam. 2014. "Nigeria Tries to 'Sanitize' Itself of Gays." *New York Times*, February 8. http://www.nytimes.com/2014/02/09/world/africa/nigeria-uses-law-and-whip-to-sanitize-gays.html?_r=0 (accessed February 8, 2016).

Nwafor, Sunday. 2017. "Come, Stay under the 'Umbrella,' 'Broom' No Longer Sweeping Well, Makarfi Tells Nigerians." *Vanguard*, October 12. https://www.vanguardngr.com/2017/10/come-stay-umbrella-broom-no-longer-sweeping-well-markarfi-tells-nigerians/ (accessed December 10, 2017).

Nwaubani, Adaobi Tricia. 2010. "Nigeria's Anger at the BBC's Welcome to Lagos Film." *Guardian* (U.K.), May 6. https://www.theguardian.com/commentisfree/2010/may/06/nigeria-response-bbc (accessed March 13, 2015).

Nwaubani, Adaobi Tricia. 2017. "LGBT Acceptance Slowly Grows in Nigeria, despite Anti-Gay Laws." *Reuters*, May 16. https://www.reuters.com/article/us-nigeria-lgbt-survey/lgbt-acceptance-slowly-grows-in-nigeria-despite-anti-gay-laws-idUSKCN18C2T8 (accessed May 26, 2017).

Nyong'o, Tavia. 2012. "Queer Africa and the Fantasy of Virtual Participation." *Women's Studies Quarterly* 40 (1–2): 40–63.

Obono, Oka. 2007. "A Lagos Thing: Rules and Realities in the Nigerian Megacity." *Georgetown Journal of International Affairs* 8 (2): 31–37.

Ochiagha, Terri. 2018. "E. H. Duckworth's Clean-Up Lagos Campaigns: The Political Use of *Ex-Centric* Colonial Discourse on African Dirt." *Social Dynamics* 44 (1): 21–37.

Ofiebor, Okafor. 2014. "Why Amaechi Dumped Tattered Umbrella for the Broom." PM *News*, November 17. https://www.pmnewsnigeria.com/2014/11/17/why-amaechi-dumped-tattered-umbrella-for-the-broom/ (accessed March 25, 2018).

Oke, David Mautin, et al. 2017. "Some Correlates of Rural-Urban Led Urbanization in Lagos, Nigeria." *Review of Urban and Regional Development Studies (RURDS)* 29 (3): 185–95.

Okere, Theophilus, Chukwudi Anthony Njoku, and René Devisch. 2011. "All Knowledge Is First of All Local Knowledge." In *The Postcolonial Turn*, edited by René Devisch and Francis B. Nyamnjoh, 275–95. Oxford, U.K.: African Books Collective.

Okoroayanwu, Emeka, and Adewale Sanyaolu. 2010. "How We Plan to Make Lagos the Cleanest City in the World, by Ola Oresanya, MD, LAWMA." NBF

News, January 11. http://www.nigerianbestforum.com/blog/tag/by-ola
-oresanya/ (accessed April 30, 2018).

Oloko, Patrick. 2018. "Human Waste/Wasting Humans: Disposable Bodies and
Power Relations in Nigerian Media Reports." *Social Dynamics* 44 (1): 55–68.

Olorunfemi, F. B. 2007. "Living with Waste: The Impact of Landfill Sites in
Lagos Metropolis, Coping Mechanisms." *Nigerian Journal of Economic and
Social Studies* 48 (3): 203–15.

Olukoju, Ayọdèjì. 2004. *The "Liverpool" of West Africa: The Dynamics and Impact
of Maritime Trade in Lagos, 1900–1950*. Trenton, NJ: Africa World Press.

Olukoju, Ayọdèjì. 2018. "'Filthy Rich' and 'Dirt Poor': Social and Cultural Dimensions of Solid Waste Management (SWM) in Lagos." *Social Dynamics* 44
(1): 88–106.

Oluwasegun, Jimoh Mufutau. 2017. "The British Mosquito Eradication Campaign in Colonial Lagos, 1902–1950." *Canadian Journal of African Studies* 51
(2): 217–36.

Omu, Fred I. A. 1974. "Journalism and the Rise of Nigerian Nationalism: John
Payne Jackson, 1848–1915." *Journal of the Historical Society of Nigeria* 7 (3): 521–39.

Omu, Fred I. A. 1978. *Press and Politics in Nigeria, 1880–1937*. Atlantic High-
lands, NJ: Humanities Press.

Onuoha, Godwin. 2017. "Shared Histories, Divided Memories: Mediating and
Navigating the Tensions in Nigeria-Biafra War Discourses." *Africa Today* 63
(1): 3–21.

Onuora, Chika. 2014. "'Night Soil Men' and Their Provocative Statements."
pointblanknews.com, November 26. http://pointblanknews.com/pbn/?s
=Night+soil+men (accessed March 23, 2018).

Osinubi, Taiwo Adetunji. 2016. "Queer Prolepsis and the Sexual Commons: An
Introduction." *Research in African Literatures* 47 (2): vii–xxii.

Otero, Solimar. 2010. *Afro-Cuban Diasporas in the Atlantic World*. Rochester, NY:
University of Rochester Press.

Ouoro, Justin. 2011. *Poétique des cinémas d'Afrique noire francophone*. Ouagadougou, Burkina Faso: Presse Universitaire de Ouagadougou (PUO).

OutRight Action International. n.d. "South Africa New Constitution Protects
Gays and Lesbians." https://www.outrightinternational.org/content/south
-africa-new-constitution-protects-gays-and-lesbians (accessed April 30, 2018).

Parle, Julie, and Vanessa Noble. 2014. "New Directions and Challenges in Histories of Health, Healing and Medicine in South Africa." *Medical History* 58
(2): 147–65.

Parris, Matthew. 1995. "Scandals in the House." *Independent* (U.K.), October 29.
https://www.independent.co.uk/arts-entertainment/scandals-in-the-house
-1579987.html (accessed April 28, 2018).

Patton, Adell. 1996. *Physicians, Colonial Racism, and Diaspora in West Africa*.
Gainesville: University Press of Florida.

Pearson, George. 1948. "The Making of Films for Illiterates in Africa." *The Film in Colonial Development: A Report of a Conference*, edited by the British Film Institute, 22–27. London: British Film Institute.

Pefanis, Julian. 1990. *Heterology and the Postmodern: Bataille, Baudrillard, and Lyotard*. Durham, NC: Duke University Press.

Perham, Margery. 1933. "The Census of Nigeria, 1931." *Africa: Journal of the International African Institute* 6 (4): 415–30.

Peters, Oreoluwa. 2016. "'When I Was Married, I Told My Ex-Wife I Was Gay'—Kenny Badmus." ynaija.com, July 8. https://ynaija.com/i-married-i -told-ex-wife-i-gay-kenny-badmus/ (accessed June 13, 2019).

Peterson, Derek, Emma Hunter, and Stephanie Newell, eds. 2016. *African Print Cultures: Newspapers and Their Publics in the Twentieth Century*. Ann Arbor: University of Michigan Press.

Peterson, Jennifer Lynn. 2013. *Education in the School of Dreams: Travelogue and Early Nonfiction Film*. Durham, NC: Duke University Press.

Pew Research Global Attitudes Project. 2013. "The Global Divide on Homosexuality." June 4. http://www.pewglobal.org/2013/06/04/the-global-divide-on -homosexuality/ (accessed March 20, 2018).

Pierce, Steven. 2016. "'Nigeria Can Do Without Such Perverts': Sexual Anxiety and Political Crisis in Postcolonial Nigeria." *Comparative Studies of South Asia, Africa and the Middle East* 36 (1): 3–20.

Pillai, Thakazhi Sivasankara. (1947) 1994. *Scavenger's Son*. London: Heinemann.

Potter, Simon. 2012. *Broadcasting Empire: The BBC and the British World, 1922– 1970*. Oxford: Oxford University Press.

Pratt, Mary Louise. 1992. *Imperial Eyes: Travel Writing and Transculturation*. London: Routledge.

Procter, James, and Bethan Benwell. 2015. *Reading across Worlds: Transnational Book Groups and the Reception of Difference*. Basingstoke, U.K.: Palgrave Macmillan.

Prunier, Gérard. 1998. *The Rwanda Crisis: History of a Genocide*. 2nd rev. ed. London: Hurst.

Public Works Department (Cape of Good Hope). 1901. *Chief Inspector's Report for the Year 1900*. Cape Town, South Africa: W. A. Richards and Sons (Government Printers).

Punch, Samantha. 2002. "Research with Children: The Same or Different from Research with Adults?" *Childhood* 9 (3): 321–41.

Quayson, Ato. 2014. *Oxford Street, Accra: City Life and the Itineraries of Transnationalism*. Durham, NC: Duke University Press.

Rais, Marina. 1988. *The Lebanese of West Africa: An Example of a Trading Diaspora*. Berlin: Das Arabische Buch.

Rashid, Ismail. 2011. "Epidemics and Resistance in Colonial Sierra Leone during the First World War." *Canadian Journal of African Studies / Revue canadienne des études africaines* 45 (3): 415–39.

Ray, Carina. 2015a. *Crossing the Color Line: Race, Sex, and the Contested Politics of Colonialism in Ghana.* Athens: Ohio University Press.

Ray, Carina. 2015b. "Sexual Panic and the State in Colonial and Post-Independence Africa." Unpublished research paper, Yale University, October 14.

Reuters. 2014. "Gambia's Jammeh Calls Gays 'Vermin,' Says to Fight like Malarial Mosquitoes." February 18. http://www.reuters.com/article/us-gambia -homosexuality-idUSBREA1H1S820140218 (accessed February 12, 2016).

Reynolds, Glenn. 2015. *Colonial Cinema in Africa: Origins, Images, Audiences.* Jefferson, NC: McFarland.

Rice, Tom. 2016. "Are You Proud to Be British? Mobile Film Shows, Local Voices and the Demise of the British Empire in Africa." *Historical Journal of Film, Radio and Television* 36 (3): 331–51.

Robinson, Julian. 2014. "Ebola Epidemic Spreads to FIFTH West African Country as Case of Deadly Virus Is Reported in Senegal—but Quarantine Is Lifted in Slum Area of Liberian Capital." *Daily Mail,* August 30. http:// www.dailymail.co.uk/news/article-2738473/Ebola-epidemic-spreads-FIFTH -West-African-country-case-deadly-virus-reported-Senegal-quarantine-lifted -slum-area-Liberian-capital.html (accessed April 11, 2018).

Rockefeller Foundation. *A Digital History: Health—Eradicating Hookworm.* https://rockfound.rockarch.org/eradicating-hookworm (accessed November 11, 2017).

Ross, Ronald. 1922. *Memoirs, with a Full Account of the Great Malaria Problem and Its Solution.* London: John Murray.

Roy, Arundhati. 1998. *The God of Small Things.* London: HarperCollins.

Said, Edward. 1978. *Orientalism.* London: Penguin.

Saint, Lily. 2018. *Black Cultural Life in South Africa: Reception, Apartheid, and Ethics.* Ann Arbor: University of Michigan Press.

Sampsonia Way. 2016. "'Love Holds Things Together': A Q&A with Jude Dibia." March 18. https://www.sampsoniaway.org/interviews/2016/03/18/love-holds -things-together-a-qa-with-jude-dibia/ (accessed June 13, 2019).

Sarbah, John Mensah. 1897. *Fanti Customary Laws: A Brief Introduction to the Principles of the Native Laws and Customs of the Fanti and Akan Districts of the Gold Coast, with a Report of Some Cases Thereon Decided by the Law Courts.* London: W. Clowes and Sons.

Sawada, Nozomi. 2011. "The Educated Elite and Associational Life in Early Lagos Newspapers: In Search of Unity for the Progress of Society." PhD diss., University of Birmingham.

Schneider, William. 2009. "Smallpox in Africa during Colonial Rule." *Medical History* 3 (2): 193–227.

Schweppe, Jennifer, and Mark Austin Walters. 2016. "Introduction: The Globalization of Hate." In *The Globalization of Hate: Internationalizing Hate Crime?*, edited by Jennifer Schweppe and Mark Austin Walters, 2–12. Oxford: Oxford University Press.

Science. 1901. Editorial. 14 (364), December 20: 982–83.

Sellers, William. 1953. "Making Films in and for the Colonies: A Paper Read to the Commonwealth Section of the Society on Tuesday 24th March 1953." *Journal of the Royal Society of Arts* 101 (4910): 829–37.

Seun, Adetiba Adedamola. 2015. "Malaria and Sanitation in Colonial Lagos: A Historical Appraisal." *History Research* 3 (6): 65–71.

Sherzer, Dina. 1996. "Introduction." *Cinema, Colonialism, Postcolonialism: Perspectives from the French and Francophone World*, edited by Dina Sherzer, 1–19. Austin: University of Texas Press.

Simone, AbdouMaliq. 2004. *For the City Yet to Come: Changing African Life in Four Cities.* Durham, NC: Duke University Press.

Simone, AbdouMaliq. 2005. "Introduction." In *Urban Africa: Changing Contours of Survival in the City*, edited by AbdouMaliq Simone and Abdelghani Abouhani, 1–26. London: Zed Books; Dakar: CODESRIA.

Simpson, William J. R. 1909. *Report by Professor W. J. Simpson on Sanitary Matters in Various West African Colonies and the Outbreak of Plague in the Gold Coast.* London: HMSO.

Sklar, R. L. 1963. *Nigerian Political Parties: Power in an Emergent African Nation.* Princeton, NJ: Princeton University Press.

Smith, Constance. 2019. "Accumulating History: Dirt, Remains and Urban Decay in Nairobi." *Social Dynamics* 44 (1): 107–27.

Smith, Constance. 2019. *Nairobi in the Making: Landscapes of Time and Urban Belonging.* Martlesham, U.K.: James Currey.

Smith, Robert S. 1979. *The Lagos Consulate, 1851–1861.* Berkeley: University of California Press.

Smith, Virginia. 2007. *Clean: A History of Personal Hygiene and Purity.* Oxford: Oxford University Press.

Smyth, Rosaleen. 2011. "Images of Empires on Shifting Sands: The Colonial Film Unit in West Africa in the Post-War Period." In *Film and the End of Empire*, edited by Lee Grieveson and Colin MacCabe, 155–75. Basingstoke, U.K.: BFI and Palgrave Macmillan.

Smyth, Rosaleen. 2013. "Grierson, the British Documentary Movement, and Colonial Cinema in British Colonial Africa." *Film History* 25 (4): 82–113.

Spitzer, Leo. 1975. *The Creoles of Sierra Leone: Responses to Colonialism, 1870–1945.* Madison: University of Wisconsin Press.

Spivak, Gayatri Chakravorty. 1988. "Can the Subaltern Speak?" In *Marxism and the Interpretation of Culture*, edited by Cary Nelson and Lawrence Grossberg, 271–313. London: Macmillan.

Spurlin, William J. 2001. "Emerging 'Queer' Identities and Cultures in South Africa." *Postcolonial, Queer: Theoretical Intersections*, edited by John C. Hawley, 185–205. Albany: State University of New York Press.

Stallybrass, Peter, and Allon White. 1986. *The Politics and Poetics of Transgression*. Ithaca, NY: Cornell University Press.

Stanley, Henry Morton. 1890. *In Darkest Africa or the Quest, Rescue, and Retreat of Emin Pasha, Governor of Equatoria*. 2 vols. New York: Scribner.

Stein, Eric A. 2013. "Colonial Theaters of Proof: Representation and Laughter in 1930s Rockefeller Foundation Hygiene Cinema in Java." In *Empires of Vision*, edited by Martin Jay, 315–45. Durham, NC: Duke University Press.

Stoler, Ann Laura. 2002. *Carnal Knowledge and Imperial Power: Race and the Intimate in Colonial Rule*. Berkeley: University of California Press.

Stoler, Ann Laura. 2010. *Along the Archival Grain: Epistemic Anxieties and Colonial Common Sense*. Princeton, NJ: Princeton University Press.

Stoller, Paul. 1992. *The Cinematic Griot: The Ethnography of Jean Rouch*. Chicago: University of Chicago Press.

Stratton, Florence. 1994. *Contemporary African Literature and the Politics of Gender*. London: Routledge.

Strelitz, Larry, and Priscilla Boshoff. 2008. "The African Reception of Global Media." In *International Handbook of Children, Media and Culture*, edited by Kirsten Drotner and Sonia Livingstone, 237–53. Buckingham, U.K.: Open University Press.

Strickland, C. F. 1940. "Instructional Films in India." *Journal of the Royal Society of Arts* 88 (4547): 204–15.

Sultana, Habiba, and D. B. Subedi. 2016. "Caste System and Resistance: The Case of Untouchable Hindu Sweepers in Bangladesh." *International Journal of Politics, Culture, and Society* 29 (1): 19–32.

Sutphen, Mary P., and Bridie Andrews. 2003. "Introduction." In *Medicine and Colonial Identity*, edited by Mary P. Sutphen and Bridie Andrews, 1–13. London: Routledge.

Teltumbde, Anand. 2017. *Dalits: Past, Present and Future*. London: Routledge.

Thompson, Michael. 1979. *Rubbish Theory: The Creation and Destruction of Value*. Chicago: University of Chicago Press.

Tilley, Helen. 2016. "Medicine, Empires, and Ethics in Colonial Africa." *AMA Journal of Ethics* 18 (7): 743–53.

Uwa, John. 2018. "Transcultural Tension and the Politics of Sewage Management in (Post) Colonial Lagos (Nigeria)." *Social Dynamics* 44 (2): 221–38.

van Dijk, Teun A. 2000. "Ideologies, Racism, Discourse: Debates on Immigration and Ethnic Issues." In *Comparative Perspectives on Racism*, edited by J. Ter Wal and M. Verkuyten, 91–115. Aldershot, U.K.: Ashgate.

van Reybrouck, David. 2014. *Congo: The Epic History of a People*. Translated by Sam Garrett. London: Fourth Estate.

Vaughan, Megan. 1991. *Curing Their Ills: Colonial Power and African Illness.* Cambridge, U.K.: Polity Press.

Vaughan, Olufemi. 2000. *Nigerian Chiefs: Traditional Power in Modern Politics, 1890s–1990s.* Rochester, NY: University of Rochester Press.

Wagner-Lawlor, Jennifer. 2018. "Poor Theory and the Art of Plastic Pollution in Nigeria: Relational Aesthetics, Human Ecology, and 'Good Housekeeping.'" *Social Dynamics* 42 (2): 198–220.

Warner, Michael. 2002. *Publics and Counterpublics.* Cambridge, MA: MIT Press.

Watson, L. 2011. "Shifting Terrains: Women Writing West Africa, 1890–1960." PhD diss., University of Southampton.

Webb, James L. A. 2013. "Historical Epidemiology and Infectious Disease Processes in Africa." *Journal of African History* 54 (1): 3–10.

Webb, James L. A. 2014. *The Long Struggle against Malaria in Tropical Africa.* Cambridge: Cambridge University Press.

White, Luise. 1990. *The Comforts of Home: Prostitution in Colonial Nairobi.* Chicago: University of Chicago Press.

Whiteley, Gillian. 2011. *Junk: Art and the Politics of Trash.* London: I. B. Taurus.

Whiteman, Kaye. 2014. *Lagos: A Cultural and Literary History.* London: Signal Books.

Whitford, John. (1877) 1967. *Trading Life in Western and Central Africa.* London: Frank Cass.

Willems, Wendy. 2014. "Producing Loyal Citizens and Entertaining Volatile Subjects: Imagining Audience Agency in Colonial Rhodesia and Post-Colonial Zimbabwe." In *Meanings of Audiences: Comparative Discourses*, edited by Richard Butsch and Sonia Livingstone, 80–96. London: Routledge.

WREC (Warwick Research Collective). 2015. *Combined and Uneven Development: Towards a New Theory of World-Literature.* Liverpool: Liverpool University Press.

Wren, P. C. 1924. *Beau Geste.* New York: Grosset and Dunlap.

Wynne, Deborah. 2015. "Reading Victorian Rags: Recycling, Redemption, and Dickens's Ragged Children." *Journal of Victorian Culture* 20 (1): 34–49.

Wyse, Akintola J. G. 1990. *H. C. Bankole-Bright and Politics in Colonial Sierra Leone, 1919–1958.* Cambridge: Cambridge University Press.

Xiang, Sunny. 2018. "Race, Tone, and Ha Jin's 'Documentary Manner.'" *Comparative Literature* 70 (1): 72–92.

Yankah, Kwesi. 1989. *The Proverb in the Context of Akan Rhetoric.* Bern: Peter Lang.

Yusuff, Ayọ. 2015. "English Loans in Yoruba Language: Linguistic Empowerment and Disenfranchisement." Linguistics Association of Ghana Annual

Conference, Kwame Nkrumah University of Science and Technology, Kumasi, July 27.

Zimbabwe Independent. 2017. "Mugabe Comes Face to Face with Gays." November 27. https://www.theindependent.co.zw/2015/11/27/mugabe-comes-face-to-face-with-gays/ (accessed March 18, 2018).

INDEX

British Empire, 43, 52, 85
British West Africa, 7, 23, 32, 34, 37,
    41, 43–44, 47, 52–60, 82, 127–28
Broad Street (Lagos), 17
broom, 123–26, 128–31, 136, 206n78
bubonic plague: epidemic in Lagos,
    50–56, 178n15; films about, 64; im-
    pact on trade, 190. *See also* "filth
    diseases"
Buhari, Muhammadu, 125, 129–30,
    143, 150, 210n57
building regulations, 21–24, 202n7.
    See also town planning
Burton, Antoinette, 14, 91

Calabar (Nigeria), 97, 205n59
Cape Coast (Ghana), 22, 26, 35, 127,
    179n35
Carter Bridge (Lagos), 128
"cart-pushers," 132, 139. *See also* waste:
    waste workers
Casablanca, 3
censorship, 46, 61, 165, 211n60
Central Africa, 1, 19, 41
cesspits. *See* toilets: pit latrines
Chamberlain, Joseph, 35
Chambers of Commerce: Lagos, 16;
    Liverpool, 16, 37
Chaplin, Charlie, 75, 76, 196n105
chiefs, 20, 60, 80, 81, 127, 162
children, 4, 37–38, 69, 82–85, 92,
    102–7, 121, 129, 135, 141, 151–53,
    185n33
cholera, 22, 152. *See also* "filth
    diseases"
Christianity, 28, 37, 63, 69, 85–86, 104,
    144–49, 153–54, 195n88
Christiansborg Castle (Ghana), 28,
    180n48
Christophers, S. R. (Dr.), 39
cinemas: commercial, 60, 63, 74,
    196n105; mobile, 62–63, 67, 72,
    82–83; propaganda films, 11, 28,

59–63, 67, 71–76, 80–85, 122, 156,
    184n19
class, xii, 14, 17, 22–23, 50–54, 116–20,
    123, 129, 159, 180n43, 212n85. *See also*
    elites, African
Clean Cooking, 68
cleanliness, 4, 12, 54, 90, 110, 112,
    117
Clifford, Hugh (Sir), 22, 28, 30,
    34–35, 40–41, 48, 180n48, 183n18
Cohen, M. E., 29
colonial archives, xii, xiv, 10–11, 14,
    20, 58–60, 80–86, 89, 117, 166
Colonial Development Fund, 63
Colonial Film Unit (CFU), 14, 63–89,
    166, 192n26, 193n33, 196n103
Colonial Office (London), 23, 30, 39,
    42, 44, 62, 67–68, 75, 77, 165
commodities, 3, 12, 28, 37, 81, 141
Communism, 54, 165
Curtis, Valerie, 100

Daily Mail, 158–59
Daily Times (Nigeria), 9, 45, 56, 133,
    189n36
Dalziel, J. M. (Dr.), 26–27
Dashit village (Nigeria), 70
Daybreak in Udi, 68, 73
deBoeck, Filip, 106
Deniga, Adeoye, 47–48, 189n26
Dettol, 126–27
Dickie, Simon, 76
disgust, 2–3, 12–13, 37, 86, 95, 99,
    100–102, 109, 111, 117, 122, 129, 136,
    143–44, 152, 154–56, 160–64
disinfectants, 22, 127
Douglas, Mary, 4, 12, 36, 111
drains, 22, 26, 27, 36, 48, 91, 98, 102,
    105, 109, 120, 125, 132, 140, 191n64,
    200n55
dumpsites, 17, 91, 109, 115–23, 128–35
Dysentery, 68, 73
dysentery, 26, 66

East Africa, 7, 143, 163, 181n68, 184n21
Ebola, xiii, 102, 124, 139, 152, 158–59, 175n5
Ebute Metta (Lagos), 37
Egan village (Nigeria), 71
Egbe people, 127
Egun people, 127, 205n59
Ehingbeti (Lagos), 17
Eko Akete, 47–48, 51, 189n32
elections, Nigerian presidential (2015), 115, 124, 129–30, 143
electricity supply, 91, 103, 146
elites, African, 9, 14, 23, 39, 44–45, 48, 50, 54, 56, 73, 81, 85, 86, 160, 165
English language, xii, 44, 55, 119, 120
Entertainments West Africa Ltd., 60
ephemera, 38, 91, 166
epidemiology, 19, 25, 33–34, 38–40, 42, 100–101, 166
Eṣu, 28
ethnicity, xii, 12, 16, 17, 24, 33, 40, 53–54, 82, 91, 93, 95, 96–99, 107, 112, 114, 127, 146, 201n99
Eurocentrism, 10–12, 17, 22, 24, 27, 54, 64, 86, 91, 115, 119, 162, 163, 181n64
European Quarter (Lagos), 17, 39

Fanon, Frantz, 126, 160–61
Fardon, Richard, 4
Fashola, Babatunde Raji, 133, 206n95
feces, 17, 21–25, 28, 35, 47, 54, 64, 96, 99–102, 121, 123, 128–29, 180n49. *See also* "shotput"
feminism, 138, 143, 151, 209n22
films: African spectators, xv, 10, 14, 58, 62–67, 74; audience responses, 59, 63, 65–77; colonial research, 13, 59, 63, 67–68, 75–78; documentary, 12, 14, 62–63, 68–69, 71–75, 85, 89, 115–19, 166; popular movies, 63, 74, 76, 165, 193n33; public health, 58, 64, 78–79, 84, 89; "Sellers technique," 65, 74; STD films, 85; war-

time propaganda, 75. *See also* Colonial Film Unit
"filth diseases," 7, 19–20, 22, 25–29, 37, 44, 48–49, 63, 152, 179n34
food, preparation and consumption, 2–3, 28, 42, 54–55, 64, 69, 71, 82, 95, 98–99, 101, 107, 122, 163
Freetown (Sierra Leone), 7, 16, 26, 127, 187n5, 189n33

Galway, Henry Lionel, 23
Gambia, 23, 191n59
Gandy, Matthew, 140
Gays and Lesbians of Zimbabwe (GALZ), 146
gender, xiii, 59, 76, 88, 92, 104–5, 138–39, 152, 184n19, 209n22, 212n81
Ghana, 22, 33, 35, 39–40, 52, 60, 68, 75, 127, 179n34, 180n48, 184n19
global cities, xiii, xvi, 2, 18, 41, 90, 128, 146, 159, 163, 165
global economy, 3, 4, 29, 51, 53, 55, 62
globalization, 2, 13, 42, 80, 86, 89, 127, 142, 144, 154–55, 162, 165
Global North, xiv, 22, 81, 112, 154, 158
Gold Coast. *See* Ghana
Gordon, David, 20
Government Reserved (or Residential) Area (GRA), 17, 41
Graphic (London), 4, 6–8
Grassi, Giovanni Battista, 32, 182n1
Griffith Street (Lagos), 48
Guardian (U.K.), 118
gutters, 92, 98, 120, 123, 137

Hall, Stuart, 161
Harcourt, Lewis (Viscount), 38–40, 186n36
Harewood, David, 116
Harrow, Kenneth, 122
Hartley, John 82
Hausa people, 17, 65, 66, 68, 77, 83, 94, 96, 97, 101, 108, 112, 132, 201n99

New Kru Town (Liberia), 158
newspapers: African-language, 47,
51, 56, 191n72; Anglophone, 9, 47,
55–56, 86; anticolonial, 9, 43–48, 50,
52, 54, 57, 187n2; conservative, 9, 46,
47, 50, 54, 159, 188n17, 190n44; editors of, 9, 46, 52, 54, 56; and public health, 9, 11, 22, 44–49, 52, 56,
119–20, 122–23, 133, 155, 158, 164
Ngũgĩ wa Thiong'o, 143
Nigerian *Daily Times*. See *Daily
Times* (Nigeria)
Nigerian Medical and Sanitary Department, 17, 51
Nigerian National Archives (Ibadan),
51
Nigerian National Democratic Party,
46
Nigerian Pidgin, xv, 12, 107–8
Nigerian Pioneer, 9, 46, 49, 50–54. *See
also* Ajasa, Kitoyi (Sir)
night-soil worker. See *agbépóò*
nonelites, African, 22, 47, 56, 57, 73,
166
northern Nigeria, 2, 65, 68, 142, 149

Obama, Barack, 145
Obasanjo, Olusegun, 143
Obono, Oka, 140
Ocansey cinemas, 60
Oke, David M., 113
Oloko, Patrick, xii, xiv, 90, 120, 122,
131
Olorunfemi, Felix, 113
Olukoju, Ayòdèjì, 123, 203n26
Olusosun dumpsite, 117–18
Oluwole, I. (Bishop), 49
Ọmọ Èkó, 17, 97–98
Onuora, Chika, 130
oral history, 83, 91, 166
Orde Brown, Granville St. John
(Major Sir), 27
Oresanya, Ola, 133, 135–39

Orientalism, 160–61
Orlu (Nigeria), 74
Oshodi Street (Lagos), 74

pan-Africanism, 45, 54
pàntí, 108, 120
parables: African, 130; colonial health,
63–64, 66, 73–84, 88
Pearson, George, 63, 67
Pears Soap Company, 4, 6, 7
Pentecostal churches, 144–45, 150
People's Democratic Party (PDP),
129–31
Peterson, Jennifer L., 87
Pew Research Global Attitudes Project, 146
Plague, 61, 64
plague. *See* bubonic plague
plastics, 109, 120, 164
Plissart, Marie-Françoise, 106
pollution, 12, 41, 98, 105, 140
póò, 96, 99–100, 105
popular literature, 38, 165, 193n33
popular sayings, 55, 99, 124–26, 129,
132, 188n25, 204n41
population, of Lagos, xi, 16, 51, 113,
141, 202n103
Porch, R. O. H., 77–78
potty. See *póò*
Prince of Wales, visit to West Africa,
48, 52
Principal Medical Officers' Conference (Lagos), 39
Private Sector Participation (PSP), 92,
132, 139, 140
propaganda, 11, 28, 59–63, 67, 71, 73,
75–76, 80–85, 156, 165, 184n19
proverbs, 12, 122–23, 127, 130, 134, 166
proximity, 4, 7, 30, 33, 35–37, 64, 72, 76,
92, 94, 95, 103, 113, 158–60, 184n21
public health, 9, 10, 19–25, 29–41, 54,
64, 66–73, 86, 91–93, 102, 112, 122,
134, 166